CW01091168

THE COMEBACK

ELVIS

AND THE STORY OF THE 68 SPECIAL

SIMON GODDARD

By the same author

ON BOWIE
Ziggyology

ON POSTCARD RECORDS
Simply Thrilled

ON THE ROLLING STONES
Rollaresque

ON THE SMITHS & MORRISSEY
Songs That Saved Your Life
Mozipedia

THE COMEBACK
ELVIS
AND THE STORY OF THE 68 SPECIAL

SIMON GODDARD

OMNIBUS PRESS

London / New York / Paris / Sydney / Copenhagen / Berlin / Madrid / Tokyo

Exclusive Distributors
Music Sales Limited
14/15 Berners Street
London, W1T 3LJ

Music Sales Pty. Ltd
(Australia and New Zealand)
Level 4, 30–32 Carrington Street
Sydney
NSW 2000
Australia

Every effort has been made to trace the copyright holders of the photographs in this book but
one or two were unreachable. We would be grateful if the photographers concerned would
contact us.

Printed in Malta.
A catalogue record for this book is available from the British Library.
Visit Omnibus Press on the web at www.omnibuspress.com

CONTENTS

v

ACT II

NOTE TO THE READER

This book concerns events in American social history in the late 20th century, including themes of race and racism. Both author and publisher would like to stress that the inclusion of certain language common to that era yet otherwise anachronistic to our own is solely for reasons of historical authenticity, and has been used strictly in context of those divisive times without wishing to cause any offence to the reader of today.

PREFACE

Welcome to the Memphian. It's midnight and the cinema is yours. Sit wherever you like. Surround yourself with whoever you like and tell them to sit where you want them to sit. Order any food or drinks you want and somebody will bring them to you. Keep ordering and they'll keep coming. Then, once you're comfortable, just call out to the projectionist and the film will start.

Tonight's film is called *The Comeback*. It's the story of what happened to Elvis Presley in the 1960s. And what happened to the 1960s with, or without, Elvis Presley.

It's a true story, in the way that one of Elvis' later favourite films, *Patton*, was a true story. The facts, people, places and pharmaceuticals are all real. But, like *Patton*, it's a film, not a documentary. A Technicolor drama, with scripted dialogue, deep focus, close-ups, montages, jump edits, special effects and music. A picture, not a lecture. That's why you're sat in the Memphian and not in class at Humes High. A story this unbelievably true really couldn't be told anywhere else.

So, if you're ready, we'll begin. Be sure to leave room for Gary Pepper on the end of the row there. And anytime you want to rerun a particular scene just holler up and they'll play it again.

OK. The lights are dimming. Roll the film...

'For what is a man advantaged
if he gain the whole world
but lose himself or be cast away.'

LUKE 9:25*

---

* A favourite verse of Elvis Presley's which he copied out by hand at the top of a page in the monogrammed Bible given to him by his Uncle Vester for Christmas, 1957 – his last before entering the United States Army.

ACT I

THE DRESSING ROOM

Eyelids closed. Darkness. White noise. Numbers. Scriptures. Methamphetamine 30. Hydrochloride 20. Genesis 1:3.

'And God said "Let there be light."'

Eyelids open.

'Fuck!'

His eyes saw the eyes of the face reflected back at him in the dressing room mirror. A face that would make anyone gasp 'fuck!', even him, born with that face but still 'fuck!'-gasping as the bliss of shut-eyed ignorance was sucker-punched blinking to the truth. That *that* – that *thing*, that masterpiece of male physiognomy – was *him*.

He was so beautiful it was almost inhuman. A convent girl's self-flagellating fancy of the face of God, sculpted in caramel. He had eyes as if the cloudless Pacific summer sky was shining straight through the top of his head, concentrated in a pair of truest blue lasers that made all who met its twinkly Medusa gaze feel as if they'd been fried to a smoky heap of diamond dust smelling of warm sugar. He looked squeezed from a tube and wet to the touch. Liquorice hair and marshmallow lips, hugged head to foot in leather glistening like tailored treacle, and that caramel God-face that made women gape with pupils big as begging mouths screaming to let them lick him all the way down to the birch-wood stick.

A jealous husband in Ohio once threw a fist at this truest blue laser caramel face because his estranged wife carried its picture in her wallet instead of his own. The husband was arrested, tried and fined 19 dollars and 60 cents, and when he couldn't pay he was sent to jail where he had to mope in a cell tortured by the thought of his ever-more-estranged wife at home, happily drooling and dreaming of her tongue lapping all the way down to the stick and being incinerated in a puff of sugar-smelling diamond dust. This is what *that* thing in the mirror did to women and men who might otherwise be perfectly sane had they not existed on the same planet at the same time to have their Sunday Schooled lives kicked into sweet chaos of 'fuck me!' and 'screw you!'

'Fuck!'

He said it again. Fuck and double-fuck for a double-fuck face. Just to know *his* was *that* face, to know *he* was *that* thing. That fuck-times-a-thousand thing. The thing called Elvis Presley.

'Elvis?'

The voice belonged to another man reflected further back in the mirror standing by the dressing room door. He was wearing smart jeans and a sweater with a loose kerchief tied around his neck, ears jutting through thick dark brown hair with square-shaped sideburns, his eyes and chin vibrating a quiet self-assuredness.

A young woman holding a powder brush stood between them, just behind Elvis, who remained motionless in front of the mirror watching the rivulets of molten caramel trickling down his forehead. The other man spoke to her. 'You'd better leave us alone.' She smiled, nodded an unspoken 'OK', lay her brush down on the table next to Elvis and left, quietly closing the door on heavy silence.

Elvis and the other man stared at one another in the mirror, saying nothing, exchanging glances slowly edging towards a conversation. The other man arrived there first.

'Joe said you wanted to see me.'

Elvis nodded but when he tried to speak the words dried up and blew away like sand. 'Steve, I…'

Steve, the other man, suspected this might happen. That at this precise minute, of this hour, of this day of all days, he could find himself called to Elvis' dressing room and be met with 'Steve, I…' sentences evaporating into nothing.

Elvis turned his chair around away from the mirror to face Steve. His body now said what his mouth couldn't. Molasses and caramel melted as one in a flesh and leather cascade of panic; to see him sweat was to see a fudge sundae in a rainstorm. His chest heaved to the tempo of tight breaths pulsing under his jacket. He rubbed his palms back and forth against his leather-holstered thighs, his right leg locked in a violent tremble like a patient in the first block-biting flick of electroshock.

'Steve, I…'

Another one crumbled. He tried again.

'I… can't.'

Elvis shook his head.

'I *can't*,' he repeated, clinging to the word like a handrail saving him from being swept overboard. 'I can't do it.'

Steve said 'what do you mean?' though he knew what he meant.

'I can't go out there, man,' said Elvis, clinging firm. 'I can't.'

It took an effort his tone never betrayed for Steve to sound as calm as he did. 'You can,' he said. 'You can, Elvis. You *know* you can. I've *seen* you can. Everything we've rehearsed. Everything you've been doing all week. You *can*.'

'But an audience, man. An *audience*. What if they don't like me? What then?'

Elvis stood up from his chair, clenching and unclenching his fists, pacing back and forth in a slither of sweat and gloss.

'It's been so long. Too long. I… I don't know what to say. I don't know what to do.'

Steve's effort cracked. '*Elvis*,' he sighed, pinching the bridge of his nose and closing his eyes. When he opened them again Elvis was stood right in front of him. He tried to begin again.

'Elvis…'

It was Elvis all right. *The* Elvis, *that* Elvis, inches from his face. Never in his life had he looked more lickable a caramel prince. There was nothing 'can't' about that face. It was a 'can' face capable of anything and everything, conceivably the face of God, in wicked schoolgirl dream or messianic reality, in flesh or in caramel, if even just the once God literally *did* make man in his own image. And since God could have chosen any face he wanted you'd surely have to question the wisdom of any God who, given the choice, chose not to look like Elvis Presley.

'Elvis,' Steve repeated, 'what you do is you go out there and you start by saying "hello". And then if you have to, you say "goodbye" and then you leave and you walk right back in here.'

Steve jabbed a finger towards the door.

'But you're going out there, Elvis. Don't you back out. Not now. Don't bail out on me, man. You've *got* to do this.'

Elvis skittered back to the mirror, leaning both palms flat on the dressing table, his elbows stiff, his arms rigid. He dropped his chin to his chest, crunching his eyelids, his nostrils flaring, deep breaths forcing his jacket to rise and fall like giant bellows.

Steve walked over behind him, placing a light hand on his shoulder.

'Elvis,' he said softly. 'Do you remember what I said to you that day you first came to my office?'

Elvis listened, his head still down, his eyes still closed.

'You asked me about your career. And I told you. I told you straight. I told you your career was in the toilet…'

Elvis opened his eyes, the mirror bouncing their truest blue light at Steve.

'... And you remember what you told me? You said to me you wanted to show people what you can really do. Those were your exact words. "What I can *really* do." You remember?'

Elvis remembered, lifting and dipping his chin enough for it to count as a nod.

'Out there,' Steve pointed at the door, 'there are people waiting to see Elvis Presley. Waiting to see *what you can really do*. And TV cameras, so the whole world can see *what you can really do*.'

Elvis turned his truest blues on himself.

'So it's your choice. You go out there and show them. What you can really do. *Who* you really are.'

Blue burning blue, diamonds and warm sugar.

'Or you don't. You stay here. You stay in the toilet.'

A pin missed its moment to drop.

'It's up to you, Elvis.'

Elvis shut his eyes, his mind spinning the dial of its crystal transistor. Scrawling through amphetamine sulphate and etchlor-vynol, shortwave, longwave, for the faintest fog of scripture, for just a crackle of Matthew, a hiss of Mark or Luke.

A voice in the static. John. Chapter 11. Verse 25.

'I am the resurrection and I am the life...'

Show the world *what* he can really do.

'... he that believeth in me, though he were dead...'

Show the world *who* he really is.

'... yet he shall live.'

Elvis opened his eyes and saw the double-fuck face of God staring back in the mirror.

Steve patted him on the shoulder. 'Good luck.'

Elvis' eyes stayed fixed on the dressing room door long after Steve had walked out closing it behind him. Minutes became eternities.

Then Elvis stood up straight, taking a last look in the mirror, turned and walked towards the door. Towards a live audience and television cameras. Towards the valley of the shadow of death. Towards fate, towards destiny, towards tomorrow.

Towards all that separated the world from being reminded of the fuck-times-a-thousand beautiful truth of Elvis Presley.

MARCH 26, 1960

He walked through the dressing room door, along the corridor, towards the stage, towards the television cameras, towards his feverish audience, with the dead legs of a man dragging the last mile to Old Sparky.

The dressing room had been his condemned cell, clock-watching every second that brought him closer to his hour of execution. In place of a priest he'd had 'Diamond Joe': Joe Esposito of Italian blood and Chicagoan heart. Normally, he could count on Joe to crack him up with Windy City tales of dating mob bosses' daughters, or shared memories of their wild nights together in Paris with Lido dancers, ice-skating redheads, and their favourite punchline about the time their buddy Lamar mistakenly chatted up a drag queen.

'She had a bigger one than Lamar's.'

But not tonight. Joe thought he knew every nuance of Elvis' many moods, the trademark twitches and restless hands, the way he'd sit with knees crossed, one foot tapping the ground, the other hanging trembling in mid-air. But this was a whole new human shipwreck. It was the awful silence that was hardest to bear. Joe tried his best but couldn't get Elvis to say anything any more. He was past speech. He was almost past life itself.

The last vapours of hope finally evaporated at 6.15 pm. Time for the dead man to take his position behind the stage. Unsteady bloodless steps found their marker on the floor behind a partition door. From the other side he could hear a band in full swing and people singing. Elvis stood and waited, heart smashing against his ribs like a barn door in a gale.

'Look and see who's comin'!'

He screwed his eyes shut, trying to suck some breath into his lungs. The partition suddenly pulled upwards, exposing him to harpoons of bright light and shrill screams.

'There he is!'

There he was. Elvis Presley.

No. It couldn't be. Not *the* Elvis Presley.

That was unmistakably someone, some-*thing* else...

THE THING

The thing called Elvis Presley had blown up over 70 million American homes in the Great Cathode Ray Apocalypse of 1956. A white-hot fireball of thermonuclear sex, joy and abandon, turning the same television screen that once framed Lassie, Lucille Ball and The Lone Ranger into a weapon of mass destruction.

The impact was devastating, the debris divine.

Hymens snapped between the legs of girls who'd never been taught they owned one, their bodies newly alive with an urgent electric hunger and a revolution begun.

The cookie-cut American housewife, too, flushed and moaned as her uterus flopped from under her apron to slide screenwards across the carpet, past the slippers of her husband now purple with shame that his sorry conjugal flappings had finally been exposed by the air-humping sonnets of this Brylcreemed Byron.

Boys, at first bewildered by these same alien spasms of hair, hips and cloth, quickly recognised the ultimate instruction manual, a holy lesson in frugging manhood they'd see through to its final exam on leatherette seats in a moonlit layby.

Between January '56 and January '57 the thing called Elvis Presley detonated a dozen times on American television. Few took notice of the first blast but by the sixth the Pentagon was on orange alert. The eighth, the one where he seemed to be trying to impregnate his microphone stand as he bucked and bawled about a hound dog, was Pearl Harbour II. In retaliation his ninth was counterattacked, Elvis ambushed into tuxedo and tails, forced to croon to a top-hatted basset hound. But by the twelfth he'd proven himself invincible to further humiliation, even as they tried to censor all commotion in his trousers by instructing the cameras to film him from the waist up. In torso, fingers and lips alone, the thing called Elvis Presley was the Rape of the Sabines in a velvet shirt.

He was sex, music and war. War on a straight white America that liked its women in the kitchen, its faggots in the jail and its niggers in the back of the bus. And as in any war, there were human casualties.

In Chicago, a gang of teenagers who didn't much care for Elvis Presley thought it would be funny to make an effigy from rags and newspapers and hang it from a lamppost. The laughter only stopped when the 14-year-old boy assigned to do the hanging was fatally electrocuted by 5000 volts.

In Redwood, California, a 15-year-old girl got into an argument about Elvis with her foster-brother. She told him she thought Elvis was a joke and he was a joke for liking him. The foster-brother settled their differences by bashing her brains out with a softball bat.

The first time Elvis played Jacksonville, Florida, he told the 14,000-strong crowd 'Girls, I'll see you backstage' and, taking him literally, they scuttled like soldier ants through an open dressing room window to claw every stitch from his body. Jacksonville was slow to learn its lesson until his third visit the following year when a local judge sat through the concert to ensure his popping-corn pelvis behaved itself. His pelvis obliged, Elvis instead transferring all lusty impulses to flex of phalange and metacarpal in his little finger. And still the women of Jacksonville went berserk.

That was the thing called Elvis Presley. 'Elvis the Pelvis.' 'The King of Rock 'n' Roll.' The creature from outer space sent to realign the thermostat of America's sanity.

But if *that* was Elvis then who – or *what* – was that thing stood on stage in Miami?

MIAMI

The thing that definitely wasn't Elvis Presley staggered forth toward the television camera pointing centre stage of the Grand Ballroom in the Fontainebleau Hotel, Miami Beach, exactly three years, two months and 20 days since the thing that definitely *was* Elvis Presley last appeared before a television camera.

Where there should have been a liquorice quiff there was a yellow-trimmed peaked cap scrunched tight to his brow. Where there should have been sideburns there were none. Where there should have been truest blue lasers there were dim flashlights. Where there should have been a velvet shirt with an upturned collar and loose Lansky's pants there was a starched U.S. Army sergeant's uniform, buttoned collar and tie. Where his body should have rippled like quicksilver it lurched like Frankenstein's monster taking its first faltering steps off the gurney, bloodless arms clumsily swinging by his sides.

This was not Elvis Presley. This was his cadaver laid out in the wrong clothes. A confused zombie in military dress.

The life-force, the magic, the caramel God-faced fuck-times-a-thousand Elvispresleyness had been bled out of him. But it was more than the face, the clothes and the stance. It was the whole scene.

The scene was Elvis, in parade dress, beside a reduced Rat Pack of Frank Sinatra, Sammy Davis Jr. and comedian Joey Bishop,

Frank's daughter Nancy mooning beside him in a cocktail dress and the sound of an orchestra meekly plinking through Frank's 'It's Nice To Go Trav'ling'. It was wrong, all of it, and it only got worse when the thing that couldn't possibly have been *the* Elvis Presley opened his mouth.

'It's very nice...'

The voice fell out like a dead body stuffed in a wardrobe. He only had 14 words to sing but in a kinder universe somebody would have shot him before the twelfth. The last two collapsed in a mumbled panic as he jerked a shoulder and girls in the audience screamed in what could easily have been mistaken for horror: the horror of seeing their once glorious Samson, scalped of his power, dragged in chains to be humiliated in the temple of tuxedoed Philistines.

Vibeless in Gaza.

53310761

The villainous Delilah who turned Elvis Presley into this sorry eunuch with a four-bar chevron wasn't a she but a they. The United States Army.

Within 30 days of turning 18 in January 1953, yet to share the beauty of his voice and visage with the outside world, as required by law Elvis registered with the Selective Service System, the military lottery that could see him drafted at any point between then and the age of 26. They waited until he was a 22-year-old millionaire to classify him 1A fit for service. With malice aforethought worthy of Delilah herself they served his call-up papers Christmas week of 1957. Hark, the herald angels wept.

He was finally inducted on March 24, 1958, the day Elvis Presley became just another shaven-headed schmuck in khaki. Private 53310761.

It killed his mother, Gladys Presley, who died just four months after an Army barber sheared off her baby's sideburns. Something of Elvis' that would never grow back died with her. Her middle name was Love and he'd know no greater. Without her the world was a television set suddenly without power and every day another lived in the reflection of its cold inanimate screen. In his unplugged grief he started to look for electricity elsewhere.

Six weeks after he first threw himself screaming upon his mother's grave the day of her funeral, they shipped him to

Germany. His father, his grandmother and two friends from Memphis went with him. He made other friends around the barracks. Some wore uniform, some wore skirts. Others came in bottles and jars. He'd found his trip switch.

After 18 months serving his time abroad, when Delilah had done her worst she sent him home with sergeant stripes, a dextroamphetamine sulphate addiction and a son's broken heart unhealed by tank manoeuvres and weekend passes whoring in Munich and Paris.

On the flight back his transit plane stopped to refuel at Prestwick Airport on the West Coast of Scotland. It would be the only time Elvis ever set foot on British soil. The blessed Scots made sure he'd always remember and the English would never forget. As he climbed from his aircraft he saw a girl screaming at him from behind a chain-link fence next to the runaway.

He shouted over to her. 'Where am I?'

She shouted back. 'I love you.'

Elvis had never been to I Love You Land before. It put a saltire twinkle in his truest blue eye.

From I Love You Land he flew straight on to New Jersey, touching down on American soil on Thursday, March 3, 1960. One of the first faces to greet him was that of Nancy Sinatra, waiting at the press conference in Fort Dix to present him with the gift of two nylon shirts. It was a goodwill gimmick to publicise his upcoming appearance on her father's network television show, the first by Elvis Presley newly returned from the Army, returned from Germany, the 'King of Rock 'n' Roll' back to reclaim his crown.

A reporter asked the obvious question that needed to be asked. *'Are you apprehensive, about what must be a comeback?'*

The word punctured his brain like a pickaxe. *Comeback.* It was the first time the whole journey home anyone had said it out loud. 'Yes,' Elvis wobbled. 'I am. I mean, I have my doubts…'

THE VOICE

He was coming back. Back home, back to music, back to television, back to the stage.

It was over two years since Elvis last sang live on stage. That was November 1957 at the Conroy Bowl in Schofield Barracks, Hawaii, before 10,000 military personnel and their families. He wore a gold lamé jacket and ended the show grinding the floor moaning about hound dogs and rabbits, the air thundering with hormones erupting in screams echoing all the way to the top of Mount Ka'ala. The local paper described him as a 'one-man hurricane'.

Schofield Barracks survived Hurricane Elvis just as it had survived two Pearl Harbours, the real one back in '41 and the fake one cooked up by a Hollywood crew who'd invaded the base a few years earlier to shoot *From Here To Eternity*. The film won Best Picture of 1953, scooping seven other Academy Awards including Best Supporting Actor, a coup all the more remarkable since the man who won it was, by vocation, a singer. Though to call Frank Sinatra a singer was like calling Michelangelo a stone mason.

They called Frank 'the Voice' for reasons no one who heard his ever needed question. Back in the Forties he'd been the closest America experienced to a warning tremor for the thing called Elvis Presley. Young women in customised sweaters framing his name in cross-stitched love hearts, kissing the pages of any magazine bearing his bony portrait would queue for hours outside theatres so that, once inside, he could play their fallopian tubes like a pipe organ till they passed out. They formed fan clubs called 'The Slaves of Sinatra', 'Frankie's United Swooners' and 'The Society For Souls Suffering From Sinatraitis'. In October 1944 a mass gathering of 'Swoonatra' fans in New York led to what became known as the Columbus Day Riots as a locust plague of besotted bobby-soxers aching to glimpse their 'Swoon Boy' swarmed upon the Paramount Theatre off Times Square. Twenty police radio cars, four lieutenants, six sergeants, two captains, two assistant chief inspectors, 70 patrolmen, 50 traffic cops, 12 police on horseback, 20 policewomen, 200 detectives and 41 temporary police convened to try and stop them reducing the ticket office to matchsticks.

They failed.

Experts in the field of psychology, psychiatry and psycho-pathology attempted to explain why the Voice affected women this way.

They concluded as follows:

'A simple and familiar combination of escapism and substitution, to be expected in times of high emotional stress.'

Because women were victims of wartime fantasy.

'Mass frustrated love, without direction.'

Because women were sex-starved and desperate.

'Mass hysteria.'

Because women were crazy.

'Mass hypnotism.'

Because women were weak-willed.

'Increased emotional sensitivity due to mammary hyperesthesia.'

Because women had tender chests and men didn't.

The Voice shook the bottle of American adolescence in the Forties ready for the Pelvis to explode in the Fifties and should, perhaps, have looked upon Elvis as a worthy heir had his ears only been able to attune to a style of music he'd describe as 'a rancid smelling aphrodisiac'. Frank never criticised Elvis by name, only in euphemistic slur of rock 'n' roll's 'cretinous goons' and 'sideburned delinquents'.

The press baited Elvis to react. 'I wouldn't knock Frank Sinatra,' he said, refusing to bite. 'I like him very much. If I remember correctly, he was also part of a trend, just like rock 'n' roll.'

But all that was back in 1957. Before Elvis became Uncle Sam-sucking Private 53310761. And before the first run of ABC's *Frank Sinatra Show* was cancelled due to such poor ratings they had to replace it with a gameshow about telepathy hosted by Vincent Price.

In 1959 the network gave Frank another chance, commissioning four one-hour specials to be broadcast every couple of months, branded by its watch-manufacturing sponsor as *The Frank Sinatra Timex Show*. By the third episode Vincent Price was being tipped off by his agent to start dusting down his old host's jacket and patter. Faced with yet another small screen flop, with one show left Frank's ego needed a dramatic ratings spike.

For a mouthful of cretinous-goon-flavoured humble pie and a king's ransom of $125,000, he'd get it.

PEACHES

Having murdered his opening line and despite looking anything but, the thing that was supposed to be Elvis Presley stalked off the stage of the Fontainebleau Hotel Grand Ballroom in his sergeant's uniform mobbed, as had been rehearsed, by Nancy, the dancing girls and Sammy Davis Jr. squeaking, 'Elvis, can I have your autograph please?'

He returned some 40 minutes later for the finale of the show looking no more reassuring a conquering King of Rock 'n' Roll in supper club tuxedo and tie, though his quiff, tall as a centurion's crest and the colour of Texas tea, had since made a bid for freedom raising faint hopes the thing called Elvis Presley as the world had once known might yet be dangling somewhere beneath.

He began by pining *'faay-mun forchin''*, silky doo wop ballad 'Fame And Fortune', then a strictly first gear swinger called 'Stuck On You' that didn't jump any red lights but caused havoc enough for a pile-up of girlish screams.

Six days earlier his record label, RCA Victor, had frogmarched him to their studio in Nashville where he recorded both songs for his first post-Army single. They'd already advance-printed over a million sleeves promising 'ELVIS' 1ST NEW RECORDING FOR HIS 50,000,000 FANS ALL OVER THE WORLD' without knowing for certain what he was actually going to sing on the day. The product and the packaging came first: the content, an obligatory after-thought.

To RCA Victor – the Radio Corporation of America incorporating what used to be the Victor Talking Machine Company, as symbolised by a terrier called Nipper cocking its head into a blunderbuss gramophone horn – Elvis Presley was canned peaches.

Though they liked canned peaches, or at least pretended to, they cared less about the taste of the peaches than the label on the can, and less about either than selling canned peaches to 50 million non-discerning canned peach fans all over the world. Their biggest fear was that having not canned any peaches in two years, the thing called Elvis Presley wouldn't taste the same or that the people who once loved canned peaches might, in the interim, have since decided they preferred canned pineapple. Which is why out of the six songs Elvis recorded that first session it was they, the label, who chose 'Stuck On You' as just peachy enough to be canned as his comeback single; choosing with the deaf ears of capitalism that heard neither words nor music, only the atonal *'ching!'* of the cash register.

Elvis himself wasn't nearly so keen on the song, hearing it for what it was: two minutes and 17 seconds punching sandbags in the gym where he should have been back breaking ribs in the ring. He didn't *feel* for 'Stuck On You' because 'Stuck On You' didn't have *feel*.

Feel was a gift, not so unique as to be a mark of genius but a shining rare enough that, used intuitively, it could become so. There've been plenty of people who could write algebraic formula but there was only ever one Einstein. Plenty of people have musical feel, but there was only ever one Elvis.

Feel was something as old as the first caveman thwack of bone on bone, an ancient voodoo haunting humanity since the dawn of time from campfire to temple to cotton-field to pew to slum to cellblock to juke-joint.

Feel first found Elvis as a young boy glory-hallelujahin' Pentecostal seizures in his local church in Tupelo, a city in Northeast Mississippi whipped by twisters and belted by Bibles. He was born there in a two-room shack, a Tuesday's child full of grace on January 8, 1935, delivered 35 minutes after his dead twin. The brother was named Jesse Garon and buried in an unmarked grave.

Elvis grew up forever wondering what would have happened had Jesse lived: whether Jesse would be exactly like him; whether God called the wrong twin home and it should have been Jesse's lower regions flabbergasting Ed Sullivan's cameras; or whether if both had lived they'd each be only half the person Elvis became as maybe he'd stolen double the life-force. Double the feel.

Outside of church, it didn't take the boy Elvis long to discover God didn't have all the best tunes. All it took was to place a curious ear to the ground and hear the S.O.S. tapping from the wrong side of Tupelo's tracks, to the woe-cussin' and ma-babin', the gut-pickin' and liquor-moanin', the bessie-wailin' and belly-leadin' thumping from Shake Rag.

To the city's middle-class white folks frowning on anything with feel from the jitterbug to Swoonatra, Shake Rag was *no-go niggertown*, a pimp and bootlegger's ghetto echo of its first freed slave settlers after the Civil War. To Elvis, too poor to know no-go, not white enough to call another man 'nigger', Shake Rag was the Promised Land, baptising him with the genie of rhythm and blues and a life's vocation to become its lamp. The day would come before the century was through when civic developers would raze Shake Rag to the dust of memory. But in the voice and feel of Elvis, a rub of the lamp, Shake Rag would stand for all eternity.

Feel was vital in the days when records were cut live in the studio, the singer and the musicians working as one trying to make each take *the* take good enough to release to the public. Elvis spent one summer evening of '56 in a New York studio recording 'Hound Dog' 31 times. The producer was happy by take 15. It was Elvis, aged 21, following the instinct of feel, waiting for 'Alakazam!' of Shake Rag, who demanded they keep going. He was proved right. The 31st take, the one with the feel he'd striven for, was the million-seller.

There was an old showbiz saying that Bing Crosby was the first to sing *at* you but Frank, the Voice, was the first to sing *to* you. Elvis, the Pelvis, was the first to sing *in* you, mamboing the loins, choir-mastering the pulse and crescendoing symphonies in every heartbeat. The same mystic power Michelangelo held in his hands, Elvis held in his windpipe. A power nobody should have been allowed to put a price on. But for the love of the *'ching!'* they did.

'Stuck On You' reached number one in the American singles chart in late April 1960 and stayed there for four weeks. It was only the beginning of the Sixties.

People hadn't yet grown sick of canned peaches.

THE PATSY

By the end of 'Stuck On You' the thing on stage at the Fontainebleau Grand Ballroom, Miami Beach, was beginning to move as if he really *were* Elvis Presley, if an Elvis Presley awakening from heavy anaesthetic after a traffic accident; staring at the hands in front of his face as if he still weren't sure they were actually his hands; stretching his limbs and bucking his hips to check nothing vital was broken. The girls in the audience encouraged his muscle memory, each shriek vibrating pelvic atoms from their two year slumber until by the end, his right arm cocked in a lightning rod to heaven, even in a tuxedo he looked just Elvis Presley enough.

Frank and comedian Joey Bishop walked on stage to join him. 'I'm glad to see the Army hasn't changed you,' said Frank. It was one of the first Great Lies of the 1960s.

'Elvis, excuse me sir,' Joey interrupted. 'Mr Presley, would you think it presumptuous of Frank to join you in a duet?'

'Yeah, that'd be great,' Frank franked.

'I would consider it quite an honour,' Elvis gee-shucked.

The Voice and the Pelvis, the two greatest singers of the 20th century, together on the same stage. Between them they could have sung Sputniks crashing down into the Atlantic. But instead, for one night only, the Voice and the Pelvis momentarily forgot they were gods to become the Shtick and the Patsy.

The song, a medley, was brief, if not brief enough. Frank – the Shtick – made insincere chumpery of Elvis' 'Love Me Tender'. Simultaneously, Elvis – the Patsy – turned Frank's 'Witchcraft' into spastic pantomime.

When it was over they stayed patting backs at the scene of their crime while Frank beckoned his daughter over to join them.

Ever since Nancy showed up at Fort Dix to welcome Elvis home with two nylon shirts the press had circulated rumours she and he were a couple, even though she was officially engaged to singer Tommy Sands. On stage in Miami, Frank attempted to make a joke of it.

'Nancy, you've met Mr Presley, haven't you?'

'Of course,' smiled Nancy. 'How are you, Mr Presley?'

'Aw, you can call me Elvis,' awed Elvis.

Frank's punchline was a 14 pound ham. 'You can call him Mr Presley on account of she's been spoken for!'

Elvis hammed back. 'That's the way the cookie crumbles,' he shrugged, sloping away in another surf of screams.

Nancy married Tommy Sands six months later in Las Vegas. The rumours weren't true. Elvis wasn't sleeping with Frank's daughter. Though in a matter of weeks he would be with Frank's soon-to-be fiancée.

HOLLYWOOD

She liked it lying on her back, spreading her legs wide, clenching both ankles, braced like a shock absorber. That's what Elvis told his buddies about Juliet Prowse.

Juliet was a dancer foremost, an actress lastmost, but Frank's girl utmost. Frank said she was 'the sexiest dancer I've ever seen.' Elvis said she 'had a body that would make a bishop stamp his foot through a stained-glass window' and saw more of it than Frank would have preferred.

It's likely Elvis and Juliet would never have crossed paths had she not been cast as the female lead in his first post-Army feature film, with some reluctance from its director who complained she was 'gawky'. It was true Juliet had a mouth wide enough to wrap around a watermelon and teeth that threatened to flee her gums whenever she opened it. But her gawkiness wasn't the film's only problem.

The director, Norman Taurog, was another. Members of his own extended family sometimes called him 'that fat Jew bastard.' Unfairly so: there were far bigger, fatter and Jewier bastards in Hollywood.

The problem with Norman wasn't that he was a bad director, just the wrong director to be shouting 'Action!' anywhere in the vicinity of Elvis Presley. Norman, slowly going blind at 61, had been born at the end of the 19th century with no better an innate understanding of rock 'n' roll than Little Richard knew how to hail a hansom cab. The film was thus doomed, but not merely because of Norman's cobwebbed vision and Juliet's refugee teeth. It was doomed the moment its palest germ of a bad idea first popped into artless heads whose ears pricked only for the cold echo of *'ching!'* and whose eyes were blind to all but sales charts, account ledgers and receipts for canned peaches; who could count on one hand the number of films Elvis had already made before the Army but not, on the other, the reasons why nearly all four had worked.

The first had worked least. It was a period Western set at the end of the Civil War and should probably have stayed that way without any Elvis. But, as his trial debut feature, it was decided to crowbar him into the cast to jiggle his pants as nobody ever would have in 1865. Elvis was naive enough to think he wouldn't have to sing in *The Reno Brothers* which, once he'd been made to pluck a guitar and pucker his lips, they renamed after its soppiest ballad, *Love Me Tender*.

The die was cast and would never be remodelled. From that day forth the movie career of the thing called Elvis Presley became solely an exercise in merchandising. The film: the billboard advertising the record. The record: the bumper sticker advertising the film. 'Love Me Tender', the song, became Elvis' third number one single. *Love Me Tender*, the film, took over $4 million at the box office, recouping over three times its budget. Celluloid or vinylite. It was all just canned peaches.

Elvis' one consolation in *Love Me Tender* was its opportunity to press his lips against those of his fantasy screen goddess. Debra Paget was five feet two inches of foaming fox musk whose saucy attitudes in *Princess Of The Nile* reduced men to maggots squirming in flip-velvet seats. Elvis called her 'the most beautiful girl in the world' and though the only kisses they shared were those on screen, her face left a permanent imprint in his thoughts, bewitching him like a primordial echo of Adam's first sight of Eve. Whenever Debra Paget's echo sounded in the eyes, lips and bone structure of another woman's face, however faint, Elvis was instantly enslaved.

This would have huge and terrible consequences.

His second film, *Loving You*, was the first anyone could properly call 'an Elvis Presley film' with rock 'n' roll music and a star who was recognisably the same star they'd seen lassoing his hips on television now doing the same twenty times larger in glorious VistaVision. This time he had the advantage of credibility, playing a Southern rock 'n' roll singer much like himself in a rags-to-riches yarn winking to the cheap seats as his 'Deke Rivers' complains of being sold 'like a monkey in a zoo.' The plot was a cartoon but that didn't matter when the songs were sublime, which they mostly were in *Loving You*. Never did Elvis sound more shamanistic a sex prophet than his jiving Kemosabe: *'Anda no-wonna hoo-drada doo-it widda hanna-yoo.'* (In white man's tongue: *'And there's no one who I'd rather do it with than you.'*)

The next, *Jailhouse Rock*, was a similar fairy tale about the path to pop stardom with the twist of having Elvis' character discovering his talent while doing time for manslaughter. It was as stupidly perfect and perfectly stupid a rock 'n' roll musical as Fifties Hollywood ever made and its title song, taking institutionalised sodomy to the top of the American singles chart, a masterpiece.

His fourth, *King Creole*, was Elvis' personal favourite. Like its immediate predecessors it, too, was about a young rock 'n' roll singer, though set against a much grittier New Orleans nightclub world of gangsters, teenage thugs, thieves and hookers.

The script was adapted from a Harold Robbins novel about a young boxer, *A Stone For Danny Fisher*, the rights originally bought with James Dean in mind. Elvis adored Dean, who'd died in a car crash in September 1955: nine months before he'd recorded 'Hound Dog', an anomaly that didn't stop at least one biographer printing the chronologically impossible myth that the neurotic young actor used to enjoy randomly ringing people up to play Elvis' hit down the phone at full volume. Elvis called Dean 'a genius' and had watched his *Rebel Without A Cause* so many times he could recite whole scenes. Since arriving in Hollywood he'd also made friends with Dean's *Rebel* co-star, Nick Adams, and briefly dated his *Rebel* love interest, Natalie Wood, the only woman in the history of bed linen to claim Elvis Presley couldn't satisfy her. Possibly because of it, he nicknamed her 'Mad Nat'.

The role of Danny Fisher was as close as Elvis had ever gotten, and ever would get, to the Jimmy Dean of *Rebel Without A Cause*. The sort of young man who'd give a prostitute a goodnight kiss in broad daylight outside the school gates then punch the first kid dumb enough to tease him about it. Had Dean the voice and *Rebel* been a musical it couldn't have been blessed with a better signature tune than the one the 'Hound Dog' and 'Jailhouse Rock' duo of Jerry Leiber and Mike Stoller wrote for Elvis' first big club scene.

'If you're looking for trouble – you came to the right place.'

Except that in *Rebel*, Dean had waltzed from knife fights to chicken runs upon the strings of Leonard Rosenman, just as Brando in *The Wild One* had frothed his beer bottle in a twangless vacuum of jazz. *King Creole* was the right teenage delinquent film with the right music, even a song called 'Crawfish' which from Elvis' lips sounded about something infinitely more pleasurable than eating fried shrimp.

It was also the first film where critics had to concede that Elvis was capable of more than yodelling *'hanna-yoo'* in flashy trousers. 'Cut my legs off and call me shorty!' exclaimed the *New York Times*, 'Elvis Presley can act.' The secret was out. But the bottom line of *King Creole*, his last before the Army, was still the sum of its songs, just as it had been in *Loving You* and *Jailhouse Rock*. The maths was simple. If you have good songs, you have a good Elvis Presley film.

It was the one golden rule everyone in Hollywood with any stake in any film starring Elvis Presley forgot the moment he returned from the barracks to the backlot.

HELLYWOOD

The canned peach salesmen had sealed his fate even before his military transport plane had left German tarmac. The return to Hollywood they'd mapped out for him was at the forefront of his mind the whole journey home, although when asked by the press he seemed unclear about the details. He knew they'd signed him up for at least another three films but seemed convinced 'they won't be the rock 'n' roll type I've featured in so far'. He also said he wanted 'to branch out and do something serious.' He used the word 'serious' a lot when discussing his acting ambitions. When a woman reporter asked if by that he'd meant maybe *Hamlet* he chuckled, 'no, ma'am, I know my limitations.'

His limitations would be immediately tested on his first film after the Army, the one with Frank's gawky girl, Juliet, as directed by Norman's 19th century eye. Not the limitations above Elvis, but those so far beneath him he'd yet to discover his spine could scrunch so low.

Since he'd spent the last two years as an American soldier in Germany, with paraplegic leap of imagination it was decided his first film after returning should be about an American soldier in Germany. It was 'art' imitating life though there were moments of existential crisis when Elvis wondered whether it wasn't the other way around – that his 700 days' cruel endurance as Private 53310761 hadn't all been one long elaborate publicity stunt to justify over 100 minutes of Technicolor horseshit called *G.I. Blues*.

Elvis had no say in the script or the songs and so, hamstrung by his contractual obligations to the peach-canners who'd put him there, did the best he could with the worst they had to offer. That included having to sing a song about ants ruining a picnic, another to glove puppets accompanied by oompah organ, and a scene where he had to wrestle a liverwurst sandwich from the clutches of a new-born baby.

The grotesque plot involved a sideburnless Elvis as khaki fool Tulsa McLean accepting a platoon bet that he can't spend the night with a notoriously aloof nightclub dancer played by Juliet, understudied by her teeth. Thus at its moral core *G.I. Blues* was a film about money and prostitution, so riddled with self-mutilating irony it had a scene in a bierkeller where the impostor Elvis, Tulsa, starts a fight with a soldier who attempts to drown out his singing with the real Elvis grunting 'Blue Suede Shoes' on a jukebox. The King eats himself and the Earth dies screaming.

Trailer trembles with Juliet helped take his mind off the daily humiliation on set. The evenings she didn't join Elvis in his sixth floor suite at the Beverly Wilshire Hotel he spent trying to chop wooden boards with his bare hands: the ancient martial art of karate, a new obsession entailing endless pain, cuts, bruises and occasional fractured carpals. The horror of *G.I. Blues* had driven its star to sadomasochism.

The small posse of friends he'd invited to lodge alongside him at the Wilshire could also entertain him with juvenile water fights, or drive him out to the Crossbow Inn, a favourite nightspot over the hill in Panorama City where Elvis kept one eye on the owner's teenage daughter, the other on Louisiana singer Lance LeGault whose house band, Lance & the Dynamics, paid homage to their guest of honour with deferential howls through 'Hound Dog'. Elvis was touched, but equally tormented having spent the day top-buttoned under tungsten lights singing about hasenpfeffer. But then he always had his blues to fight the blues. And pinks, and reds, and yellows, and whites, and greens, and blacks.

And he always had the Girl In Germany to talk to. The one the press had photographed waving him off from Rhine-Main air base. The one who Elvis had to be careful not to talk about in public because she was 14 years old. The one he called 'Little One' who'd speared his Achilles heel with her vague but fatal resemblance to Debra Paget, who he now rang up long distance to spill his guts about how much he hated *G.I. Blues*. That he'd already been paid and was 'locked into this thing' only to realise, as he told her, 'it's a joke.'

He was still under the joke's lock and key the night of Thursday May 12 when ABC finally aired the *Frank Sinatra Timex Show* he'd filmed over six weeks ago. Elvis watched it in his suite at the Beverly Wilshire, grimacing at his awkward entrance in sergeant stripes before it cut to a word from its sponsor, filmed at Florida's Marineland, featuring a porpoise called Nellie made to leap over obstacles in a pool while carrying a Timex watch in her mouth to demonstrate its amazing waterproof durability.

Elvis gazed through eyes of fizzing Dexamyl blue, transfixed by the sad spectacle of an intelligent creature forced to perform degrading tasks in order to make others' money. Seeing himself then the porpoise, seeing the porpoise then himself, until he no longer knew which was which.

PSYCHO

Every performing animal has its trainer, every peach factory its foreman, every prison its gaoler.

The fiend who held the keys to the cell of Elvis Presley was his personal manager. A crooked-lipped Humpty Dumpty with a patty of pork mince for a head, asphalt for eyes, a medieval torture device for a brain, a stack of casino chips for a heart and blood of ice cold piss he wouldn't spill to save a burning orphanage.

He called himself Colonel Thomas A. (for Andrew) Parker of West Virginia. He wasn't a real Colonel, nor a real Tom, nor an actual Parker, nor born in West Virginia but approximately 4000 miles away in Breda, a fortress town in the Netherlands.

His real name was Andreas Cornelis van Kuijk, an anatomical pack of lies schooled by the masters of hypocrisy, greed and ritual humiliation, the Catholic Church. Further enlightenment came from the travelling fairground and the sermons of its gypsies, fortune tellers, illusionists, sharpies, flimflammers, animal trainers and every known permutation of sucker-fleecer who convinced young Andreas the only gateway to Paradise was the con and the only God its rewards of silver.

Reaching adulthood, he was sent away to live with his uncle in the port of Rotterdam when he very suddenly and very mysteriously vanished. Weeks passed before his family received an explanatory letter that he'd somehow stowed away to America and was now lodging with another Dutch family in New Jersey. Then just as suddenly, just as mysteriously, Andreas returned home to the Netherlands, only to abscond to America yet again. The second time he never came back.

Nobody knew why he left, or whether it had anything to do with the murder of a local greengrocer's wife the night he disappeared. The crime was never solved, hindered by the fact that the body had been deliberately surrounded by pepper to confuse police dogs from following any scent. The sort of trick a killer might have picked up had they, like Andreas, spent any time training animals in travelling fairgrounds.

As an illegal Dutch immigrant he tried hustling a living in carnivals and holy-rolling Chautauquas until poverty, desperation and the promise of bed and board forced his chinless blubber into the United States Army. How he managed to enlist without betraying his alien status, or why he settled on the specific alias of 'Thomas Andrew Parker' would remain two of his better closeted skeletons. In doing so he'd erase Andreas Cornelis van Kuijk from history in a single stroke of ink. A perfect murder: possibly not his first.

Private Parker made a poor soldier, crazy enough to desert and crazier still to surrender himself after five months running away with a circus in Florida. His punishment was two months solitary confinement. When they opened his cell door at the end of it the Army realised, as he had after 60 days of only his own company, that Private Parker was certifiably insane. In the assessment of the military doctor who placed him on an observation ward for another two months – a 'constitutional psychopathic.'

They trolleyed him on to a federal lunatic asylum in Washington D.C. The nuthouse eventually spat him back out to civvy street. Tom Parker was discharged as too emotionally unstable for Uncle Sam, but just about sane enough for Joe Public. This, the same man who one day would refuse to allow Elvis the comfort of the Special Services entertainment branch, insisting he serve two full years of misery and depression overseas in the United States Army.

A deserter. An illegal alien. A constitutional psychopath.

It was the Psycho, Tom Parker, who first made canned peaches of Elvis Presley.

The Psycho, who made him a star and having made him a star, bigger and brighter than any the record business had ever witnessed, sucked every cent from its sparkle like a nickel-fanged vampire.

The Psycho, who in 1956 signed a licensing deal with the same Hollywood merchandiser flogging branded tat for the Three Stooges and Lassie, so turning the thing called Elvis Presley into hats, t-shirts, blue jeans, scarves, bobby-sox, sneakers, skirts, blouses, belts, purses, billfolds, wallets, charm bracelets, necklaces, mittens, bookends, glow-in-the-dark statuettes, dancing dolls, monogrammed guitars, pencil sets, greeting cards, three-ring binders, suitcases, photo-albums, pillowcases, rings, crockery, table mats, glass tumblers, lockets, scrapbooks, a board game, portable typewriters and lipsticks available in six different colours including 'Tender Pink', 'Hound Dog Orange', 'Love Ya Fuchsia' and 'Tutti Frutti Red'.

The Psycho, who transformed himself into a human sandwich board, plus-sized clothes pasted with rosettes so he could parade the queues at Elvis' concerts in a trail of cigar smoke like a bloated choo-choo train, selling 'I Love Elvis' badges to the ones going inside and 'I Hate Elvis' badges to the ones jeering outside.

The Psycho, who, damning Elvis to the Army, merchandised dog tag bracelets, anklets and keychains, all embossed with his military serial number '53310761' and blood group, 'TYPE O'.

The Psycho, who some thought possibly controlled Elvis with hypnosis, not realising he needed no simpler, no more deadly, no more effective a power over him than the power of fear.

The fear in Elvis that he could slip back into the gutter of shoeless, squirrel-eating poverty he'd long escaped, knowing it was the Psycho's brokering with record labels, film studios and bottlers of 'Teddy Bear' *eau de parfum* that had given him the keys to his mansion and the Cadillacs in its driveway, the 24-hour maids in his kitchen skilleting egg, bacon and biscuit on demand at 5 am, the Noritake porcelain he ate off, the TVs in his bedroom, the crystal chandelier in his dining room, the sapphire on his finger and the amethyst in his tiepin. Fear of losing it all, as he'd feared he'd lost it all the moment he became Private Presley 53310761. Fear of becoming so poor he'd repeat the sins of his father, Vernon, who when a starving young man was sent to prison for forging a cheque, condemned to nine months of hard labour, buggery and the lash of 'Black Betty' that scarred him so bad he'd never remove his shirt in public. Fear of ghettoes, soup kitchens, alcoholism, tuberculosis and a pauper's grave.

Fear, and only fear, was how a constitutional psychopath from the Netherlands was able to imprison the will of a poor momma's boy from Mississippi.

MEMPHIS

One Mississippi winter's day in 1948 when Elvis was 13 years old, his family – being his mother Gladys, his father Vernon and the snuff-nosed grandma Elvis nicknamed 'Dodger' (Vernon's mother, Minnie Mae) – packed up their belongings into a green Plymouth sedan and took the highway northwest out of Tupelo bound for Memphis, Tennessee.

From the moment his feet first touched its sidewalk Elvis became a born again Memphian. He was Tupelo raised, but Memphis made. He'd never forget his birthplace, nor could he with his twin brother's bones rotting beneath its turf and the rumble of Shake Rag forever in his eardrums. But it was Memphis – the lockers of Humes High, the noise of Beale Street, the cut of Lansky's, the backrow of Loew's State Theatre and the wiggle of the waitresses at the Arcade restaurant – that taught him how to walk, dress, pose, pout, flip, flop and fly like the thing called Elvis Presley.

Memphis was home, and home was an eight-bedroom mock-colonial mansion in 14 acres of land on Highway 51 South. The estate was named 'Graceland' after its owner's daughter. Her niece's family built the house of the same name at the end of the Thirties. It became home to the Presleys in 1957 when Elvis bought it for a little over $100,000. Among the first things he installed were a kidney-shaped swimming pool and wrought iron entrance gates decorated with crotchets, double-quavers and his own guitar-strumming silhouette.

Elvis spent just one Christmas in Graceland with his mother before she died. The few weeks he'd managed to spend there since his return from the Army felt like living in her mausoleum. His counsellors fell into two categories: the ones that came in bottles and jars; and the ones who took from the same bottles and jars to keep pace with him.

They were his sentries, his wheels, his caddies, his linebackers, his fixers, his busboys and his jesters. They were the water balloons hurled down the corridors of the Beverly Wilshire, the out-of-hours call to the drugstore owner, the girl's chauffeur home, the flab between idol and autograph book, the midnight pizza and the knock on his trailer when alone with Juliet cry-wolfing 'Frank's coming!' They wore jeans when he wore jeans, black tie when he wore black tie, and sunglasses when he wore sunglasses, shielding their dilated pupils from the lights of Las Vegas where they'd spend regular weekends of chips, chicks and tricks. They did as he did, played when he played, ate when he ate and slept only when he slept. He was the cymbal, they its splash.

They jokingly called themselves 'El's Angels'. The press saw only a mob of misshapen hillbillies, bumpkin cousins to Frank's Rat Pack, and so flexing their alliterative wit christened them 'the Memphis Mafia'.

The West boys, both Memphis born, supplied the muscle. Robert 'Red' West, so-named because of his hair, had been Elvis' protector since high school. He also sang and played guitar but had since moved to Los Angeles to work as an extra and stuntman. Red's equally capable younger cousin Delbert West Jr., known as 'Sonny', had just been recruited that year to add some more Tennessee brawn.

Lamar Fike was a former disc jockey the size of a grain silo and looked a cross between a teddy bear and a dead Raymond Burr. Lamar and Red had been the two loyal friends and the only non-family members Elvis invited to live with him in Germany.

Alan Fortas met Elvis in 1957 through their mutual friend 'G.K. the D.J.', local disc jockey George Klein. Alan was a stocky Jewish kid with a fixed grin that seemed to stretch wider than the face supporting it. Elvis nicknamed him 'Hog Ears'.

Joe Esposito, alias 'Diamond Joe' from Chicago, met Elvis in Germany where he was serving in a different regiment. After their discharge Elvis hired him as his personal road manager, group foreman and proverbial right hand.

Charlie Hodge was a sweet-voiced munchkin from Alabama who'd enjoyed white gospel success with the Foggy River Boys before being drafted and sent to Germany. Elvis liked Charlie for his music. Charlie liked Elvis because he was Elvis and stuck to him like gum to a boot heel you couldn't shift with gelignite.

The Smiths, Elvis' cousins Gene and young Billy, were also part of the gang who kept Elvis entertained night and day, neither knowing nor caring which was which. Day could mean water-skiing on nearby McKellar Lake or endless games of touch football making sure that Elvis always won. Night could entail hiring out his favourite cinema, the Memphian, the Fairground Amusement Park or the Rainbow Rollerdrome, the staff working until whichever hour of the dawn he finally tired of *Ben-Hur*, Scrambler rides and boisterous skate-congas 'popping the whip'.

Fortified by the blues, pinks, reds, yellows, whites, greens and blacks, his playful angels – Red, Sonny, Lamar, Hog Ears, Joe, Charlie, cousins Gene and Billy – kept his body and mind from the Elsinore of grief and sin befallen Graceland.

His mother dead not two years, that first summer home Elvis' father remarried. He'd met Davada 'Dee' Stanley in Germany. Dee was nine years younger than Vernon, if ten years older than the famous son she'd tried to seduce first. Elvis hoped he'd suffered the last of their violent mating cries at his Goethestrasse home off base in Bad Nauheim. But now that the ink on her divorce was dry, Vernon was marrying Dee and inviting her and her three sons to live with him in Graceland, forcing Elvis to consider the same slutty moans travelling down the staircase his mother had trodden.

Elvis didn't attend their wedding in Alabama, pointedly staying at home in Memphis. The next day, his first as a stepson, he rode alone on his motorcycle to Forest Hill Cemetery where Gladys Presley laid to rest. There he dismounted next to her white marble cross, kneeled on the ground, stroked his fingers over her name and sobbed as if she'd just that moment died afresh in his arms.

PSYCHO (2)

With no friends, no prospects and an army severance cheque of just $117 to bail him out of the Depression, the Psycho, Tom Parker, gravitated back to the only things that had ever given him any happiness. Tent pegs, candy apples, bearded ladies, shrunken heads, strongmen, tarot cards, alligator boys, sword boxes, midget races, dancing ponies and the prospect of cheating smalltown chumps out of every filthy dime in their pocket.

Carnival life provided colours to paint upon the otherwise blank personality spat out by the army asylum, a pristine crib in which 'Tom Parker' could be born anew behind a griddle peddling the great Foot-Long Hot Dog scam. Two tiny pieces of sausage sticking out either end of a foot-long finger bun that was otherwise stuffed with cheap slaw and onions. If the mark ever came back to the stand to complain, the Psycho would point to a preplaced frankfurter in the dirt directly below the counter. The one they'd evidently dropped by accident.

Years after he'd robbed his last sucker of their weiner he was still bragging about the Foot-Long Hot Dog, usually when warming up to deliver his self-mythology's greatest hit.

'Tom Parker's Dancing Chickens.'

It worked best at a crowded meal table and better still if chicken was dish of the day. He'd begin by describing how he rigged an electric hotplate hidden with a thin covering of straw inside a cage with a half dozen hens. A waiting audience would watch as the cage was wheeled out to the old folk song 'Turkey In The Straw'. Parker would flick the secret switch and in the intermittent agony the birds would start hopping in an aimless frenzy, seemingly 'dancing'. He finished by explaining how he started each week with six chickens but usually ended it with only one. 'Well,' he'd chomp, drumstick in hand. 'A fella's gotta eat.'

There never were any dancing chickens. But he told the story so often, enough people believed it. He wanted them to believe it. Not just because it was bullshit, and he the Bard of Bullshit, but because it was the lie that in its fabricated cruelty, cunning, greed and inhumanity somehow told the truth about the psychopath Tom Parker.

His soul was married to the con, but his body, needing hot meals and clean shirts, decided it should marry a woman. Like seeing like, he took for his bride a con artist.

Marie Mott was in uneven portions a kleptomaniac, a grifter, a mother and a divorcee. She also knew how to woo a psycho. They made courtship of defrauding the bereaved, travelling town to town with a box of beat-up Bibles, checking the local obituary notices then turning up on the doorstep of the grieving widow or widower demanding outstanding payment for the deluxe new Good Book the deceased 'had ordered' shortly before they passed away.

It was love at first scam.

Until he met Marie Mott, Tom Parker had shown little interest in sex. Like music, clothes and honest living it was something absent from the chemical composition of his DNA. Whether the Psycho and his swindling bride ever actually consummated the marriage was anyone's guess. Those who got to know the couple guessed not.

THERE'S NO TOMORROW

The Psycho's wife had a favourite song and it was the Psycho's wish that Elvis should sing it. 'Are You Lonesome Tonight?' was a sugar mountain of hankie-dabbing schmaltz from 1920s vaudeville. Later versions by bandleader Blue Barron and Al Jolson modified its design, axing two explanatory verses to instead loop its chorus and add a spoken interlude based upon Shakespeare's 'All the world's a stage' speech from *As You Like It*. The same arrangement Elvis would obligingly record in the witching gloom of 5 am, the studio lights dimmed, his voice deep sea diving in reverb full fathom five to the abyss of melancholy. It was more beautiful than the widow-robbing Marie Parker ever deserved.

That same Tennessee night Elvis recorded another ballad of his own choosing. He'd probably learned it as a boogie-woogie number, 'There's No Tomorrow', on the flipside of one of his favourite singles by one of his favourite black vocal groups, the Clovers. Before that it was a Forties crooner's tune based on the old Neapolitan standard 'O Sole Mio'. Partly in a misunderstanding over copyright, his A&R man commissioned new words for Elvis, changing the title to 'It's Now Or Never', keeping the same *carpe diem* romantic hysteria and smoothing its rhythm to a gentle rumba.

The peach-canners were especially pleased, hearing in its soft melody the golden *'ching!'* of the lawn-sprinkling middle classes.

They, like others, would entirely misunderstand Elvis' intentions, believing 'It's Now Or Never' a wilful act of self-castration in penance for all his rock 'n' roll sins, his cowed plea to tinkle the same cocktail cabinets as Percy Faith and Pat Boone. It wasn't.

'It's Now Or Never' was *Don Giovanni* in blue jeans. Elvis recorded it in Nashville but as the tape rolled, eyes closed, he sought the spotlight of Naples' Teatro di San Carlo and on take four he found it, with Krystal burgers on his breath but Caruso in his lungs. Elvis never made a secret of his love for the great Italian tenor Mario Lanza, who'd famously played Caruso on screen, and whose soundtrack to *The Student Prince* had been a well-worn sonic salve on homesick Army nights in Goethestrasse, helping to drown out any obscene ululations from his father's room. The press might not have believed Elvis loved Lanza to then hear him sing, *'Anda no-wonna hoo-drada doo-it widda hanna-yoo.'* They'd believe him after 'It's Now Or Never'.

The two ballads, the one he recorded for himself and the one he recorded at the behest of the Psycho's wife, were released in turn as his next singles after 'Stuck On You'. Both went to number one, both selling millions, with 'It's Now Or Never' going on to become his biggest selling single ever. Elvis had only made it to prove to his critics the King of Rock 'n' Roll wasn't some yodellin' greaseball but a pomade Lanza with a voice to atomise marble.

Unknowingly, he'd just signed his abdication.

ELI, ELI, LAMA SABACHTHANI?

There come moments in a man's life when they are forced to stop and question their beliefs. Their belief whether God actually exists, and if he does then whether he's a saviour or a sadist; whether God's more interested in rewarding faith and easing human suffering or an indiscriminate punisher for his own sick celestial amusement; whether we're all just his game of jacks doomed to an inescapable agonising death on whichever Calvary he chooses to forsake us; whether bedside kneeling and table grace is all a waste of time because God has already decided ever since his first sarcastic breath stirred Adam upright that he hates the whingeing bones of all of us.

Elvis would have many such moments in his life, and though they all occurred at different times, in different years, they usually occurred in that crucible of the damned where even the most desperate prayers can be guaranteed the engaged tone of divine disinterest. Hollywood.

It had happened before, when forced to dance with a glove puppet on the set of *G.I. Blues*. And it happened again in a recording studio on Santa Monica Boulevard where Elvis stood faced with a microphone and a lyric sheet instructing him to yodel like a halfwit hayseed about gals in britches.

As a cow led to an abattoir believing it to be their new barn, so Elvis returned to Hollywood to fulfil his next film commitment, assured that this one, called *Flaming Lance*, would finally be the 'serious' non-singing role he'd been campaigning for in the press ever since his Army discharge. He would play Pacer, a 'half-breed' Indian son of a white rancher, caught up in a bloody race war between his maternal Kiowa tribe and his father's hostile cowboy neighbours. The studio, 20th Century Fox, had originally developed the film for Marlon Brando and, on paper, the script allowed Elvis to frown, punch and stagger like Stanley Kowalski in cowboy chaps. Until someone insisted on adding songs about gals in britches.

That someone was the Psycho, quick to remind the studio that an Elvis Presley film without music was a billboard without canned peaches and thus made no economic sense. In a private internal studio memo, Fox's publicity department noted with mild concern that the Psycho seemed 'more interested in selling records than he is building a motion picture career for Elvis Presley.' The Psycho was brash enough a Foot-Long Hot Dog salesman to agree, boasting to the press that no Elvis film would ever win an Oscar.

'All they're good for is to make money.'

The Psycho made money with no end of caveats and percentages, writing himself into every contract, obliging an on-screen credit as 'Technical Advisor' for a film he would sabotage with his dogged demands on music, a script he refused to read and a set he would disrupt with a cashbox and trestle-table to sell Elvis records and memorabilia to members of the crew. As the keeper of the thing called Elvis Presley the studio had no choice but to allow him to do exactly as he pleased.

The Psycho's Midas touch was only ever called into question when early test screenings of *Flaming Star*, as it had been renamed, had audiences sniggering the moment Elvis broke the drama to start crooning accompanied by an invisible band. Two songs, including 'Britches', were mercifully cut, but another similarly daft hoedown stayed, enough to emasculate what might otherwise have been Elvis' best chance of a gold statuette cluttering Graceland's mantelpiece.

Ensuring no Elvis film ever won an Oscar now became the Psycho's matter of personal pride, applying the same 'Technical Advice' on Elvis' next. As with *Flaming Star*, Elvis had been under the impression there'd be no songs in *Wild In The Country*, a contemporary drama about a misunderstood youth whose affections are torn between three women including his probation officer who eventually kills herself. Clearly not the sort of film requiring Elvis to warble *'I guess that love is a banana peel'* with a simpleton's grin while driving a truck. Or so he'd assumed with a naivety dissolving quicker than an icicle up Satan's ass.

'Eli, Eli, lama sabachthani?'

An early scene in the script where Elvis' character faces a parole board required him to recite some scripture in Aramaic then in English.

'My God, My God, why hast Thou forsaken me?'

Elvis didn't have to act.

He was back in Graceland for Christmas, his first there since his mother had died. His dad had moved into the separate garage apartment with his new wife so Elvis wouldn't have to hear their sacrilegious shenanigans, nor entertain the three new stepbrothers he called 'Dee's brats' any more than was civilly necessary.

He was home, he was miserable and he was Christmas number one on both single and album charts. The single was the Psycho's wife's favourite, 'Are You Lonesome Tonight?'. The album was the soundtrack to *G.I. Blues*. The film had been a shocking box-office success with the tie-in album outselling both his studio albums that year, one of rock 'n' roll, the other gospel music. The message to his peach-canners being the public evidently preferred him singing about cold showers and pumpernickel than sex or God.

★

Beyond Graceland's iron gates, far away in Palm Beach, America's young president-elect, 43-year-old John F. Kennedy, was busy drafting his upcoming inauguration speech.

In Atlanta, the pastor and activist Dr Martin Luther King Jr., not long out of prison for his part in a peaceful sit-in at a segregated lunch counter, freed thanks to the intervention of Kennedy and his younger brother Bobby, was writing an optimistic article on the new presidency signalling 'a radical new approach' for race relations.

In Louisville, the Olympic gold medal won by boxer Cassius Clay spent its first winter deep in the Ohio River where he'd tossed it in disgust after being refused entry to a whites-only restaurant.

In Pasadena, 16-year-old Jordanian Sirhan Sirhan was spending school recess fermenting his resentment to fellow students at John Muir High.

In Missouri State Penitentiary, professional criminal James Earl Ray was ending his first year of a 20-year sentence for armed robbery and dreaming of escape.

And in Memphis, Elvis Presley shook out a handful of red bullet-shaped capsules manufactured in Indiana by Eli Lilly –

'Eli, Eli, lama sabachthani!'

– popping as many as it took to evacuate his mind of Hollywood, God and his dead, dead mother –

'Why hast Thou forsaken me?'

– and dream of nothing.

TOXICOLOGY

They came from Eli Lilly & Co of Indiana, Smith, Kline & French of Philadelphia, Abbott Laboratories of Chicago, Stragenburgh Laboratories of Rochester, Breon of New York, Endo of Richmond Hill, Parker Davis & Co of Detroit and CIBA Pharmaceuticals of New Jersey. They were medicinal miracles, long-acting, slow-release, distributed in hundreds of minute pellets packed into ampules, spansules, capsules, kapseals, pulvules and tablets of different shapes, colours and sizes, each stamped or embossed with its company initials or insignia. They were manufactured to be prescribed by qualified physicians for depression, obesity, insomnia, hyperactivity, cardiac pain, compulsive eating or as a sedative counteracting psychosis and hysteria.

They came to Elvis through the doctors, dentists and drug dispensers he'd met in Hollywood and Las Vegas willing to sell him prescriptions or the drugs themselves by the quart jar at a dollar a pill. He took them because he could afford them, because he liked them and because being Elvis Presley meant being in another dimension to the rest of the human race, a parallel world with its own atmosphere, its own speed, its own temporality, its own colours, its own gravity and its own perspective. It was lonely being the only person living in the dimension of Elvis Presley and so he took the pills both to cope with the loneliness and to keep him there, safe in his room-for-one twilight zone of Elvisness lest he should suddenly fall out of it and become just another nine-to-five fink unplugged from the cosmos. And because he was wretchedly addicted.

He bought in bulk and stored them in a safe in his bathroom in Graceland, or wherever he happened to be living in Hollywood. He made sure when he travelled cross country from Memphis to Los Angeles and back, or on weekends to Vegas, that he carried enough of a supply with him, entrusting the magic bag to one of his Angels. He also kept separate smaller supplies of pills by his bedside, and on his person in a dark blue felt box that he sometimes shared out as a kid might a bag of jujubes.

He studied them with the obsession of a birdwatcher and the devotion of a Benedictine monk. His field guide and bible was the medical professional's *Physician's Desk Reference To Pharmaceutical Specialities And Biologicals*: a hard-backed volume published every year listing the different drugs from different manufacturers, explaining their composition, actions and uses, side-effects, precautions, contraindications and overdose symptoms, with a handy plate section to help identify the different brands, colours and shapes. Elvis kept a copy by his bedside, like a Sears catalogue next to the very pills it had helped him choose.

To live permanently in his special dimension of Elvisness, Elvis seesawed his body chemistry with uppers and downers, speeding up and slowing down from consciousness to unconsciousness in a perpetuity that couldn't be described as 24/7 since there were neither 24 hours in an Elvis day nor seven days in an Elvis week. Time was all one unquantifiable abstraction of Elvis o'clock.

The uppers were mainly diet pills, each its own cocktail mixing amphetamine sulphate, dextroamphetamine sulphate, sodium chloride or methamphetamine hydrochloride. They came in pink triangles (Benzedrine, Dexedrine), blue triangles (Dexamyl), pink tablets (Ritalin), white capsules (Eskatrol), green capsules (Desbutal) and 'black beauties' (Biphetamine). Their side-effects included hyper-excitability, agitation, flushing, sweating, restlessness, heart pain, dizziness, increased reflexes, circulatory collapse and overt psychotic behaviour.

The downers were prescription opiates, sedative compounds of barbiturate, pentobarbital sodium, acetaminophen, dihydro-morphinone hydrochloride, dihydrohydroxycodeinone hydro-chloride, dihydrohydroxycodeinone terephthalate, homatropine terephthalate, acetylsalicylic acid, acetphenetidine and ethchlor-vynol. They came in white tablets (Amytal, soluble Dilaudid), yellow tablets (Percodan), white and blue kapseals (Carbrital), red and blue bullets (Tuinal), 'green meanies' (Placidyl), 'red devils' (Seconal), 'yellow jackets' (Nembutal) and pink mottled tablets providing sedation 'unsurpassed by morphine' (Demerol). Their possible side-effects included flushing of the face, dryness of the mouth, sweating, over-excitement and, in rare cases, coma.

Elvis picked the colours of his chemical rainbow with a scholar's care but a gastronome's appetite; his knowledge acute, but his hunger blind to the one recurring gospel of the *Physician's Desk Reference* he failed to remember.

'WARNING: May be habit forming.'

PSYCHO (3)

It was the spurs that eventually did it. The spurs, the Stetsons, the hay bales, the saddles, the horses and the covered wagons. Without them, the morbidly obese shadow of the Psycho Tom Parker may never have darkened the corridors of the American phonograph industry. He might have stayed in Florida where he'd settled with his wife, working as a dog catcher, pet cemetery racketeer and animal welfare defrauder. He might even have gone back to the midway and become the world's first Foot-Long Hot Dog millionaire, if they didn't tar and feather him first. But then he saw the spurs.

The Psycho had a kink for cowboys. Something about their ten-gallon hats, their britches, their holsters, their lassos and their smell of the Wild West. They made his granite heart skip and put a shine in his tarmac eye. Even the ones that sang.

He didn't like music but he liked cowboys and a singing cowboy, even though he played music, was still a cowboy with spurs. Which is why the Psycho Tom Parker's dead ears first pricked to the yodel 'n' twang of country and western package tours rolling through Florida, chasing their trail back to the source in Nashville and setting up 'office' at a payphone in a hotel foyer.

He'd had some experience of talent booking in his carnival past representing has-been crooner Gene Austin. That was enough to impress rising star Eddy Arnold, nicknamed 'The Tennessee Plowboy', into hiring him as his exclusive manager.

The Psycho's promotion methods for Arnold were no different to those he'd once used to drum up footfall for 'the Wild Boy from the Jungles of Borneo' and other carnie freaks: traipsing tired circus elephants through towns, dishing out free publicity photographs as a loudspeaker blasted his client's fiddlin' weepies: *'It's a sin, ma darlin', how I love yooo!'* The Plowboy was embarrassed. As the Psycho pointed out, he was also number one in the country charts. The elephants traipsed on.

The music business, as the Psycho fast discovered, was no different to the carnival; an unsentimental sewer of backstabbers, thieves, whores, mountebanks, conspirators, slavers, bloodsuckers, bailiffs, calculating cutthroats and cutthroats with calculators.

They were his kind of people.

People like Jimmie Davis, a country singer best known for 'You Are My Sunshine', a song he claimed he'd written after purchasing the copyright. He was now the Governor of Louisiana, paying more attention to Hollywood than home, spending as much time in California playing himself in his own musical biopic than behind his desk in Baton Rouge. To a man like Davis status and showbiz were one and the same and in the Psycho he recognised a monster after his own billfold. And so, abusing full power of governorship, it was Davis who promoted Parker into the American Southern gentry, granting him an honorary rank in the Louisiana State Militia. The illegal immigrant, army deserter and certified psychopath Andreas Cornelis van Kuijk thus became 'Colonel Tom Parker.' His staff and industry associates were told from now on they must address him accordingly.

'The Colonel' wouldn't answer to any other name.

THE PRISONER

The Colonel conceived it, the Colonel announced it, the Colonel organised the support acts – including circus acrobats and a tap dancer – and the Colonel's name was printed alongside Elvis' in the press ads so at first glance anyone might think he'd be there on stage beside him.

They'd be the first proper Elvis concerts in over three years. Two shows, matinee and evening, taking place in Memphis as fundraisers for multiple local charities including the Crippled Children's Hospital, the Lions School for Visually Handicapped Children, the Les Passees Treatment Centre for Cerebral Palsied Children, St Jude Children's Hospital and the Home for Incurables. The kid from Lauderdale Courts they'd once called 'the Memphis Flash' had become Saint Francis of Tennessee. Nobody could accuse a young man of lewd behaviour while he was actively healing the sick and clothing the poor and, as the Colonel relished telling reporters, even Elvis would pay for his own ticket.

In gratitude, the city fathers decreed the day of the shows, Saturday February 25, 1961, 'Elvis Presley Day' and hailed him one of their 'most outstanding citizens'. The Colonel, who lived 200 miles away in Madison, a suburb of Nashville, took it as a given they meant him too.

Elvis Presley Day started at 12.30 pm with a charity luncheon at $100 a plate amidst the exotic decor of the Balinese Room of the Hotel Claridge. It was another of the Colonel's ideas. All 225 seats sold out.

Elvis made a tradesman's entrance through a back alley to avoid the crush of fans outside the main foyer, taking a service elevator to the second floor kitchen, finally emerging through a pantry door in a black mohair suit, white shirt and silk tie, a blue sapphire ring sparkling on his finger and pink Dexedrine sparkling in his brain. He took his place as guest of honour at the head table, the city Mayor on his left, the state Governor on his right. He ate candied sweet potatoes, broccoli and a French tossed salad with roll washed down with ice water. Dessert was a crème de menthe parfait.

The Mayor made a speech praising Elvis' conduct both 'as an entertainer and a soldier'. The vice president of RCA Victor then presented him with a diamond-encrusted watch and a special plaque to commemorate 75 million record sales. That included one million of his latest peach, 'Surrender', another bionic remake of an old Neapolitan tune hoping to can the same operatic juice as 'It's Now Or Never'. The trophies continued, one from the TV show *American Bandstand*, another from *Billboard* magazine, trophy after trophy from all around the world: Australia, Britain, Belgium, Brazil, Denmark, France, Germany, Norway, Sweden, Japan and South Africa. They even announced a trophy from the Netherlands. The Colonel didn't once twitch.

At 1.45 pm on Elvis Presley Day, Elvis was still at the hotel addressing the press ahead of his afternoon matinee. He admitted he was nervous about performing, that he hadn't had much of a chance to rehearse with his band and that it had been so long since he'd sung in public he had trouble remembering the words to his old hits.

They asked him about his love life.

'Well it hasn't progressed any,' he smirked, saying nothing about Juliet nor his other co-stars, nor the various wardrobe and make-up assistants, nor the girls in Hollywood he liked to watch making out through his two-way mirror in a secret closet, nor his steady girl in Memphis called Anita he'd been cheating on for the past four years, nor the Girl In Germany he still drip-fed his sweetest long-distance nothings.

'It's about like it was. Nuthin' serious.'

They asked him about his next film. He told them it was called *Blue Hawaii* and shooting started in three weeks. Other than that he knew nothing except that it was 'a kind of drama'. Which it was, in the way a train crash was a kind of rollercoaster.

They pressed him about his films and whether he enjoyed playing more dramatic roles.

'I would like to,' he said as Tulsa McLean began twisting his arm.

'But I'm not ready for that...'

It kept twisting.

'... Until I'm ready for it, it would be foolish to undertake something very dramatic.'

A female reporter asked if that meant he'd continue making musicals. 'Probably so, honey,' he yielded. 'It's up to the studio, mostly. You can rest assured there'd be music in almost all of them.'

He was ready to cry uncle.

'There has to be.'

They asked him why he hadn't done any television since the Frank Sinatra show. 'Because of the movie contracts I have.' It was Elvis' voice but the Colonel's answer. 'I'm pretty tied up in movies right now and too much television kind of hurts movies a little bit.'

Someone suggested he'd become more conservative since leaving the Army.

'Well,' he flushed, 'I'm getting a little older, y'know.'

They asked if he missed his once-trademark sideburns.

'Not especially.'

They asked if he liked playing live best. Elvis said he did and that he hoped to arrange a European tour. He turned to the Colonel for back up. 'Are we gonna be doing any?'

The illegal immigrant and unsolved-murder suspect who could never leave the jurisdiction of the United States of America because he'd never be allowed back in smiled his psychopath smile, removed the stogie from between his teeth, drawled 'We're waiting for a good offer', then replaced it with the same twisted leer.

The questions continued: about his superstitions ('breaking mirrors'), how many cars he owned ('four'), whether he still practised karate ('quite a bit') and ate cheeseburgers ('I don't eat many'). Then the Mayor spoke up, asking if it felt like coming home every time he came back to Memphis.

'Yes, sir,' said Elvis. 'It does.'

The whole room applauded.

The applause was louder still when, around 4 pm, Elvis walked out into the coloured spotlight at the North Hall of Ellis Auditorium. He wore a silver tuxedo with a black handkerchief in the upper pocket, a white ruff shirt and black pants with a white stripe down the side. Behind him were his band, labelled 'The King's Men', and a chain of stuffed hound dogs suspended from the rear stage curtain.

The crowd mewled like cattle trapped in a burning barn, a noise hideous and absurd, drowning him in its swell. He swayed, laughing, his head adjusting to its current. Then, taking a deep breath, he grabbed the mic stand in his right hand, swung it like a lever, cocked a hip and sang.

'Well, since my baby left me...'

And Memphis melted.

The faster they melted, the fiercer he roared, every scream more tinder to his fire until, by the closing 'Hound Dog', there wasn't a button, brace or carpet tack unscorched.

Five hours later the inferno raged again. For his evening performance Elvis was introduced by Hollywood's veteran 'Toastmaster General of the United States' George Jessel. Years earlier Jessel had his own TV show interviewing former celebrities who'd overcome alcoholism, cancer or general obsolescence. It was called *The Comeback Show*. But Jessel could see this was no comeback. When Elvis walked on stage, the Toastmaster kowtowed at his feet. This was a coronation.

The King of Memphis had changed his silver jacket for another of pristine white. The white of the centre of a supernova hurtling Elvis through time and space to the lost thrill of *what was* made only more thrilling by realising *this is*. And what *this is* was not U.S. Army Sergeant 53310761 or Tulsa McLean but as close as any human might ever witness to a striptease by God.

He stormed 16 songs with thunder voice and lightning flow, striking his very first record, the Shake Rag boogie 'That's All Right', knowing that its producer, Sam Phillips, the first to share Elvis with the world on Sun Records, was there in the audience watching with a parent's eye and an ex's pulse. He howled another of his blues favourites, 'One Night', reinstating the mattress-bound filth he'd had to censor from his own single version. He purred one of his smoochiest Leiber and Stoller ballads, 'Love Me', and rolled with its punching ricochet of so much snapping elastic. He cracked jokes, introducing 'Heartburn Motel' and his band, 'the Unwashables', and sent up 'Are You Lonesome Tonight?' mid-monologue hamming *'you seemed to change – you got fat!'* and *'now the stage is bare – and you've lost your hair.'* And just before the final fiery apocalypse of 'Hound Dog', he rained holy kerosene with 'Swing Down Sweet Chariot.'

'I've got a home,' hollered Elvis, *'on the other side.'*

The squeals of six-and-a-half thousand reminded him he was already there.

The two concerts raised over $50,000. In reward for all his generosity, the following week the Governor invited Elvis to a special ceremony in Nashville where he would officially honour him before the Tennessee State Capitol with the title of 'Colonel'. Meaning, if he wanted, he could start calling himself, like his boss, 'Colonel Presley'.

The Colonel chose not to attend.

Elvis drove to Nashville with Diamond Joe, Hog Ears and Sonny in his new Rolls Royce Phantom: a present to himself after being told the Colonel had negotiated a Mint-sapping new studio contract for another five films on top of the five he'd already negotiated. Ten more shots of Tulsa McLean. If he wasn't going to enjoy them, he would their paycheque.

He appeared in smart suit and tie before a Wednesday session of the State Legislature and a packed public gallery. Governor Ellington told the assembly that Elvis was 'that type of man unaffected by fame, the great popularity, but with a sincere desire in his heart to help all he comes into contact with.'

'Truthfully,' said Elvis, 'this is one of the nicest things that has ever happened to me in my entire career.' The Governor shook his hand to a boom of applause. Elvis stepped down from the podium and, exercising his first privilege as Colonel Presley, demonstrated his sincere desire towards all he came into contact with by whisking the Governor's pert 'n' purty blonde daughter away.

Tennessee State Prison wasn't Ann Ellington's idea of a normal date but then Elvis Presley wasn't her normal suitor. With her father's permission they'd been granted a special visit to meet one of Elvis' favourite singers currently serving ten years for robbery and attempted murder. Johnny Bragg had seen his first cell as a 14-year-old car thief. He was barely 18 when he was arrested on a rape charge. Bragg claimed he was innocent but by the time he went to trial he'd been identified, wrongly he'd insist, as the culprit in five other cases. The jury found him guilty on all six counts of criminal assault and the judge sentenced 99 years for each without parole. Unless he lived to be 611 Bragg would die behind bars.

After serving 16 years his sentence was commuted by a new Governor, Frank Clement, a campaigner for penal reform who admired the vocal group Bragg had since formed with fellow inmates calling themselves the Prisonaires. They'd also caught the attention of Sam Phillips who recorded them for his fledgling Sun Records in 1953. The Prisonaires' debut disc was an original by Bragg and convicted burglar Robert Riley, 'Just Walkin' In The Rain'. It became Sun's first big hit on the R&B charts.

In 1959 Bragg was approved for parole after his tariff was commuted to a standard life sentence. The day of his release, the sun shining on Nashville, Bragg posed for photographers on the prison steps with an umbrella in homage to his signature song.

A year later he was back before the judge accused of forcing a woman into his car at knifepoint then driving her to a secluded spot to rob and molest her. After a mistrial he was tried again and acquitted. Then a second woman came forward and accused Bragg of trying to choke and rob her at knifepoint in a park. The jury found him guilty.

Elvis didn't know the gory particulars of Bragg's rap sheet, only that he loved his sweet tenor and cherished his copy of 'Just Walkin' In The Rain' among his most well-worn singles. He just wanted to meet Bragg and offer him what help he could.

When he arrived the prison guards had to apologise to Elvis that, being a woman, they couldn't allow the Governor's daughter inside. He told Hog Ears to wait with Ann in the car while he, Joe and Sonny were admitted through to see Bragg. The famous Prisonaire was gracious, if without hope. He thanked Elvis for coming and said it had been a pleasure to meet. But he was a convicted negro in Klan country, where black men still vanished overnight from their cells, never to be seen or heard of again. There was really nothing Elvis could do for him.

An hour later they came back out, saying their goodbyes to Ann and to Nashville before turning the Rolls back towards Memphis.

Elvis thought a lot about Bragg on the drive home in the Tennessee twilight, picturing how the same sky might look through window bars in a cold lonely cell. It must be the worst feeling in the world. To be trapped, confined and helpless. A prisoner with no control.

He was still dwelling on Bragg as he opened his felt-lined travelling box and pushed a couple of coral blue spansules to the back of his throat.

PSYCHO (4)

The Psycho became the Colonel and, thanks to his number one country star Eddy Arnold, the Colonel became a success. But being the Colonel, being a psychopath, a gambler, a grifter and a glutton, one star wasn't enough.

He breached his own contract with Arnold to promote yodelling rival Hank Snow. It looked a stupid move when Arnold fired him. Not so stupid when the Colonel countersued Arnold for a five-figure release fee. The severance left him free to manage Snow, already a hit recording artist, and free to merge their respective talent booking agencies as one: 'Hank Snow Jamboree Attractions'.

The Colonel thus became Snow's man.

And, simultaneously, *the* Snowman.

He always liked the word 'snow'. It wasn't like 'scam', 'mug', 'cheat', 'con', 'swindle', 'dupe', 'rob', 'rip-off' and 'fiddle'. 'Snow' was soft and Christmasy. He could declare himself the 'First High Potentate Snower' and people might think him some jovial old wizard in a way they wouldn't if he printed up business cards with 'Last Low Filching Scumbag'. As the Snowman he could wear his duplicity in public as a badge of honour, freeing himself from the shackles of hypocrisy and subterfuge. He was still a thief, but a thief knocking on the window in stripy top and bandit mask pointing to an open sack marked 'SWAG'. The world would see him coming, and if he cleaned them out, more fool them. And there were always so many more fools them.

Just as the story of the Dancing Chickens was the lie that told the truth, the Snowman was the joke that told the truth of the psychopath Tom Parker.

He printed up membership cards for an imaginary union punning the Showmen's League of America – 'the Snowmen's League of America' – featuring, on the front, his cartoon insignia of a snowman in top hat and scarf with a stogie in its mouth and, on the reverse, a quote from the Renaissance scholar Fra Giovanni Giocondo: 'There is nothing I can give you which you have not. But there is much while I cannot give you, you can take.'

Membership of the Snowmen's League was entirely at the Colonel's discretion. Those admitted were usually chosen because they'd already been snowed by the High Potentate.

Or soon would be.

Each new recruit received an accompanying members' rulebook, the *Confidential Report Dealing With Advanced Techniques Of Member Snowers*: the inside pages were blank. A separate enrolment letter bore the League's motto – *'Let it snow, let it snow, let it snow!'* – and a list of Parker's services as High Potentate: 'free advice at reasonable rates', 'choice mosquito manure', 'housebroken cockroaches' and 'unactive radio activity.'

Somewhere within the upper storeys of his psychopathic mind the Colonel kept a trophy room, upon its walls the mounted heads of those he'd snowed. On that wall, Eddy Arnold. Over there, Sam Phillips. To the left, the United States Army. And there, just above the fireplace, the biggest moose of all. His favourite snow – Hal Wallis.

The studios called him 'the Starmaker'. Wallis made his name at Warner Bros producing Bette Davis, Errol Flynn and Humphrey Bogart. It was Wallis who came up with Bogey's closing line in

Casablanca: 'Louis, this could be the beginning of a beautiful friendship.' He later moved to Paramount where he made hit comedies with Jerry Lewis and Dean Martin. Wallis was as big a big time as the hands of Hollywood's clock knew to tell. He was ripe for the snowing.

In 1956, Wallis struck a deal with Paramount Pictures to be the first Hollywood producer to make a film starring the thing called Elvis Presley. It wasn't anything like the deal the Colonel felt he deserved. Irrespective of Elvis' million record sales, Wallis offered a typical contract for a new actor for one feature film, with the option of six more. There'd be no script approval. Elvis would film whatever Wallis and Paramount wanted. The agreed fee for the first film was $15,000: the Colonel had gotten more from Ed Sullivan for ten minutes of Elvis on television. But the contract wasn't exclusive. Under its terms, Elvis was free to make one film per year with any other studio. A small loophole just big enough for the Colonel to steam his snow plough through.

Before Wallis and Paramount had time to decide what to do with Elvis, the Colonel exercised the non-exclusivity clause with *Love Me Tender*, Elvis' debut film made at 20th Century Fox. The Colonel had tried pokerfacing Fox for his fantasy fee of $1 million. In the end he settled for $100,000. It was still over six times what Wallis had paid. It meant when Wallis finally called on Elvis to make the film for Paramount he'd originally signed for, the Colonel could tear up the contract. Less than a year after Wallis signed Elvis for $15,000, the Colonel snowed him for over ten times that figure, quintupling the total again through bigger deals with rivals Fox and Metro-Goldwyn-Mayer. That sum, like all of Elvis' Hollywood income, to be split with the Colonel. Fifty-fifty.

That's how the First High Potentate Snower and psychopath Tom Parker played the table of Tinsel Town. Studio against studio, fee against fee, increment against increment, selling shares in the thing called Elvis Presley one 70mm frame at a time. It was all just chips, shills and parlays. Elvis was the wheel, he the croupier and the house – *his* house – always won.

By the time Elvis returned from the Army the Colonel had snowed Wallis $175,000 up front for *G.I. Blues*, with the option of three more films for close on another half a million. But being the Colonel, the gambler, the grifter and the glutton, it still wasn't enough. He wanted Wallis' head stuffed and mounted. He wanted that $1 million movie contract.

It became one of Tom Parker's Greatest Hits. The story of how he finally took that sonofabitch Wallis for six zeroes. He told it with the same dinnertime zeal as his Foot-Long Hot Dogs and Dancing Chickens, with napkin stuffed in neck, grease on his lips and specks of meat bouncing on his tongue, a main course comedian holding cutlery-frozen court, relishing his favourite gag.

The gag went like this. A fat man dressed like a country hick walks into a Smug Hollywood Jew's office to talk business. Though the Fat Hick is wearing an expensive suit he's deliberately changed the labels, sewing in that from a cheap department store. When he sits down he takes off his jacket and deliberately throws it over his chair with the label showing, knowing the Smug Hollywood Jew will see what a nickel-poor loser he's dealing with and privately laugh his Smug Hollywood Jewish laugh.

The Fat Hick then says he wants to talk about his client's picture deal. The Smug Hollywood Jew smiles, listens and makes his offer.

The Fat Hick gasps. He tells the Smug Hollywood Jew he's insulted and stands up from his chair. As he walks towards the door he warns the Smug Hollywood Jew that, if he makes it out of the room, his client's price automatically goes up an extra $50,000. Then for every extra minute he spends waiting in reception he'll add another $50,000.

The Smug Hollywood Jew assumes he's bluffing. But a minute passes and the Fat Hick doesn't return.

After sweating $100,000, the Jew folds, running to the door. The Fat Hick in the pretend cheap suit gets his money. The Snowman wins again. Cymbal splash. Applause.

Like the Colonel's Dancing Chickens story, not everyone who heard it believed the one about Wallis, the suit and the $50,000-a-minute standoff. But enough did to repeat it in crisp earshot over lunch at the Brown Derby, dinner at Romanoff's and cocktails at Bar Marmont, the details and sums sometimes misremembered but the punchline essentially the same. On Hollywood's gaming table of dollars and cents, nobody fucked with the Colonel.

Elvis and the Colonel took their million for five more films with Paramount, starting with the 'kind of drama' mentioned at the Memphis press conference, *Blue Hawaii*. The new deal tipped the scales of Elvis' income so hard it snapped the axis. On basis of earnings, as of 1961 he was now principally a movie star – one who could still make another half a million a year in pocket money as an occasional pop singer. But only if he really needed to.

HAWAII

The Pan-Am flight carrying the millionaire movie star and occasional pop singer Elvis Presley landed at Honolulu International Airport just after midday. He stepped off the plane in a black suit to the screams of three thousand. The first lei was over his neck before his feet touched the tarmac. By the time he reached his limousine he looked like a man with a bouquet for a head.

He arrived at the Hilton Hawaiian Village, Waikiki Beach where more fans blockaded his entrance, the police struggling to restrain them as they scratched, clawed and garrotted him with more flowers, all of them too blinded to be so close to Elvis to recognise his were the wild amphetamine eyes of barely conscious artifice.

The Colonel was waiting at the hotel with the overbaked tan of someone who'd already been there two weeks, his hotel suite a war room decorated with Elvis posters and stuffed hound dogs to prepare for the imminent filming of Wallis' *Blue Hawaii*, and another charity concert that evening.

The idea was the same as Elvis' recent fundraisers in Memphis, but with the added prestige of military patriotism. The Colonel had read about the struggling memorial fund for the USS Arizona, sunk in the attack on Pearl Harbour with the loss of over a thousand lives. The memorial, designed to allow visitors to walk above its rusting hull, still visible in the clear Pacific waters close to shore, was short of its $200,000 target and behind completion. The Colonel decided Elvis would help raise the remainder needed with a charity concert at the Bloch Arena in Pearl Harbour's Navy Yard. Tickets for the show would range from $100 ringside to $3 at the rear and everyone, including Elvis and the Colonel, would pay for their ticket. It would make a national hero of Elvis and the uncanny coincidence of being in Hawaii to make his next film a publicity blitz no studio could buy. It was a stroke of genius by the measure of any Army-certified psychopath and deserter.

Elvis looked and sounded many hundred milligrams below functioning at the afternoon press conference, mumbling a droopy-eyed 'thankoo' when presented with an Award of Honour by the USS Arizona Memorial Commission. But after a pep talk from the lid of his blue felt box, five hours later he was a different beast.

Rear Admiral Robert Campbell had seen war in the Pacific but he'd never heard a noise like the one greeting him as he walked on stage at the Bloch Arena to introduce 'a fine American'. A noise to shake the sunken Arizona bobbing back to the surface.

'He has had many starring roles,' persevered Campbell. 'In one of these roles, his role as a soldier in the U.S. Army, his performance was outstanding. And it's a great pleasure to welcome him here and present to you...'

The Kraken woke in black slacks and a gold lamé jacket. He rose in roars, grunts and giggles, in sliding knees, catapulting thighs and slamming groin against floor and mic stand, suspending the human bliss found only in that slither of a second between the ache of desire and the joy of fulfilment between the eyes and ears of the blessed 4000 for a full 45 minutes. Until the blinding light vanished, the dust settled and the all-clear sounded.

'Elvis has left the building.'

★

Two days later he started filming *Blue Hawaii*. There wasn't much of a plot because Wallis hadn't asked for one, only a 'framework' for a dozen songs 'and lots of girls'. The songs weren't worth the framing. There was one solid ballad, 'Can't Help Falling In Love', which the script had Elvis singing to his girlfriend's grandmother. Others were old Hawaiian and European folk tunes, some borrowed from Bing Crosby and Andy Williams. The rest were tailored to the story of a returning G.I. who upsets his dad's hopes of inheriting the family fruit business by becoming an island tour guide. They included a calypso about a fat Polynesian with an eating disorder who *'even eat de shell of de coconut'* and a blues pastiche about canned pineapples. Elvis recorded the best with a passion not all deserved and the worst with hurried indifference. There didn't seem any point protesting. The contract was signed and the Rolls Royce paid for.

Elvis spent the next four weeks location filming. Evenings he liked to stand on his balcony overlooking Waikiki Beach, gazing out into the Pacific. Except that when he did, girls usually gathered on the sands below yelling his name and flashing their bikini tops.

And so he mostly stayed in, with his co-star Joan Blackwood, or whichever other member of the cast or crew he was sleeping with that night. Hidden from view, staring through the balcony doors to the blue Hawaii beyond, bluer than his eyes, bluer than the felt that lined his travelling pill box. The sort of wild expansive blue that tortured the cell dreams of captive men like Johnny Bragg.

Apart from when required on set, Elvis never once left the building.

KEN®

The public loved *Blue Hawaii*. They loved it senselessly and rapturously. They loved its tranquilising blueness and fantasy Hawaiian-ness, its Wahinis and hula skirts, its surf and swaying palms, its postcard pictures and bad back-projection. Most of all they loved its plucked Elvis in white swimming trunks singing *'Darling, I love you so'* to an overegging lap steel. They especially loved its soundtrack album, the one that bragged '14 Great Songs' on the cover even though it contained, at most, one. They loved it over everything else Elvis fired at the charts that year, even over the greatest aim of 'His Latest Flame', a jilted jungle jive reminding the universe of one of rock 'n' roll's most treasured truisms: when in doubt, make it sound like Bo Diddley. But the public didn't want Heathcliff Elvis rooting for his heart in the skip where some green-eyed harpy had cruelly tossed it. Not as much as they wanted ukulele Elvis singing *'even eat de shell of de coconut'*.

The album, *Blue Hawaii*, went to number one in early December 1961. It was still there 20 weeks later. The public had chosen his fate. Life sentence of white swimming trunks.

The peach-canners sent him straight back to Hawaii to make the same film all over again. He landed at the same airport to the same wild halloo and brutal noise, the same choking tower of leis around his neck, the same violent crush of fans as he fought his way into the same hotel, only so much worse, falling on Elvis like an over-stuffed piñata at a Mexican picnic. Only after he'd taken the same elevator to the same suite on the same fourteenth floor could he assess the extent of their scavenging: his watch, a gold tie-clasp, a diamond ring and his favourite yachting cap. He'd spend the next three weeks there, the same walls echoing with the same nightly moans and cracking karate boards as outside from his balcony the same Pacific sparkled with its same teasing blue.

The same film had the different name of *Girls! Girls! Girls!*. It was Elvis' seventh since returning from the Army two years earlier. None of the previous six had lost any money but only two, *G.I. Blues* and *Blue Hawaii*, had made the kind of profit that had the peach-canners licking their lips. Both were musical comedies produced by Hal Wallis and directed by half-blind Norman from the 19th century, both had borne number one soundtrack albums and both cast Elvis as the singing equivalent of a new doll just launched by Mattel Incorporated of California.

The doll was created to save Barbie® from spinsterhood: 12 inches of polished vinyl and flocked hair named Ken®. He was blue-eyed, the average end of the handsome spectrum with a shiny broad chest, skinny limbs and swimming trunks stuffed of flat nothing where his genitals ought to bulge. Stick Ken® in khaki he'd be Tulsa McLean. Stick a lei round his neck, he'd be *Blue Hawaii*'s Chad Gates. The thing called Elvis Presley had become the thing called Ken®. Smooth, safe and dickless. Elvis was now Elvis®.

He'd be Ross, Josh, Lucky, Charlie, Johnny, Rick, Guy, Ted and three different Mikes. But even if he'd never be a Ken, he'd always be a Ken®.

He'd be a boat skipper, a pilot, a lifeguard, a racing driver, a carnival worker, a frogman or a water-ski instructor. In this one he was a tuna fisherman and occasional nightclub singer.

He was always an occasional nightclub singer.

The plot followed his attempts to buy back his fishing boat while being pursued by several beauties.

There were always several beauties.

He had to sing a dozen songs, mainly about love and girls and a few about fishing. A couple weren't bad but they were mostly terrible.

The songs were always mostly terrible.

The Colonel, Wallis and the other peach-canners were only concerned with repeating the arithmetic: Elvis + lots of girls + lots of songs = box-office hit + number one soundtrack album. It didn't matter they weren't good films nor good albums. A foot-long hot dog bun stuffed with onions wasn't a good hot dog but the suckers still bought it. One more with relish. *'Let it snow, let is snow, let it snow.'*

And so Elvis learned his lines, arrived on set on time and smiled into the lens as directed. A Ken® of utmost professionalism. Apart from one overexcited scene tangoing with his young blonde co-star when his tight black pants bulged where no Ken® should bulge. Either the studio didn't notice in the dailies or didn't care to waste money on a reshoot. The dick stayed in the picture.

The similarly oblivious Colonel, its 'Technical Advisor', spent most days on set puffing his stogie in a white greengrocer coat emblazoned all over with 'Elvis' and 'Girls! Girls! Girls!' in different colours. He looked moronic, but nobody ever had to ask twice the name of the film or who was in it. When bored, he'd pull a watch and chain from the same coat and entertain himself 'hypnotising' Hog Ears, Cousin Gene or whichever one of Elvis' constant shadows happened to be around at the time. Nobody was ever sure whether it was real or just an act to keep the Colonel happy and their ass on the payroll. But when he told them to quack like a duck every time he pulled his ear, when he pulled his ear, they quacked. One by one, the Colonel had them clucking like hens, barking on all fours and cocking their legs like pissing dogs.

The Colonel never once tried it with Elvis, but then he had no need. He already had half his income and Elvis' face in Technicolor sat beside a bucket of dead fish singing *'Goodbye, Mama Shrimp'*.

You could only humiliate a man so much.

COCONUT HEAD

He had money to buy whatever he wanted. More diamond rings and tiepins to be torn from his body by molesting maidens. A bigger, faster speedboat. A bigger, better tour bus for the long drives back and forth between Hollywood and Memphis. Gold hub caps for the outside of his Cadillac, and for the inside a gold electric razor, gold hair clipper, chrome brush, ice box, record player and backseat television. Money to buy more of anything and double of everything. The cheque was as blank as his barbiturated brain.

And so he bought a chimpanzee.

Elvis collected animals the way he collected cars, in all types, shapes and sizes. He had peacocks, chickens, pigs, a dog called Muffin, a turkey called Bowtie and a caged mynah bird near his kitchen which squawked 'Elvis isn't here right now' whenever Elvis was there right then.

He'd once had a spider monkey which he liked to show to dates so he could play the piano while it sat on the lid singing along. It sang like Satan's own gargoyle. Elvis missed that monkey.

It was Hog Ears who found a replacement. Its previous owner was a cartoonist calling himself Cap'n Bill. The Cap'n and his chimp had their own children's show on local television. The chimp even had his own fan club. But now the Cap'n wanted to break up the double act and if he couldn't find his chimp a new home he'd have to put him in the Memphis zoo. When Hog Ears heard, he invited the Cap'n to bring his chimp to Graceland.

Elvis bought him on the spot.

The chimp's name was Scatter. He came with certain idiosyncrasies which the Cap'n, in his shrewd salesmanship, thought best not to mention, leaving his new master to discover for himself when he took Scatter out West on his next trip to Hollywood.

Elvis hadn't long taken the lease of a new Spanish-tiled mansion on Bellagio Road next to the Bel-Air country club, with mirrored master bedroom, marble hallway and a bowling alley in the basement. The house also came with a butler, and the butler with ten fingers, one of which Scatter tried removing with his teeth.

Scatter was a biter. He was also a beer drinker, a bourbon swiller, a shit-thrower, a curtain-ripper, a skirt-peeper, a blouse-unbuttoner and a chronic masturbator, especially when there were girls around. At Bellagio Road there were always girls around.

As the one who'd brought Scatter into their midst, Hog Ears was assigned his keeper, cleaning his cage, preparing his food and furnishing his wardrobe. His favourite was Scatter's chauffeur costume, worn cruising around Hollywood in Elvis' Rolls Royce when Hog Ears liked to slip under the wheel with Scatter above his head. Any passing car or pedestrian would have seen a chimp in a chauffeur cap driving a Phantom V down Sunset Boulevard.

Elvis called Scatter 'Coconut Head' when he was good, 'Coconut-Headed Motherfucker' when he was bad. He was more often a Motherfucker.

Scatter was banned from Elvis' film sets after going missing one day only to be found swivelling in the chair behind the studio boss' desk. The director was relieved the boss wasn't in the office that day: Elvis was more relieved Scatter hadn't Jackson-Pollocked the walls with monkey shit as he usually did motel rooms.

Another time, Elvis knocked Scatter cold with a pool cue after he wrecked the furniture. But however destructive his monkey business, Elvis always forgave him, if only for the time he bit his stepmom, Dee. That's when Elvis knew ol' 'Coconut Head' was a friend for life.

And so Scatter stayed, and yet more girls came to Bellagio Road. And after Elvis had picked out the ones he'd be taking upstairs that evening he'd give the word to 'let him out!' And Scatter would hurtle out of his cage, arms up, whooping and hollering, and the girls would scream as he swung on the curtains, chugged on a beer bottle, squeezed their tits and rubbed his dick.

And Elvis would laugh till he cried. A 27-year-old millionaire film star getting his kicks from watching a sex-crazed alcoholic chimpanzee made to hump a stripper on his living room floor.

It was almost as if something was missing from his life.

NUNGEN

That something flew into Los Angeles in a prim white blouse and skirt rarely worn beyond earshot of a school lunch bell. Beneath their buttons was a girl a few weeks past her seventeenth birthday. She had light hair tied back in a ponytail, a cherub's pout and brattish blue eyes demanding the world to dazzle her. Five feet of soft teenage clay, aching to be kneaded and sculpted. But only one sculptor would do. Which is why she'd flown five-and-a-half-thousand miles to feel his chisel.

She hadn't felt it in two years, three months and 15 days. Not since waving Elvis goodbye at the Rhein-Main airbase in Germany the day she was photographed and captioned by *Life* magazine as 'the Girl He Left Behind.' Not for two years, three months and 15 days of physical and mental torture.

She'd been 14 when his lips last kissed hers. In between there'd been infrequent letters to her family home in Wiesbaden, sometimes packaged with copies of his latest records, and sporadic phone calls when they baby-talked and he'd call her his 'Nungen' and those two syllables alone were enough to convince her she really was his Girl He Left Behind.

But then he'd hang up and the torture would recommence. The longing, the need and the suffocating paranoia stoked by every gossip magazine's conflicting rumours of his latest off-screen romances. Elvis would ring to reassure her that the stories were all made up, which they usually were. He just didn't tell her the truth was unprintably worse.

The Angels who'd been with him in Germany already knew about her. Those who hadn't been, he told about in private. Some thought it a bit strange: as he described her, 'a little girl'. Stranger still why after two years he should suddenly beg her parents to let her visit him in America.

The girl's adoptive father was a U.S. Air Force Captain, straight as the flagpole on Capitol Hill. Elvis reassured him that his daughter would be entirely safe in his care in California. Naturally, it would be improper to stay with Elvis in Bel-Air. Instead she'd lodge with the Barris', the home of the man who customised Elvis' cars, way over on the other side of town in Los Feliz. Elvis would show her Hollywood by day and at night she'd be chaperoned back home to the Barris'. All would be strictly respectable.

Once satisfied with these arrangements, that summer recess her parents waved their eldest daughter goodbye from Frankfurt, bound for Los Angeles. There she spent a single night under the same roof as Mr and Mrs Barris and the rest under the same sheets as Elvis.

On her second day he took her to Las Vegas where she spent her remaining two weeks. Before leaving Bel-Air she pre-dated letters to her parents that Elvis' Scatter-bitten butler could send on at intervals with a Los Angeles postmark. When the first landed on her father's doormat she was already at the blackjack tables of the Sahara Hotel, dressed in the satin gown and sandals Elvis had chosen as her eyes shone first acquaintance with the contents of his blue felt box.

Her clay was yet supple and the sculptor intended to make her his masterpiece. *Debra Paget de Milo*. A woman who would wear whatever clothes he wanted, wear her hair the style and colour he wanted, paint her face how he liked a woman's face painted, and

say whatever he wanted only when he wanted her to. A Barbie®
tailored to satisfy his Ken®'s every need.

One drowsy Tuinal dawn of an afternoon in their Vegas hotel
suite Elvis played her a copy of his new album. A proper album,
not a soundtrack, called *Pot Luck*. The sleeve looked like a pack of
gravy mix endorsed by some Pillsbury Doughboy Elvis, but the
songs, though mostly ballads, were mostly good and his voice, free
ranging ever since the Napoli revolution of 'It's Now Or Never',
magnificent throughout. Elvis asked her what she thought. She
told him she liked it though she still preferred it when he sang
faster rock 'n' roll songs. Like he used to do.

It was Barbie®'s first mistake.

Hours later, after he'd called her an amateur whose opinions
didn't count for chicken shit, after he'd stormed into another
room, after she'd begged his forgiveness, after they'd kissed and
made up and she was his 'Nungen' once more, he explained why
he'd been so upset. He was proud of the songs he'd played her
because they were *songs*, not the short-order junk about rainbows
and tuna fish they were forcing him to sing in his films. And his
films, as he told her, were 'getting worse and worse.'

She was on the flight home all too soon and cried all
five-and-a-half-thousand miles back to Germany. Her parents were
there to greet her. She'd gone to America dressed like a Junior
High hockey player. She stepped off the plane with her hair dyed
so black and beehived so high that in her lipstick and mascara she
looked like a transvestite bombardier.

His 'Nungen' lingered on Elvis' mind as he took his customised
bus home from Hollywood to Memphis. Maybe Nungen was the
One. But maybe she wasn't. Maybe there were other Ones still out
there. Maybe there was no One. In any case he didn't have to
make any decisions just yet. He had his own way of learning
things.

'I have my own way of learning things.'

His own way of thinking.

'I have my own way of thinking.'

And nobody else could change him.

'And nobody else, regardless of their intelligence or their belief can change me or make me think a certain way if I don't feel that it's right. There's not an intellectual son of a gun walkin' the face of this earth that could make me believe a certain thing or something unless I really thought it, so I don't try to surround myself with a group of intellectuals. It's more important to try to surround yourself with people who can give you a little happiness. Because you only pass through this life once, Jack! You don't come back for an encore...'

'COOL!'

'Play it again!'

It was becoming a familiar cry to the projectionist. Elvis had hired out the Memphian cinema every night that week. He sat in his usual seat, front middle, surrounded by his Angels around him, local fans behind him, Krystal burgers, fries and shakes beside him.

'Play it again!'

The reel to be played again was from *West Side Story*. Elvis had been watching it on repeat every night this past week. Its leading actress was his old girlfriend, 'Mad Nat'. Elvis could have been on screen beside her had the Colonel not stubbornly refused him the studio's offer of the lead role of Tony; Elvis the Jet clicking fingers through upper Manhattan in tight jeans and a baracuta jacket; Elvis fighting jetés with Loco the Shark played by young Puerto-Rican dancer Jaime Rogers; Elvis serenading Mad Nat with 'Maria' and, oh, what beautiful sounds *he* could've made of that single world.

'Play it again!'

The scene he liked best was the one where the Jets regroup after a bloody showdown, finger-poppin' through a song like 'Trouble' from *King Creole* made grand ballet.

The snap of their fingers. *Click! Click! Click!*

'Boy, boy, crazy boy!'

Click! Click! Click!

'Get cool, boy!'

Cool: like Elvis used to be.

The reel ended and in the blink of a sedated eye he was back on a Hollywood soundstage. The final week on set he spent half an hour rambling into the tape machine of a reporter from a Sunday magazine. They asked him about his screen capabilities. Elvis slurred and squirmed as the tape spool clicked sharp as a Jet's fingers.

Click! Click! Click!

'If I can entertain people with the things I'm doing, well, I'd be a fool to tamper with it, to try to change it. I can't...'

Click! Click! Click!

'... It's ridiculous to take it on your own and say, well, I'm gonna some... I'm gonna change. I'm gonna apply...'

Click! Click! Click!

'... I'm gonna try to appeal to a different type audience, I'm gonna...'

Click! Click! Click!

'... Because you might not... you might not...'

Click! Click! Click!

'... and if you goof a few times, you don't get many more chances in this business. That's the sad part of it...'

Click! Click! Click!

'So you're better off if what you're doing is doing OK...'

Click! Click! Click!

'... You're better off stickin' with it until time itself changes things.'

The time was September 1962.

In Hayes, Middlesex, the EMI record factory was preparing to press the debut disc called 'Love Me Do' by a new guitar group from Liverpool.

In London, the young 'Rollin' Stones' were waiting for a consonant, a proper bassist and a better drummer on stage at the Ealing Jazz Club.

In New York, 21-year-old college dropout Bob Dylan was waiting to go on stage at Carnegie Hall to debut a new song called 'A Hard Rain's A-Gonna Fall'.

The Sixties were becoming THE SIXTIES.

And in Los Angeles, Elvis Presley stood in Studio B of Radio Recorders on Santa Monica Boulevard singing about marsupials.

'How would you like to be, a little kangaroo?
A hoppin' up and down, and I could hop with you...'

SIESTA FIESTA

Nungen came back that Christmas for her first visit to Graceland. Her welcome gift from Elvis was 1000 milligrams of Placidyl. She was there for 23 days and, thanks to the Placidyl, spent the first two in a coma. The rest she spent resuming her audition for the role of his Ideal Woman and made slavishly excellent progress; had he told her how she should piss she'd have learned to adjust her bladder accordingly.

She made just two mistakes. The first was becoming jealous when he brazenly flirted with another girl in front of her. The second was to tell him. But she was still 17 and in his landslide of anger found a pebble of praise when he yelled at her calling her 'woman!' It only made her a more dedicated pupil.

For Christmas, Elvis gave her a six-week-old poodle she christened 'Honey'. She gave Elvis a musical cigarette box that played 'Love Me Tender' when the lid opened. He told her he loved it. She told him she loved him. He told her he loved her. He still wasn't sure he believed it. Beyond the halogenated carbinol power of Placidyl he wasn't sure of much these days.

Nungen went back to Germany in January and Elvis went back to Hollywood with his Angels and his pills in his blue felt box, but without his beer-guzzling primate. The last trip West, Scatter gate-crashed a neighbour's cocktail party, molesting the guests and chasing a gardener into the pool. The gardener told the Bel-Air

Homeowners Association, who in turn told Elvis his chimp was no longer welcome. Poor ol' Coconut Head would have to stay behind in Memphis.

They built Scatter his own climate-controlled cage at the back of Graceland. Elvis waved him goodbye through the bars, told him he'd be back in a couple of months and tried not to linger on the all-too-human abandoned brown eyes pleading unspoken 'help me!'s. The kind of look that comes back to haunt a man like a punch in the face when he least expects, stood looking at the studio control room window and seeing in its reflection the bars of his own monkey cage.

'No Room To Rhumba In A Sports Car – Take One!'

He didn't need a take two. Nor did the song. Monkey sing, monkey do.

The new film was called *Fun In Acapulco*. For Elvis it was the same misery in California. The script was another witless falderal about a trapeze-artist-turned-singing-lifeguard. Elvis was 'Mike' just like in his last film, and just like in his last film spent much of it accompanied by a precociously cute child. The opening scene had him in a boat wearing the same yachting cap he'd worn in his opening scene in another boat two films ago. And like every film it had sand, swimming trunks, bikinis and back projection. For the difference it made they could have called it *Blue G.I. Girls! Hawaii*.

The only new change was an abundance of sombreros and Mariachi brass. Its Latin chintz hid weak songs strengthened only by virtue of Elvis' vocal chords. Without them they were cheap cut 'La Cucaracha' and boiled dry 'La Bamba'.

The cutters and boilers were the usual script-serving composers filtered through the Colonel once he'd carved a fat sliver from their publishing. Maestros of mediocrity rhyming 'siesta' with 'fiesta' and 'peso' with 'say so' over an off-the-peg melody as the action demanded. Court minstrels in a kingdom of the bland, its soil so ploughed by repetition hit singles now rarely took root. Given yet another infertile crop, the peach-canners were forced to pay extra for an existing tune by Leiber and Stoller inspired by a new Brazilian dance craze, 'Bossa Nova Baby'. It was the best thing about *Fun In Acapulco* by several miles. About 4000: the distance between Rio and Acapulco.

Elvis finished the film without once setting foot in Mexico. It kept the budget down, which pleased the studio. It also kept the Colonel from having to explain why his illegal alien hide couldn't travel across the border: a secret triumph his *Psycho* genius later commemorated with his idea for the film's promotional flyer.

The one that looked just like a passport.

THE LONELY LIFE

The night his tour bus rolled back into Highway 51 South and turned into Graceland a vigil of local fans was waiting outside. They'd been summoned on collective instinct, a strange stirring in the breeze as if they somehow smelled his approach like the first pollen of spring and had no choice but to flock to its gates. Some of them were always there, so often that the guards in the gatehouse knew them by name and they, in turn, knew the names of the guards. If they came by in the daytime, it was usually Elvis' Uncle Vester or Uncle Travis. In the evenings, it was Elvis' Cousin Harold. The nightshift was usually the father of Elvis' 'little pal', Gary Pepper.

When Elvis first came home to Memphis after the Army the first hand he shook belonged to Gary Pepper. 'I think a lot of Gary,' Elvis told one reporter, 'we've had some swell times together.' Those times were usually gone midnight at the cinema, the fairground or the rollerdrome where Elvis liked to speed around the rink pushing Gary Pepper in his wheelchair. Gary Pepper couldn't walk due to severe cerebral palsy. He lived in Memphis with his mum, his gateman dad and a poodle named after his and Elvis' new favourite actress, 'Brigitte Bardot'. He was Elvis' number one fan, though preferred the word 'Tanker'. Gary Pepper had started his own fan magazine while Elvis was in the Army, using the nickname of his battalion, *The Tankcaster*. Its readers, the fans, were the Tankers, and Gary Pepper was the biggest Tanker that ever lived. His bedroom was decorated with pictures of Elvis, his bedding was embroidered with the names of Elvis' films, he wore his hair like Elvis and some of his clothes were castoffs given to him by Elvis. Nobody loved 'the Big E' more than Gary Pepper.

It was after midnight when Gary's dad, Mr Pepper, in his peaked cap and guardsman coat embroidered with 'E.P.' across the chest, opened the gates, the fans squealing like royal trumpeters as Elvis' bus curved up Graceland's driveway lined with poplar, cherry and oak trees, their trunks and branches silhouetted like black paper cut-outs against the portico lights of his distant mansion. Then the gates closed behind him, the crowd hushed and the city exhaled like a satiated lover. He was home.

Whenever he was home Memphis slept a little sounder and woke a little happier, eager to start the day with a perkier spring in its step. The morning mechanics in the Fairground Amusement Park running the track of the Zippin Pippin went about their brake checks with a louder, more tuneful whistle in their cheeks. The rink men at the Rainbow Lake Rollerdrome buffed the maplewood floor until the sweat from their brow ran to their lips and they savoured the taste of a job well done. The projectionist at the Memphian cinema dusted the lens, wiped down the glide rollers and oiled the sprockets with the not-to-be-hurried delicacy of a French polisher. The manager at Krystal made meticulous stock check of their square patties, buns and dill pickles as if he were auditing gold bullion. The cosmetic counters at Lowenstein's and Gerber's became candy stores to young girls queuing for Maybelline, Max Factor, Revlon, Peggy Sage, Cutex and other magic potions to mask their immaturity in hope of catching a kingly eye in Red On Red, Breezy Peach, Wild Mango, Eye

Velvet, Gay Whisper and Cleopatra Pink. And not one of them aware they had terrifying new competition in town.

When he climbed off the bus and walked up his steps, past the stone lions, between the reassuring splendour of his Corinthian pillars and through his front door, it was straight into the arms of Nungen. She was back, and back to stay.

Her father had flown over with her a few weeks earlier to visit Elvis in Hollywood. A deal had been brokered to allow her to permanently move to Memphis on two strict conditions. The first, that she finish her last two months of education at a suitable Catholic school. The second, and most important, that she not live at Graceland with Elvis. Her father was assured on both counts. She would enrol at the all-girls Immaculate Conception Cathedral School and she would live with Elvis' dad Vernon, his wife Dee and her sons in their home on Hermitage Drive, just behind Graceland but not part of the grounds. Her father took her to Memphis to inspect the arrangements and, once placated, bid his daughter a cautious farewell before flying back to Europe.

Her first two weeks were spent miserably pining for Elvis to return from Hollywood while the Sisters of Immaculate Conception searched for signs of life in her vacant mascara-blind eyes, and quietly prayed for her soul. The eyes grew droopier once Elvis came home and the Sisters' words fell on ears deaf from Dexedrine nights of rollerdromes and rollercoasters. Before she graduated he bought her a lipstick-red Corvair Coupe so she could drive herself to school, and gave her a .25 automatic pistol to keep in the purse she took to class.

The day of the ceremony he was waiting outside to pick her up in his Rolls Royce. The same week she'd finally turned 18. She spent her graduation night as she now spent most every night. In his bed, at home, in Graceland.

★

'The act of sex, gratifying as it may be, is God's joke on humanity.'

Elvis was reading. These days he was always reading. When he wasn't sat in a booth at Vanucci's with his favourite meatball sandwich, or whisking Gary Pepper around the Rainbow Rollerdrome, or watching *The Nutty Professor* at the Memphian with a sack of Krystals, or enjoying the 2 am rush of the Zippin Pippin, or playing touch football, or rolling around the bedsheets, or stock-taking the quart jars in his bathroom safe, he read.

He was reading more than he'd ever read in his life. Books about science, philosophy, karate and history. Joke books, atlases and autobiographies. He read for information, for wisdom, for fun, but mainly for answers. He read a book called *Strange People* about giants, midgets, psychics and two-headed children. He read *The Little Prince* because it had been given to him by a fan and was a favourite of James Dean. He read Bette Davis' *The Lonely Life* because it sounded a lot like his own.

'A good percentage of our lives is spent doing things we loathe. Marvellous! It puts starch in your spine.'

Whenever he read, Nungen would silently watch him, wondering how the words on the pages were turning the cogs inside his head.

'The act of sex…'

Wondering how long it would be until he put the book down.

'… God's joke…'

Took her in his arms and kissed her.

'It's all we've got…'

And told her that she was his 'Nungen' and that someday soon they would be m—…

'… It is not, however, sufficient reason for matrimony.'

Some nights he was just too engrossed in Bette Davis to notice her.

Memphis noticed her. From the first startled sight of her on the other side of the Graceland gates, from her first day at school among corridors of a thousand whispers, from the first time she was seen riding pillion on Elvis' motorbike to grab milkshakes at Chenault's when he told a reporter she was merely 'a friend of the family'. Memphis noticed and when Memphis noticed, Memphis talked. Over the sugar dispensers of diners, in the back rows of movie theatres, in supermarket aisles and steam baths, at lunch counters and shoe-shine stands, wherever coffee, soda or liquor was served with a shot of gossip on the side. Memphis talked about the Girl In Graceland. But nobody beyond the limits of Shelby County was listening.

She spent one full month of bliss when time melted into a long woozy now-and-foreverness; adrift in the undisturbed tactile stupor of his bedroom, its draped windows lined with aluminium foil blockading the slimmest chance of sunlight. They played records, they watched television, they made foreplay of pillow fights and popped pill after groggy pill. Until one day he told her he'd be leaving again for California tomorrow and time froze solid once more.

Elvis told her he couldn't possibly take her with him. She could come out and visit him in a few weeks. Perhaps. But she wasn't his Girl In Germany any more. She was his Girl In Graceland now and that's where she belonged. There in Memphis.

The day he left he kissed her on the steps and told her to 'be a good girl'. She watched his bus of Angels roll down the driveway, past the oaks, cherries and poplars, through the gates opened by Cousin Harold to the shriek of waiting fans, turning right to head north up Highway 51 until it disappeared. She let out a soft moan and Memphis moaned with her. He was gone again.

She stayed in his thoughts almost as far as Little Rock when someone cracked a joke about Scatter, reminding him of the last time he'd ever looked in those poor brown eyes.

Scatter became lonely in his Graceland cage without Elvis, the limo drives with Hog Ears, the beer, the girls and their peek-a-boo skirts. The only women he ever saw were the maids who brought him his meals. Out of boredom he attacked one named Daisy and tore off her wig. A few days later they found Scatter lying on his cage floor, stiff as sheet metal. Daisy had been the last to feed him.

'Daisy. *Goddamn!*'

Elvis chuckled staring out the window as the bus cruised on West down Interstate 40.

Yep. He sure did miss ol' Coconut Head.

FLIP-FLOP

Memphis then Hollywood. Hollywood then Memphis. Sure as Percodan followed Benzedrine one followed the other. Sometimes an extra shot of Nashville in between, but increasingly less so. Elvis had been back there just once in the last year for the usual play-till-the-cock-crows studio all-nighter to record a new single and, he assumed, new album. The single was a sassy frug of bitch-shaming hellfire with a schizophrenic tempo called '(You're The) Devil In Disguise'. It was his best in two years. The album never materialised.

Swishing the peach-canning abacus back and forth, it seemed to the Colonel there wasn't much point. Elvis' albums sold, but not as much as the soundtracks. Any record that didn't sell a film, like a film that didn't sell a record, was a waste of time. It was the same reason the Colonel had turned down all offers for Elvis to tour, including Europe, or return to television. Why bother chasing nickels when there were dollars to be made staying put in Hollywood.

And so Elvis flipped back and forth faster than a square patty on the Krystal griddle. Memphis, Hollywood, Memphis, Hollywood. The weeks and months going on with regularity over and over, each indistinguishable from the next. A long continuous chain.

Then suddenly – there is a change...

RUSTY

She hit him like a bolt of golden lightning, kindling a blaze deep in his groin, its bright orange fire spreading through his arteries along every limb, corkscrewing like a lit fuse up the length of his spine to ignite his head like an Olympic torch. She had a face like the sound of a muted trumpet, its melody plaguing any man who saw it for the rest of their lives. She had a body that moved as if her muscles and bones were at permanent war with one another as to whether to go forwards or back and in their vacillating stalemate created the most wondrous motion in all human anthropology. When she danced she was a steam train running off the rails, her legs its wayward coupling rods, her rump the cabin rocking wildly on its axel, her torso the smokestack popping white hot rivets while her tumbling red hair licked the sky like flames. She was the sex of a thousand bordellos concentrated in five feet and four inches of Swedish-American aged 22 years and weighing 110 pounds.

Her name was Ann-Margret. She was Elvis: The Woman.

The whole cosmos knew it would happen. From the moment the casting of his next film was announced and she was named as his female co-star. His Angels teased Elvis the whole ride from Memphis that it was going to happen. The press speculated it would happen. His Nungen feared it would happen and he tried to reassure her it wouldn't, just as he reassured her when any other actress' name came into conversation. But it happened.

The first day they met for pre-publicity photographs he wore a suit and tie and she a double-breasted coat buttoned-up to the neck. The clothing loosened the next time they met in the studio to record duets for the soundtrack. By the second week of filming the clothes were on the bedroom floor.

The film was called *Viva Las Vegas*. When shooting moved to Sin City itself, after the day's work was done and they retired to his suite on the 28th floor of the Sahara Hotel they sinned all they could in the name of civic pride. They sinned the life out of one another for days at a time. They sinned so long and so hard that the speculation on the physical mechanics involved pushed the curiosity of others beyond the limits of imaginable pornography. When his guys reached their limits they next reached for cutlery, buffing butter knives to a mirror shine to then crawl on all fours outside his room, slipping the blades under the door in the pathetic hope of catching the tiniest peep of sinning in their reflection. They saw nothing and in desperation instead pushed burning newspapers under the door, praying it would frighten them into a sudden naked exit. But the fire under the door was nothing to the fire under the sheets. On they sinned in blissful oblivion.

If Bette Davis was right and the act of sex, gratifying as it may be, was God's joke on humanity then none told it better or laughed harder than Elvis and Ann-Margret. Each the extra neutron to the other's nuclear reactor. Their act of sex a supernova.

Sex?

No. Sex is a word to describe the dismal wriggles of awkward mortals. This was the stuff of opera cycles. A new adventure in the evolution of human intercourse. *Homo-superior coitus-magnanima.*

The congress of Gods.

Sometimes it almost scared Elvis, just how much she reminded him of him. The fuck-times-a-thousand him he used to be, and was starting to be again now that she'd smashed into his life like love's own meteor. The unstoppable meets the immovable, both cancelling out the other in yin-yanging sublimity. The male and the female things called Elvis Presley, united.

He called her 'Rusty' like her character in their film. Sometimes 'Rusty Ammo'. Sometimes 'Scoobie' because that's what she called him back. Sometimes 'Bunny' for reasons his tittering Angels never had to ask.

They both enjoyed sex. They both loved motorcycles. They both breathed music. He played her one of his favourite blues tunes by Jimmy Reed and she felt it as much as he did. From now on it would be Their Song. They would stretch out on the floor and purr its words back and forth, crawling over each other like mating panthers.

'You got me peepin'…'

'… You got me hidin'.'

And as they peeped and hid and purred and crawled in their infatuated Eden, back in the real world they'd left behind half a million feet marched towards the Lincoln Memorial in Washington D.C. And when the feet stopped marching the ears started opening to Peter, Paul & Mary singing Bob Dylan's 'Blowin' In The Wind', to Bob himself singing 'When The Ship Comes In', and to Mahalia Jackson singing 'How I Got Over'. And when Mahalia had gotten over and Dr Martin Luther King Jr. began to speak, it was she who nudged him to 'tell them about the dream.' And Martin looked across the calm black sea speckled with white faces and white banners proclaiming 'IN FREEDOM WE ARE BORN, IN FREEDOM WE MUST LIVE' and told them about his dream.

And while Martin shared his dream of 'a beautiful symphony of brotherhood' singing '*free at last!*', in Memphis a girl with tear-pickled eyes stared at the telephone that would not ring.

Nungen had come to realise in Elvis' absence that being His Girl did not necessarily make him Her Man. She'd ventured up to the Graceland attic and while rummaging around trunks of old clothes found a stash of love letters from his old girlfriend, Anita. They'd been sent to Elvis while he was in Germany, the later ones coinciding with the beginnings of their own courtship. She read every perfumed page in silent hysteria.

It was after she'd discovered the letters that the first gossip columns wagged reports of Elvis and Ann-Margret as the hottest romance in Hollywood. She fell on the newsprint like a bed of nails.

When Elvis finally came home to Memphis, he reeked of sin. Nungen confronted him about the press stories. He told her it was the usual lies drummed up by the studio as publicity for the film. He was a very good liar. But the smell of sin was much too strong.

The telephone that would not ring for her now rang for him all the time. She became suspicious and the phone calls suddenly stopped, just as Elvis suddenly started disappearing from Graceland for hours at a time. She never knew where he went and didn't think to look nearby in his father's house where Scoobie was curled up with the receiver sweet-talking his Rusty.

She began obsessively scrutinising magazine pictures of her redhead nemesis. The puckering lips and the heart-shaped face weren't so very different from hers. With careful cosmetic study they'd be less different still. Aiming for the impossible, she marshalled her body as best she could to move like she'd seen Ann-Margret move, her jealousy seizing imitation as the sincerest form of hatred. She would kill the bitch by assimilation, even at the cost of destroying herself. That's if she had any self left to destroy.

She was flesh, blood and bone but as a person she'd long ceased to exist. She was an actress starring in a fantasy directed by Elvis Presley. Not a woman but a role. The Girl In Germany. The Girl In Graceland. Always a noun, never a name.

Even though she had one…

'Priscilla!'

When the time came for Elvis to go back to Hollywood, Priscilla insisted on coming with him.

He'd tired of the mansion with the butler on Bellagio Road and resumed the lease on a futuristic ranch house he'd last rented two years earlier the other side of Bel-Air Country Club, on Perugia Way. From the outside its encircling concrete ring looked like a flying saucer had just landed above the eighth hole of the golf course below. That or a giant bagel. Elvis' furnishing touches included white and tangerine shag carpet, a jukebox, a pinball machine, a pool table and his secret closet with a two-way mirror so he could watch his Angels grope their dates in the parlour next door. Only Priscilla's arrival meant no more cruising Sunset Strip cherry-picking girls from sidewalks and drugstores to herd back to the boss. Nor any more trysts with Rusty.

Nobody asked aloud, but everyone wondered how long before Priscilla would get bored or be asked to leave.

It took a month.

It wasn't a happy month for Elvis. His new film was a new low called *Kissin' Cousins*: a braindead farce about possum-eating mountain folk ripped off TV's *Beverly Hillbillies*, with Elvis playing two roles, one requiring him to wear a blond wig that made him look like something from a horror film he'd recently seen at the Memphian about platinum-haired monster kids called *Village Of The Damned*. The wig made him look like the Damned Village Idiot.

The Colonel had capped the budget as creative punishment for *Viva Las Vegas* exceeding costs and impacting on his own profit margins. It didn't matter that *Viva Las Vegas* proudly wore its expense in slick Panavision cinematography and slicker choreography by David Winter, one of the 'coolly cool' cast of *West Side Story*. Financially, it was still a foot-long hot dog wasting too much meat with not enough cheap slaw. The Colonel made sure *Kissin' Cousins* was all slaw.

The shoot only took 15 days. Elvis hated every one. Priscilla only hated the one where he came home to Perugia Way after another day's wigged misery carrying a newspaper. The newspaper carried a story about his Rusty attending the London premiere of her latest film. The story carried a quote. The quote carried the information that Rusty was 'in love' with Elvis and together they were considering marriage. The information carried from Priscilla's white-hot brain to the tips of her shaking fingers as they picked up a vase. The vase carried flowers which scattered against the wall in a shower of porcelain as she threw it across the room with a scream. The scream carried the length of the house and into the garden where its ring petered out somewhere over the Bel-Air Country Club.

The Bel-Air Country Club carried on as normal.

The sound of Elvis yanking Priscilla's clothes off her wardrobe rails and tossing them in the driveway didn't carry anywhere near as far. Nor him telling her he was sending her back to her parents in Germany. Nor her tears. Nor his eventual confession.

Yes. He had been seeing Rusty. He'd even bought her a bed – a round one, with pink sheets. But they'd long stopped seeing each other and they weren't planning to marry. He had no idea why she'd tell the press such a thing and the worst of it was that now there'd be reporters hanging outside Perugia Way hounding him for a response.

That was why he'd decided she should return to Memphis until the fuss died down. He told her he needed a woman who could understand that 'things like this might happen'. It was up to Priscilla to decide if she was 'that woman'. And if she wasn't then – 'hell, yes!' – he'd be sending her pea-pickin' ass back to Germany.

The next day Priscilla did as she was told and went home to Graceland.

Elvis stayed in Hollywood and finished his film. When it was over he chose to stay in Bel-Air a little longer before going home. Long enough for Rusty to return from Europe. Priscilla hadn't been gone two weeks when Scoobie and Rusty were once more crawling and purring across his bedroom carpet to Their Song.

If Rusty ever noticed, she never said anything about the missing vase.

After yet another midnight rhapsody of peepin' and hidin' they awoke in Perugia Way late one Friday morning. Rusty was first to slip out of bed, throw on a robe, slide open the secret wall partition and flop on the couch in the alcove off the circular den.

She pressed the remote, switching on the television. The screen flickered to life but all she saw was death.

When her Scoobie came through and sat beside her, seeing the same horror she saw, he held her tight in his arms. Neither of them able to move, nor speak: only weep silently and uncontrollably for a slain President. It was November 22, 1963.

Six days later the film *Fun In Acapulco* opened its invitation to Americans poleaxed with grief: to take what solace they could from Elvis Presley singing '(There's) No Room To Rhumba In A Sports Car.'

THE FOUR SCOUSERS
OF THE APOCALYPSE

The ricochet of Dallas bullets rang coast to coast, ocean to ocean and kept on ringing. The world had gone mad and in its madness America self-medicated in popcorn stupor of *It's A Mad, Mad, Mad, Mad World*, in couch paralysis of *My Favourite Martian*, and in the numbing strummings of the Singing Nun. America needed saving: from nightmares of the brain-splattered lap of a pink Chanel suit every time it closed its eyes; from black headlines, half-mast flags and widow weeds; from the pious Gallic twitter of *'Dominique-nique-nique.'*

Salvation came the very last week of December. A perfect prescription dispensed by four English mopheads: the label on the bottle, 'I Wanna Hold Your Hand'.

Five weeks later it was number one. Six weeks later its creators stepped off a Boeing 707 onto American tarmac and straight into a press conference where a reporter pitched the criticism they were 'nothing but a bunch of British Elvis Presleys'. Ringo, the silly one, answered with a mock Elvis tremor. John, the sarky one, joined in. Paul, the crafty one, and George, the distant one, laughed along. The press laughed with them.

They called themselves the Beatles. They weren't a bunch of British Elvis Presleys but a bunch of British Elvis Presley fans. John would admit as much one of the few times in his life when he ever opened his mouth and didn't say anything sarcastic: 'Without Elvis, there would be no Beatles.' Even if they didn't look, or sound, anything like him.

Their suits were tight, their hair was fringed and their faces four trials and errors of masculine beauty next to Elvis' perfect specimen. Their songs were pretty rather than sexy, their rhythms a squeaky rocking chair to Elvis' hammering brass bedstead. But the day Elvis first excited cathode rays to liberate the loins of youth suddenly felt like a long time ago. Eight years to be precise. America's kids were itching again. The Beatles knew where to scratch.

Two days after landing, they drew first blood on *The Ed Sullivan Show* watched by 73 million: 13 million more than had watched Elvis' debut on the same programme.

'Something very nice happened,' Sullivan told the audience, 'and the Beatles got a great kick out of it. They just received a wire from Elvis Presley and Colonel Tom Parker wishing them a tremendous success in our country. I think that was very, very nice.'

Youth's new infestation of Beatlemaniacs didn't. Outside the band's New York hotel, mounted police grappled with biblical plagues of screaming girls. Some of them waved handwritten signs.

'ELVIS IS DEAD – LONG LIVE THE BEATLES!'

The following week Elvis, not yet dead but fading from public memory, made a rare public appearance in Long Beach, California. He was there to donate a former presidential yacht to a Memphis children's hospital so they could sell it on as a fundraiser. The Colonel arranged a press call so journalists could ask him about the hospital, and the yacht. The journalists had other questions.

'What about the Beatles?'

'The who?' Elvis laughed nervously. 'Heh. I knew this was gonna happen.'

'What do you think of them?'

'Ah.. well…' Elvis stammered. 'I wished them the best of luck over here. Because if these young people can come over here and do well, regardless of what crowd they impress, well more power to them, really.'

The assembled heads smiled and nodded. The Colonel, already starting to regret that telegram, also tried to smile. Until the same reporter piped up again.

'As long as they don't take any of your fans.'

Elvis had no reply.

Having torn off America's mourning veil and stamped it into the dirt, the Beatles flew home to England to start work on their first feature film called *A Hard Day's Night*. The same month Elvis was back in Hollywood to start on his sixteenth called *Roustabout*.

This time he was 'Charlie', an all-singing, daredevil-biking hired hand in a travelling carnival. The film was no celluloid masterpiece but after *Kissin' Cousins* it felt like *Citizen Kane*. It still had its obligatory nonsense: lyrics about pink lemonade and suddenly bursting into song on Ferris wheels. But Elvis at least got to show off his karate in a fight scene, ride a motorcycle and, for the first time on screen, wear the rock 'n' roll armour of a black leather jacket. It was *almost* cool.

The Colonel paraded its carnival set in private nostalgic reverie in another of his white coats decorated with the names of Elvis, the film and its co-stars. The very coat he'd lend to a visiting disc jockey from England who came to have his picture taken with Elvis and take a recorded message back home to the *New Musical Express* Poll Winners' Concert in London. In the brief message Elvis thanked his fans, and the disc jockey.

'It was very nice seeing Jimmy Savile while he was visiting over here.'

The readers of the *New Musical Express* voted Elvis their 'World Male Singer' and 'World Musical Personality'. The same readers voted Jimmy Savile their favourite disc jockey.

Elvis closed his message wishing the Beatles 'much continued success.' His wish was instantly granted when they won both 'British Group' and 'World Group', while the best 'New Disc Or TV Singer' went to somebody called Mick Jagger: a name still unfamiliar to most Americans.

That, like everything else in 1964, would change.

RASPUTIN

The biggest change in Elvis started from the scalp inwards. His weight, circling viciously through burger binge to Benzedrine, now varied from film to film. So did his hair, much to the growing concern of his Hollywood peach-canners. Though always roughly the same in silhouette, its sheen, volume and texture differed: sometimes flaring at the temples; sometimes flat; sometimes loose and oily; sometimes set like concrete; sometimes glossy like jelly from a mould; sometimes dull as though carved from coal.

The comb of blame pointed toward Elvis' Hollywood stylist, a man called Sal from the salon to the stars on Fairfax Avenue named after its boss, Jay Sebring. Sebring thought of his staff not as 'barbers' but as 'hair architects', adopted the Egyptian ankh as his company logo and hired a team of similar occult-minded oddballs, Sal included. Elvis never went to the salon, instead hiring Sal to cut his hair at home in Perugia Way where, between snips, he'd tell Elvis about the goings on at Sebring's and its many characters. In particular this one 'interesting guy' who was especially well read on spiritualism and different religions. Elvis always liked to hear about a fellow reader.

When Sal quit Sebring's, Elvis was suddenly without a hairdresser, just as one was needed for some new studio publicity shots. In emergencies he had his 'little sister', a sexy dark-haired Jewish girl from London, England named Pat who'd started hanging out with his ever-changing choir of Angels at Perugia Way, sometimes cutting their hair, sometimes styling Priscilla's. But Pat worked for free and refused to go on his professional payroll. Elvis needed a new Sal.

That's when he remembered the reader. He told Hog Ears to ring up Sebring's and ask if they could send over whatsisname. 'The Interesting Guy'.

The Interesting Guy came to Perugia Way that afternoon. He was typically well groomed with hooded eyes, strong bones and a voice like suntan oil. A faint purr of marijuana hummed through the musky cologne clinging to the collar of his suede jacket. Just how interesting a guy he was Elvis would discover once the shampooing, cutting and setting was done and he told Elvis, because he'd asked, exactly what he was interested in. He practised yoga and meditation. He read ancient philosophy, metaphysics, theosophy, Freemasonry, the Bible, Kabbala, Buddhism, Taoism and Judaism. He wanted to understand the grand design of creation. He wanted to know the meaning of life. He was searching for God.

Elvis listened, the smell of pomade in his nostrils, the sulphate surge of dopamine in his brain, and in the smell and the surge and the search for God he suddenly thought of June.

June Juanico, the girl from Biloxi.

Back in the 'Hound Dog' summer of '56, June had given him a book. She'd cherished it because reading it made her feel calm. She gave it to Elvis, then 21 and pinballing into fame's unknown outer space, because he looked like he needed calming. And because she truly loved him.

It was a piece of philosophical fiction called *The Prophet* by Khalil Gibran and, as June hoped, Elvis loved it for the same reasons she did. 'It helps me to relax,' he told her, 'and forget everything.'

Elvis didn't forget June though he lost her, partly because June lost him, partly because he lost himself. But he always had *The Prophet*. He bought copies to give away as presents, often inscribed with his scribbled notes in the margins, just as he did on his Bibles. Like the copy he gave to Gary Pepper.

'WHEN THE STUDENT IS READY THE TEACHER WILL APPEAR.'

He wasn't ready in '56. He was now.

He looked across at the Interesting Guy standing in his Bel-Air bathroom and saw, for the first time in his life, his Teacher.

Elvis, the Student, started to speak. Private thoughts he thought all the time that he'd never spoken aloud to anyone before. About how lost he felt, in spite of all his riches. His belief there had to be a God. That everything that happened had to be part of some divine plan. That there were reasons why Jesse Garon died but he lived, why his momma died when she did and why God had chosen him, and him alone, to be the thing called Elvis Presley. He just needed someone, or something, to help him find them.

The Interesting Guy said he might be the one to help.

'Man,' smiled Elvis. 'I've finally found someone who understands what I'm going through. Someone I can talk to.'

Elvis asked the Interesting Guy whether he'd consider quitting Sebring's salon and working for him, full time. As his personal hairdresser. As his spiritual adviser.

The Interesting Guy said he'd be honoured.

That night Elvis told his Angels the Interesting Guy would be joining them from tomorrow on the payroll. His name was Larry Geller and they were all to make him welcome. They all assured Elvis they would, and tried hard not to let it show on their faces they already hated every inch of the bastard.

Larry's first day on the job, he arrived with a bag of products: bottled ones for the hair, bound ones for the head. The book titles teased with grandiose cosmic truths to be discovered within:

Autobiography Of A Yogi, The Initiation Of The World and, the one that really bulldozed Elvis' logic, *The Impersonal Life*. Its author, a mystic named Joseph Benner, first published it anonymously claiming he was merely an oblivious pen-gripping conduit for the voice of God. Benner's message, or rather God's, was that he, God, existed not outside but inside man. The text was a solemn mess of screaming capitals – *'I AM'* – titillating questions – *'Are you ready?'* – and divine disclosures:

'I have always been with you, but you did not know it.'

The Impersonal Life was the craziest of wolves in profound sheep's clothing. Elvis heard only the bleat of wisdom. He read, and re-read it, underlining favourite passages and pressing copies upon his Angels, friends and co-stars, swearing it would change their life. Just as he'd once done with *The Prophet*.

Elvis now called Larry his 'Guru'.

The Angels called him 'Rasputin'.

Rasputin was delighted with the progress of his Russian Empress and encouraged Elvis to expand his library with more baffling masterworks of mumbo-jumbo to vandalise with biro scribbles as he saw fit: *The Tibetan Book Of The Dead, The Rosicrucian Cosmo-conception, The Secret Doctrine, The Secret Path, The Secret Teachings Of All Ages, The Fourth Way, The Fifth Dimension, The Mystical Christ, The Urantia Book* and *Adventure In Consciousness*. The books had the same blissful effect on Elvis' head as the contents of his blue felt box. They helped him forget, just when he needed, who and where he was.

He was the thing called Elvis Presley in the United States of America, 1964. He was on a Hollywood set of a Florida motel pool serenading girls in bikinis with a song about the local Chamber of Commerce. He was 2500 miles away from the real motel pools of Florida where white men were throwing acid in the water to scare out black bathers protesting about segregation. He was a white millionaire 2000 miles from his home state of Mississippi where three civil rights activists were murdered by the Klan. He was in a land whose charts were being swamped with Beatles, Pacemakers, Dave Clarks and Dakotas while he was in a recording studio singing 'Do The Clam'. He was the last can of peaches past its sell-by-date on a shelf fast filling with fresh tins of English rhubarb. He was chopped onion in the Colonel's slaw, the decimal point in other people's paycheques, someone else's mansion, limo, swimming pool, champagne, cigars and rhinoplasty. He was a man in love with the sexiest redhead in Hollywood, living with a 19-year-old bottle-brunette Army brat. He was three parts Dexamyl, two parts Seconal, a pinch of Eskatrol, a dash of pomade, a squirt of Brut and a twist of Joseph Benner.

'I have always been with you, but you did not know it.'

God, and only God, could help him now.

JUDAS WRITES

'The situation regarding Elvis' records gets worse and worse. Here we have an artiste, the first in the world, being slowly but surely – as a chart prospect – killed off by inches through sheer stupidity... But here's the rub: it isn't really Elvis at fault, is it?'

– ALBERT HAND (EDITOR), *Elvis Monthly*, April 1964

'After reading your article "How To Kill Elvis By Inches" I found myself agreeing with you entirely. I think the *real* trouble behind El's releases and failures following these, both film and disc-wise, is his bad management. Of course I refer to Col. Tom Parker. In the past he has proved an excellent manager to El, but lately the discs released have been sub-standard (Elvis-style) and his films have all run on the same lines. In my opinion all this points to Col. Parker... The Colonel is gradually drawing into a shell and taking Elvis with him. He is such a shrewd businessman, thinking only of *his* needs and not of the FANS (surely the latter are more important? They keep a star going). I think Elvis is quickly becoming a legend like Garbo.'

– VALERIE WHITE (FAN), *Elvis Monthly*, June 1964

STRANGELOVE

When Elvis came home again, briefly paroled from Hollywood, he spent most nights in the dark of the Memphian watching his fellow inmates. He watched war films, westerns, crime thrillers and comedies; a film about a man who thinks his wife might be an alien; a film about preserving Hitler's brain; a film about a lunatic asylum; a film about a gentleman's club for sexual debauchery; a film about revenge, and another about how to escape from a prison camp. And over, and over, and over again he watched a film about the end of the world.

'*Mein Führer! I can walk!*'

'Play it again!'

'*Mein Führer! I can walk!*'

'And again!'

'*Mein Führer! I can walk!*'

Elvis laughed at *Dr Strangelove* for reasons his Angels didn't fully understand. But when he laughed, they laughed, and the whole of the Memphian laughed, even Gary Pepper sat on the end of Elvis' row, laughing his gurgling spastic laugh in his wheelchair at the Sieg-Heiling madman in the wheelchair up on screen. Everyone laughing with Elvis, and Elvis laughing, they guessed, at Dr Strangelove's queer voice and self-strangling hand, not knowing if Elvis might really be laughing at his world, their world, the whole world, going KA-BOOM in an Atomic mushroom cloud like the film's end credits. These days, it took an apocalypse to make him laugh.

'Mein Führer! I can walk!'

After the Memphian, he usually went to the Fairground Amusement Park, spending hour upon hour smashing dodgems in his favourite 'Number 1' car, his scarlet shirt purpling with sweat, the invited fans marvelling at his vitality and stamina with starry eyes blind to the Desbutal effervescence of his own.

The Angels loved the dodgem pile-ups too: all apart from Larry.

Before Larry arrived in their midst, the Angels spent their evenings with Elvis 'trolling' for girls, chucking fireworks at each other or filling his pool with camera flashbulbs to shoot with air-rifles for the thrilling spark and bang. Once Larry showed up Elvis stopped the throwing and the shooting and started giving them headshrink books to read as homework, or made them sit around and examine which parts of the Old Testament were really about flying saucers, or listen to him while he randomly picked words from a dictionary which they had to discuss like a college seminar, breaking each one into its individual syllable components until they fully understood its meaning. Elvis told them it would be good for their personal development. And that it was Larry's idea.

It was a rare night on the dodgems Larry didn't limp away with whiplash.

Elvis had invited Larry to come out from California back with him to Graceland. Graceland welcomed Larry with open scabbards.

Vernon hated him the moment Elvis announced he wanted a Star of David added to his mother's grave. Vernon knew he hadn't married no goddamn Jew but he couldn't stop Elvis from calling the stonemason. He also knew which shampoo-and-set Jewish mindfuck was to blame.

Priscilla hated him from the first night Elvis became more interested in studying Larry's library of gobbledygook about dead Indian yogis than the flesh of her still-teenage body. He would recite her his favourite passages aloud in bed. For his sake she smiled and acted as if she, too, enjoyed the books when she'd have rather a cane toad sit and spawn in her ears.

Larry knew all of this. That they hated him, that he was 'Rasputin', 'the Swami' and 'the Brain Scrambler', that the swords were drawn and pointed at his back, that they all resented him for taking Elvis, *their* Elvis – the lover, the son, the flashbulb-popping Peter Pan – away from them. But he also knew Elvis needed him: to find God, to find truth, to find himself. Larry wasn't going anywhere. Apart from the hell the Colonel had already picked out for him.

'Larry, you missed your calling in life. You know how to hypnotise people. You would make a *great* magician on the stage.'

The Colonel said it loud enough so everyone around him could hear. So the Angels knew that he had Larry nailed in his first blink as nothing but a flimflammer, a bunco, a scammer, a quacksalver, a sharpie, a chiseller, a shamster, a hokum-peddling pettifogger.

It took one to know one.

When the Colonel looked at Larry it was with eyes screwed tight as a gun barrel pointing from the sixth floor of a Texas book depository aiming straight at six feet of motorcading bullshit. He just hadn't worked out when he was going to pull the trigger yet.

He'd already tried squeezing it once and it backfired. He'd called Elvis to his office on the MGM lot in Culver City, the one that looked like a farmstead kitchen with oilcloth table and chairs, the walls decorated floor to ceiling with pictures of Elvis and a sign on the door reading 'Elvis Exploitations'. The Colonel politely asked him to sit down and, once settled and a new stogie lit, told Elvis the truth. It was an absurdly un-Colonel thing to do. He'd regret it immediately.

The truth was he'd been hearing things around the studio, on and off the set, about Elvis' sudden change in behaviour; things which, now brought to his attention, he had to act upon. The trouble, as the Colonel saw it, being Elvis' new 'kick'.

'This *religious* kick.'

Elvis stiffened, a righteous fire scalding his cheeks. By 'kick' he knew the Colonel meant 'guy', and by 'guy' he meant 'Larry', and by 'Larry' he meant the one person helping Elvis find something of any meaning in his life beyond dressing like a red velour Ken® singing *'oops, shoopa, doo-wah'* over a tune not even Fabian would have dragged from the drain four years ago.

The Colonel had shown his hand too soon. He realised so even before Elvis walked from the table, back outside into his waiting limo to sonofabitch to Diamond Joe, who was driving, and Larry, in the backseat, the whole way home.

'My life,' he raged, 'is *not* a kick!'

It wasn't a kick. More a sliding tackle on the edge of a precipice, slipping through a mud of crazy books, uppers, downers, meatballs, mashed potatoes, sex, karate and Pepsi. A life more God than Colonel, more Rusty than Priscilla, more Larry than reason, more sitting on the lawn out back of Perugia Way looking at the Los Angeles night sky convinced he could move planets with his marinated mind than caring about the young uprising ten miles down the hill in Santa Monica.

Ten miles down the hill in Santa Monica, thousands of kids were exercising their civil right to scream at the stage of the Civic Auditorium where the sounds of black and white mixed as one, not in greys but in the brightest colours of the pop rainbow. The Motown violets of Smokey Robinson, Marvin Gaye and the Supremes, the California blue of the Beach Boys, the Mersey browns of Gerry & the Pacemakers and Billy J. Kramer, the Chicago silver of Chuck Berry, the wild London jade of the Rolling Stones and the furious flame-red of James Brown.

The concert was the first Teenage Awards Music International event, an all-star extravaganza being filmed over two days for immediate theatrical release as *The T.A.M.I. Show*. Hosted by mentholated surf duo Jan & Dean, it also featured a troupe of go-go dancers choreographed by *Viva Las Vegas*'s David Winter, and a band led by Jack Nitzsche, the man who arranged Phil Spector's hits, its musicians a hit squad of Wall of Sound regulars including guitar player Tommy Tedesco and drummer Hal Blaine. Overseeing the film was a young director already starting to make his name in television. He was called Steve and this was his first feature.

None of the T.A.M.I. teens filing inside the Auditorium noticed the stationary Harley Davidson parked nearby, nor paid any attention to the two men astride it watching them with gently lewd curiosity. One was Hog Ears, the other a young kid from Memphis called Jerry who'd just earned his Angel stripes. The bike belonged to Elvis. They'd borrowed it for the night to clear out of Perugia Way while the boss was home peepin' and hidin' with Rusty, deciding to drive out to Santa Monica to check out the big concert. Where there were rock 'n' roll bands, there were usually girls.

The girls were a little on the young side for them: long bobs, short skirts, go-go boots, Alice bands, Beatles buttons, smelling of gum and Pretty Peach. So were the boys: moptops, white jeans, polo shirts, sunglasses, smelling of pimple cream and big brother's Old Spice. All of them chewing and fiddling with compacts or combs, giggling nervously about 'Diana Ross' and 'Mick Jagger'. The sight, sound and stench of young America, 1964.

Hog Ears and Jerry hung around until they'd gawped, heard and smelled enough, turning the bike back to Bel-Air leaving the Rolling Stones to shake Santa Monica out to sea on electric waves of 'It's All Over Now'.

When they finally got home to Perugia Way, Elvis never did ask where they'd been.

Nor did they think they'd seen anything worth telling him.

PSYCHO (5)

It had been ten years. Ten years since the Colonel first heard the words 'Elvis Presley'. Ten years since the Baron walked into his Nashville office frothing from every pore about the kid he'd seen in Memphis.

The Baron. The poor bastard.

They used to call him 'the Baron of the Box Office'. Oscar Davis was a salesman who got so excited about the sell he'd usually forget who and what it was he was selling. The joke around Nashville was that he'd still be promoting one of his shows two weeks after it had happened. Except that when the Baron started managing the greatest country singer who ever lived, the laughing stopped.

Hank Williams was six feet of lonesome genius. He was also six feet of gun-totin' alcoholic morphine addict who pissed in the middle of the street and shot up hotel rooms for kicks. One night in Ontario the Baron watched Hank drag his genius centre stage on all fours, haul himself up on the microphone stand and slur the same lyric a dozen times before toppling into the audience. As the Baron sped him out of town chased by angry fans, Hank lay in the back seat flicking a middle finger through the rear window. Eighteen months later they found Hank lying in the back of a different vehicle, a 29-year-old corpse petrified by booze and barbiturates. The Baron's confidence died in the same car.

Demoted to the Earl of the Empty Aisles, he took any work Nashville was still prepared to offer and was grateful when the Colonel and Hank Snow's joint Jamboree Attractions hired him as an 'advance man', sent to cities ahead of their package tours to drum up publicity.

That's how the Baron found the boy first.

Although the Colonel had contractually two-timed Eddy Arnold, he'd snowed him good enough to retain a share of his promotions in certain territories, including Memphis where the Baron was sent ahead of Arnold's show at the Ellis Auditorium on Halloween 1954. That same weekend a local disc jockey, Bob Neal, invited the Baron to check out a new singer at a small club just outside the city limits called the Eagle's Nest: a 350-capacity sweat box above a swimming pool where punters cheated licensing laws by smuggling their own liquor in brown paper bags to mix with soft drinks from the dry bar. The gig was hosted by another disc jockey, 'Sleepy-Eyed John', and headlined by mediocre yodeller Chuck Reed. But it was the act before Reed that Bob wanted the Baron to see. A good-lookin' white kid in Beale Street cat clothes who'd caused a minor earthquake at the local Overton Park Shell a few months back by rising up on the balls of his feet and flapping his trousers while he sang. The city's womenfolk, Bob told him, hadn't been the same since. That night the Baron saw the kid, and the trousers, for himself. Never before had he better understood womenfolk.

Two days later the Baron drove back to Nashville, eyes spinning like a one-armed bandit with dollar signs and the face of his next Hank Williams: even better that this kid was a 19-year-old pill-free Pepsi drinker. The Baron almost could've cashed his jackpot, too, had he not made one stupid mistake. He went and told his boss.

It was from the lips of Oscar Davis that the psychopath born Andreas Cornelis van Kuijk first heard the name 'Elvis Presley'.

The Baron. The poor bastard.

That was ten years ago. Ten years of crushing all who came between the Colonel and the boy like peanut shells under a road roller. First the Baron. Then the Memphis disc jockey, Bob Neal. Then his own partner, Hank Snow. Then the man who already had the boy's signature on a contract, Sam Phillips of Sun Records. It was Phillips who'd once said that if he could find 'a white man with the negro sound and the negro feel' he could make $1 billion. The Colonel snowed him out of Elvis for $40,000.

Ten years of snow, and the snow was still falling. The Colonel had just signed another Hollywood deal for Elvis for his dream fee of $1 million per picture. He'd beaten the house and broken the bank. He ought to be sleeping like an overfed sultan.

The Colonel lay wide awake.

It wasn't his conscience. He hadn't any. It was something else. It was the boy.

The boy wasn't right. The Colonel had seen to it that Elvis was now richer than he'd ever been in his life. But – *the ungrateful sonofabitch!* – he wasn't right.

He still did what he was told, but he did so with a necromanced glaze in his eyes that hadn't been there before, sparkling on the surface but murky beneath, the body present but the mind drifting on its own balloon string in strange orbits elsewhere.

He was complaining like he never used to complain, about the films, about the songs, when the films still made him money, as did the records of the songs. His latest soundtrack, *Roustabout*, had just given him his first number one album in three years. Even if it made no sense why young Americans mashed-potatoing to 'I Feel Fine' by the Beatles and the Supremes' 'Come See About Me' should suddenly want to ring in 1965 with Elvis a-hooing '*I got wheels — wheels on ma heels'* he ought at least be glad about it. But he wasn't.

And so the Colonel couldn't sleep for thinking about the boy. What was *wrong* with the boy? He had fame, he had fortune: what else did he need?

What more did he *want*?

JESUS IN THE SKY WITH STALIN

Elvis wanted God and he wanted him now.

He'd wanted him since turning 29 a year ago. Twenty-nine does strange and horrible things to the human brain. The handmaid of regret and serf of shame, 29 starts composing end credits to a film that hasn't yet finished its first reel as it dwells in shiftless misery on that first reel's worst scenes. It turns the eyes upon life's windscreen from the road stretching ahead to the one stretching behind in the rear-view mirror to an unrectifiable past. It took Elvis to be sat in the driving seat of 29 to realise there was something missing in his life that didn't come in high heels or a quart jar. And when he met Larry last spring, he realised that something was God.

Now, all of a sudden, Elvis was 30 and he wanted God even more. Only it was worse than want. It was the cold turkey of desperation.

He'd always been too impatient with his passions. When he discovered karate, he wanted to be a black-belt before he'd broken his first board. When he discovered the kick of prescription medicine, he wanted to open his own drugstore. When he started reading Larry's books about the search for enlightenment, he wanted God's ex-directory hotline number. Words on paper and meditation weren't enough. Elvis wanted signs: burning bushes, parted seas, the disembodied hand of God writing on the walls of Graceland. Once, he thought he'd seen the Angel of the Lord floating out the back of Perugia Way. Priscilla had been there too. She'd only seen the Bel-Air Country Club's lawn sprinklers.

After a year of dedicated study he had nothing to show for his daily mental labours other than shelf upon shelf of strange ologies and isms and a sexually frustrated young lover. There'd been too many nights when he'd fallen asleep sat upright in bed beside Priscilla, pen in hand, book in lap, ethchlorvynol in brain. She'd sit listening to his breathing, staring at his eyelids, his nostrils, his lips, willing them to open, inhale and kiss. Every second she stared at her insensible Adonis was oxygen to the forest fire between her legs, fidgeting beneath the sheets as it burned her flesh until the capsules newly inside her fully dissolved and she, like him, collapsed into dreamless oblivion.

'Larry, what's *wrong* with me?'

He was in a motel room in Texas. Elvis and his Angels had been driving back from Memphis to California in his customised Greyhound bus when they pulled in for a rest. Only Elvis couldn't rest. He had to talk to Larry about his crisis with God and why it was God still hadn't spoken to him directly.

'Oh, man,' he moaned. 'I want it so bad. What *the hell* is wrong?'

And so Larry told him. It wasn't God: it was Elvis.

He wasn't talking to God, he was stalking God. He was two prayers a day short of a celestial restraining order. Elvis was mistaken to believe God was ignoring him. God would speak to him only when he knew he was ready, and clearly Elvis wasn't. He was too full of want. He needed to empty himself. Of his want, of his ego, of his *self*.

'Become empty,' hushed Larry, 'so God can have a place to enter.'

The bus rolled on westwards. Larry sat next to Elvis, behind the wheel, eyes trancing out as he tried to empty himself as Larry had described. Emptying his head the way he emptied the jars from his bathroom safe into his travel case, the case which he then emptied into his mouth, flushing into his stomach, into his system to empty out his brain. Shaking it all out, slowly draining, emptier and emptier. Emptying himself ready for God.

Rolling through Albuquerque. Empty roads.

Rolling through Gallup. Empty desert.

Rolling through Flagstaff. Empty mind.

And then he saw it. Alone, in a Super Technirama sky by William Wyler, the strings of Miklós Rózsa surging between his ears in Westrex Sound. All big, white, fluffy and dictator-looking.

A cloud like the face of Joseph Stalin.

That's when Elvis knew. This wasn't just a likeness of the former General Secretary of the Central Committee of the Communist Party of the Soviet Union in a mass of suspended water vapour. This was...

'GOD!'

His hands trembled upon the steering wheel as he jolted the bus to a jerking stop at the side of the empty highway. Before any of the Angels knew what was happening Elvis had run out of the bus and away into the cacti and scrub of the twilit Arizona desert. Larry instinctively ran after him. When he caught him up, he saw Elvis was weeping and laughing. His breath was sharp, his voice croaky, his eyes fiery swirls like Catherine Wheels in the descending dusk.

'It's... it's God!'

Then he told Larry exactly what he'd seen.

First, the face of Joseph Stalin in a cloud.

A cumulus communist.

Then Stalin's face transformed into that of Jesus.

A meteorological messiah.

Then the cloud Jesus smiled at Elvis.

God had spoken.

'Now I know,' blubbed Elvis. 'God loves me!'

He was no longer empty. He'd been filled by God, just like Larry said he would be. Larry and Elvis hugged each other tight, their embracing silhouettes visible from the bus where the Angels watched in five vexed shades of 'what the *fuck?*'

Elvis remained quiet for the rest of the journey, replaying his vision over and over in his mind like a kid's flicker book from Stalin to Jesus and back again. There had to be a reason God had first come to him in moustachioed shape of 'Uncle Joe' and by the time the bus pulled into Perugia Way he thought he had it all figured out. He summoned Larry to his bathroom straight away to share his revelation.

'I've got to do something *real* with my life,' said Elvis.

'Sure,' said Larry.

'I *know* now what I want.'

Larry made a soft 'um-hm' sound.

'I want to become a monk,' smiled Elvis, 'and join a monastery.'

Larry didn't say anything. His windpipe had been cut by the thought of Elvis Presley in a rope-belted habit and tonsured head.

Elvis didn't like Larry's silence.

'*Tell me!* What should I do?'

Larry cleared his throat and told him Elvis the monk wasn't such a great idea.

The disappointment registered in every muscle of Elvis' face. It was as if Larry had suddenly yanked a plug-chain and some of the God he'd just drunk in the desert was slowly leaking out from under him.

He felt better once Larry had meticulously elaborated on the workings of God as he'd always understood them. Everything happened for a reason, and that reason was God, which Elvis agreed. Now if God had wanted Elvis to be a monk, why would he have bothered blessing him with his incredible gifts? That *voice*? That *face*? Elvis owed his fame and fortune to God, and God alone. By singing and entertaining millions of people he was doing the precious work God had planned for him. Would God have wasted such a face on a *monk*? God wanted Elvis to *sing*. God, Larry reminded him, loved him best when he sang.

Elvis thought about what Larry had said. A large part of him wondered what kind of blessed work God was trying to achieve by making him sing 'Do The Clam'. But he couldn't argue with Larry. Nor did he want to anger God.

'OK,' said Elvis.

The monastery was never mentioned again.

Elvis went to bed still loaded to the eyeballs with God, replenishing any God that might have drained away with that always on hand in his blue felt box. He lay on his covers with another of Larry's books, *Through The Eyes Of The Masters*. He read about love and Jesus while waiting for the last 500 milligrams of God to crescendo in his brain. *'There shall come one,'* said the book, *'a dearly beloved disciple and messenger of mine'*. He underlined the sentence in red felt tip. *'One who shall heal the afflicted and open the ears of the deaf to the secret melodies of the divine spheres.'* His drowsy hand grabbed another pen. He used it to print big spidery black ink capitals at the foot of the page.

'GOD LOVES YOU BUT HE LOVES YOU BEST WHEN YOU SING.'

He tried reading it aloud.

'Goluvzoo buluvzoo bezzed wenoo zing.'

Amen, to dreamless oblivion.

The next day, Godspeeding with God and speed, Elvis reported to the studios of MGM to continue the Lord's work. He had the afflicted to heal, deaf ears to open, secret melodies to sing. For he, Elvis, was the beloved disciple and messenger. His divine message: *'Shake the li'l tambourine! Shake a-ring a-jing-jing a-ling!'*

The new film was called *Harum Scarum* and was supposed to be an Arabian fantasy musical: a kind of pop *Kismet* for the Sixties recycling the same costumes worn in the *Kismet* of the Fifties and, before that, the non-musical *Kismet* of the Forties. When they costume fitted Elvis for a keffiyeh and a turban he realised these, too, were all part of God's grand design and that, therefore, God must be purposely drawing a comparison between himself and that great Sheik of the silent cinema age, Rudolph Valentino.

Accordingly, he practised Valentino's Sheik poses in his mirror, kept his turban on around Perugia Way, even at meal times, and took a late-night drive nine miles across town to Hollywood Forever Cemetery to visit Valentino's mausoleum. By the time pre-production was over and the day came to chalk the first slate, Elvis *was* Valentino. Except had Valentino lived to have been offered a choice between his untimely death following complications after abdominal surgery aged 31 or appearing in *Harum Scarum*, he would have still chosen death. After the first day of filming, Elvis wished he had too.

The Colonel was on set every day in another of his white coats splattered with the name of the film and its cast to make sure Elvis did whatever rum Ali Baba business was asked and supply what credited 'Technical Advice' he could. His main advice, once he'd seen the final edit, being the film was so weak a glass of Scheherazade they could only lend it more fizz by recutting with an added narrator: specifically, 'a talking camel'.

The studio chose to ignore him. The Colonel didn't care. They had Elvis squirming on screen in an orange cummerbund and green pyjama trousers singing 'Shake That Tambourine' to a midget pickpocket. He had his $1 million.

THE BURNING OF LOS ANGELES

Burn, City of Angels! Burn!

Burn so your angel wings melt like Icarus. Burn black and bitter smoke till it rises thicker than night to snuff out the Hollywood sun. Burn till the flames lick so high they tickle the sky like fingers, one for Watts, two for Compton, three for Willowbrook. Burn your cars, your homes and your businesses. Burn your unemployment, your poverty and the LAPD. Burn until the rest of America chokes and gasps on your fumes. Burn for six days until they have to douse with batons, curfews and the National Guard. Burn until 34 bodies lie in the morgue. Keep burning, City of Angels!

'Burn, baby! Burn!'

When the chants of 'Burn, baby! Burn!' had stopped and the looters were no more, when the last gun had been fired and the last rock thrown, when downtown Watts was nothing but scorched bricks, spilled blood, ash and broken hearts, Dr Martin Luther King Jr. arrived. He came not to judge the violence he abhorred but to see and hear. What he saw and heard was sorrow and anger. What he gave was hope.

'I mean it, at the bottom of my heart, that black and white *together* – we shall overcome.'

As Martin was speaking in Watts, half a world away America's black and white together were dying in the unfamiliar fields of South Vietnam. President Johnson had sent the order and the ground war had begun. 'Operation Starlite'. The cannon-fodder poor from Kentucky, New Jersey and South Carolina lying crippled, killed or charred beyond recognition while back home their families waited to be told they'd lost sons, husbands and brothers as the radio played 'I Got You Babe'.

And as Martin wept for Watts, as young marines listened to the screams of limbless friends for whom morphine wasn't enough, as Sonny sang to Cher and Cher back to Sonny, Elvis was laughing in paradise.

Within weeks of *Harum Scarum*, he'd been frogmarched into his next film, *Frankie & Johnny*. The best thing that could be said about it was that it wasn't *Harum Scarum*.

The month after *Frankie & Johnny*, he was poked bayonet-in-back into *Paradise, Hawaiian Style*. The best thing that could be said about it was that it, too, wasn't *Harum Scarum*.

His schedule meant Elvis recorded three soundtracks, 33 songs, in the space of six months. Six months when Bob Dylan rolled 'Like A Rolling Stone' and the Rolling Stones moaned '(I Can't Get No) Satisfaction'. Six months when Elvis Presley was made to puff 'Petunia, The Gardener's Daughter' and 'Queenie Wahine's Papaya'.

The peach-canners who'd never conceived a single original idea between them in the first place had run out of the few they believed they once had and thus saw no reason not to send Elvis back to Hawaii. Which is why, as Los Angeles burned, he was stood over 2000 miles away laughing in Laie. Laughing, because it was his last day of grass skirts and bamboo stamping tubes, because his head was a Mai Tai of methamphetamine, and because he was being interviewed at the wrap party by a funny little English guy with a squeaky voice.

His name was Peter but most people called him 'Herman'. He was the singer with Herman's Hermits, another British group who'd just ram-raided the American charts. He sounded funny because he was from a place called Manchester, and squeaky because he was only 17.

Peter asked Elvis to name his favourite group, 'after the Beatles?'

Elvis laughed. The sort of laugh that preceded bed-straps and a big syringe.

'I would zay your group,' slurred Elvis.

Peter's squeaky little heart danced, waiting for Elvis to say the magic words Herman's Hermits.

'Zuh Rolling Zdones.'

When Peter returned to England the British papers asked him what it was like to meet *the* Elvis Presley. He thought about whether he should tell them the truth: that he couldn't understand Elvis' mumbles, that he found him distant, strange and not altogether there. But better to print the legend. Peter told them he was spellbound.

'It was as if God had come down from Heaven.'

ABOVE: Demob Unhappy. Sgt Presley endures a Rat Pack reception from (left to right) Joey Bishop, Frank Sinatra, Nancy Sinatra and Sammy Davis Jr, Miami, March 26, 1960.

LEFT: The Cowboy and the Tanker. Elvis with his friend Gary Pepper on the set of *Flaming Star*, 1960.

RIGHT: That Sinking Feeling Elvis and his film career prepare for another dive in *Fun In Acapulco*, 1963.

LEFT: Sex On Fire. Elvis and Rusty vertically rehearse their hottest horizontals in *Viva Las Vegas*, July 1963.

TOP: The Almost-Wild One. Elvis' first outing in black leather with Barbara Stanwyck in *Roustabout*, 1964.

BOTTOM: Four Strings Good. Elvis in Graceland, 1965, with the same Fender Bass he played with the Beatles.

LEFT: Pluck Buddies. Elvis bumps while Nancy Sinatra grinds in *Speedway*, July 1967.

RIGHT: Caught In A Trap. Elvis weds Priscilla at the Aladdin Hotel, Las Vegas, May 1, 1967.

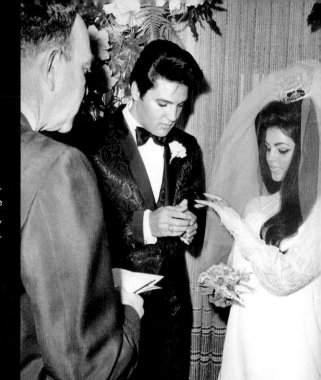

BELOW: Tomorrow Is A Long Time. Elvis drowns the sorrows of a dismal decade in *Stay Away, Joe*, late 1967.

THE PILGRIMS

The limousine to Heaven was a black Cadillac. Blacker than the summer night sky above. It waited in Benedict Canyon for another limousine to lead the way and then together they caravanned down Beverly Hills, turning right along Sunset Boulevard, winding up through the pearly gates of Bel-Air.

The road grew ever steeper, swerving and curving, the four men in the backseat swaying amidst smoke and giggles. The youngest had already lost focus. Where were they going?

'Where are we going?'

Then he remembered: they were going to Heaven to meet God.

The two cars twisted and turned higher and higher, snaking into the hills until they stopped outside another set of gates surrounded by screaming cherubs waving Instamatic cameras. The gates swung open just wide enough for the cortege to slide past, rolling to a stop on Heaven's driveway. The four men fell quiet. They'd arrived.

The passengers from the first vehicle led them through a glass door overhung with ivy. Heaven wasn't anything like they first expected. Not white clouds but futuristic furnishings with soft red and blue lighting. Not harps but the faint sound of electric guitars. They followed where they were led, through the circular hallway, past suntanned saints and bouffant angels, the celestial music growing louder with each footstep. They walked as if in a dream, every tread in slow motion, four wide-eyed babes in Wonderland.

And then in a flash of white couch and the ricochet of a jukebox, they saw him.

'*Who is the coolest guy, that is, what am?*'

He wore a red shirt under a high-collared black bolero jacket, sat opposite a colour television flickering with its sound turned down, music humming from the record machine and an amplifier beside him with a jack-lead running to the white Fender bass in his lap.

BOM-BOM!

This was *Him*.

BU-BU-BU-BOM!

This was God.

BOM-BOM!

And God was playing bass.

The four guests froze. God looked up and smiled, put his instrument down and stood up.

From behind them another voice spoke.

'Elvis, meet the Beatles...'

Zooooooomph!

A warp in space time. The crashing of two galaxies into one another. An event of such cosmic ferocity it would scorch the recollections of all who witnessed, leaving only debris of misremembered myth; rubble reshaped by hindsight, jagged pieces of different jigsaw puzzles impossible to piece together into a truthful whole. A rock 'n' roll *Rashomon*.

Elvis had returned to Perugia Way after filming in Hawaii. The Beatles were on tour in America, renting a house in Los Angeles where they were playing two nights at the Hollywood Bowl. A journalist friend of theirs, Crispy Hutch, who'd been covering their tour for the *New Musical Express*, appealed to both the Colonel and the Beatles' manager, Mr Epstein, to capitalise on the rarity of time and proximity by orchestrating a meeting between their boys. After delicate negotiations, smoothed by Crispy's diplomacy, both decided it was indeed feasible. But only on certain conditions.

It would have to be strictly informal and off record. There would be no photos, no interviews and nothing taped for posterity. The Colonel, furthermore, insisted that the Beatles come to see Elvis, not vice versa. Mr Epstein cordially agreed.

And so, alongside Crispy, the Colonel and Mr Epstein, John, Paul, George and Ringo walked through the front door of Elvis' home at 525 Perugia Way on the night of Friday, August 27, 1965. That much is undisputed.

The rest is the broken jigsaw of fable.

The Beatles stepped into the den where Elvis was playing bass along to his favourite new song, 'Mohair Sam', by Charlie Rich. He invited them to sit down: John and Paul on one side of him, Ringo on the other, while George squatted cross-legged at his feet. All four of them were silent, unable to stop gawping, so close to God they could actually *smell* him.

God smelled of pomade and Brut 33.

'Look, guys,' God told them, half-laughing, 'if you're just going to *sit there* and stare at me, I'm going to bed.'

The tension diffused, the fantasy commenced.

Elvis asked his Angels to pass around some instruments so he and the Beatles might risk the greatest jam session in the history of vibrated string. With Elvis on bass and John, Paul and George on guitars they played along to records on his jukebox by Chuck Berry, Ray Charles and even their own 'I Feel Fine'.

(Or they hardly played a note.)

John's first words to Elvis were 'So zis is ze King?' Elvis recognised his voice as that of Dr Strangelove and soon the two were trading self-throttling, Nazi salutes, the King and the Beatle laughing, 'Mein Führer! I can walk!'

(Or they did no such thing.)

Priscilla was there and sat up the whole time with Elvis and the Beatles.

(Or she was barely present, a mute spectre in a purple dress only briefly flitting in and out.)

George slipped out to the garden and spent most of the evening smoking marijuana and talking about Eastern religion with Larry.

(Or George got stoned alone.)

Elvis maybe or maybe didn't drink 7-Up.

The Beatles maybe or maybe didn't drink scotch and bourbon.

Ringo maybe or maybe didn't leave the den to play pool with the Angels while their girls drifted back and forth from the kitchen.

Elvis probably did have 'You're My World' by Cilla Black on his jukebox and the Beatles probably did tell him she was their pal, 'Cyril'.

The Colonel probably did spend all night gambling and very likely, as he bragged, did take Mr Epstein for every cent.

And John, in the insane *now* of being sat beside Elvis Presley, probably did feel the dizzying headrush of *then*. The magic then of being 15 years old, the taste of Senior Service, the smell of warm vinegar and chip paper, the sound of his friend Mike's Dansette, the vision of spinning blue HMV POP 182 and its 78 holier-than-holy revolutions per minute.

'Well, since my baby left me…'

The voice of God, only bigger than God, bigger than all existence. And now here he was, 24 years old – *top of the world, ma!* – at God's right hand, able to ask him *anything*. Able to hear whatever sacred words he wanted straight from the mouth of the Almighty. And so for the love of feeling so lonely he could die, for the love of a bellhop's tears and a desk clerk dressed in black, for the love of God, *his* God, and HMV POP 182, John seized it.

'Why,' he asked Elvis, 'don't you go back to making rock 'n' roll records?'

Zoooooomph!

Heaven cried, God was rumbled and his kingdom collapsed.

Elvis strung together an answer but the words weren't his own. He'd learned them from the script of a picture he'd been making every day of his life for the last five-and-a-half years. About how he was too busy with his film schedule, but that didn't mean to say he wouldn't, or couldn't, make any more rock 'n' roll records.

'In fact,' he toyed, 'I might just do one soon.'

John smiled. 'Then we'd buy that one.'

Thus the Master was slain by his most devout disciple.

Before they left, the Colonel gave each Beatle the gift of a table lamp shaped like a miniature covered wagon, a gun holster, a gold leather belt and a set of Elvis' latest records: the non-rock 'n' roll sort they otherwise wouldn't buy.

John returned the invitation, asking Elvis to visit them at their rented house in Benedict Canyon while they were still in town. Elvis said he'd let them know. John knew that meant he'd never see him again. He didn't.

Elvis came out to the driveway to wave them goodbye, watching their limousine vanish past the same screams and flashing Instamatics that first greeted them, through the security gates, turning downhill, back into the arms of the world that loved them. Some of the screams had even been for Elvis, but he hadn't heard. He could hear only the needle sticking in a brand new disc now spinning in his head, over and over, each jump-scratch like an oyster knife shucking into the base of his skull.

'Why don't you go back to making rock 'n' roll records?'
SHKKKK!
'Why don't you go back to making rock 'n' roll records?'
SHKKKK!
'Why don't you go back to making rock 'n' roll records?'

THE ACID KING

The scratch that entered his head that night in August, pecking away at his brain like an angry cockerel with a Scouse accent and a stainless-steel beak, would not go away. He needed an adrenalin booster shot of God to remove it, another low-lying Stalin coming in from the east. But though he still spent hours sat staring at the skies on the grass outside Graceland and Perugia Way, apart from the occasional glimpse of a flying saucer others might have dismissed for a shooting star, God would not answer.

In God's silence, Elvis tried anything and everything. He joined a Los Angeles yoga cult called the Self-Realization Fellowship where he was initiated by its leader, Daya Mata, an ex-Mormon in her early fifties who reminded Elvis a little of his mother. The Fellowship had been founded by the Indian spiritual master Paramahansa Yogananda to promote the yogic path to enlightenment and included in its monastic vows a surrender of all money and possessions. Elvis surrendered them a cheque for $5000. It enlightened the Fellowship most agreeably.

Inspired by the landscaped grounds of the Fellowship's Mount Washington headquarters he built his own 'Meditation Garden' at Graceland, with brick arches from Mexico, stained glass from Spain, marble statues from Italy, ionic columns, cherubs, monks and planters set around a fountain with underwater lights and over a dozen different sprays.

At the same time he built a slot-car room over the Graceland patio so he could be his own God over an electric world of miniature speeding Firebirds and Chaparrals; his latest attempt at mental distraction beyond the usual karate, dodgems and Memphian nights endlessly rewatching *Dr Strangelove*.

He experimented with new pills, including Quaaludes and improved compounds of codeine sulphate.

He tried smoking marijuana but found he preferred eating it baked in space cakes and ate enough of them to float to Betelgeuse and back.

'Why don't you go back to making rock 'n' roll records?'

But still the cock pecked.

There was only one thing left. The thing that he'd nearly tried earlier that summer except he'd been too scared so he made his Angels be his guinea pigs instead. Larry had gotten it for them from a cute student named Bonnie who hung around outside Perugia Way and it was there, in the same den where he met the Beatles, that Elvis made the West boys, Red and Sonny, take windowpane acid while he watched its effect.

'O nobly born, listen well: You are now in the magic theatre of heroes and demons...'

The West boys had sat on the circular couch while Elvis read aloud from a book. Larry was there as sober back-up in case either of the lab rats freaked out.

'Giants, Angels, Bodhisattvas, dwarfs, crusaders, Elvis... Elvis, woah!'

He'd chuckled.

'Wait, now. *Elves...* E, L, V, E, S. OK... *Elves, Devils, saints and sorcerers.'*

The book was another of Larry's recommendations, Timothy Leary's *The Psychedelic Experience*. Elvis wanted to see if acid could open a gateway to God and, not wishing to risk a bad trip, had selected Red and Sonny to be his special envoys to Shangri-La.

He'd hoped that by reading them passages from Leary he'd speed its onset. He'd also suggested Red kept a guitar in his lap to see what sort of music he could write under its influence.

'Do not be afraid of them.'

If the experiment was a success then he'd be willing to try LSD for himself.

'The whole fantastic comedy takes place within you.'

Sonny's eyes went first, Red's seconds later, four whirligigs of wonder.

Elvis told them to 'think about God'. They still remembered what 'God' meant but 'think' had lost all meaning.

Red watched the guitar coil itself around his body like a liquid-wood serpent.

Sonny ran to the toilet where he thought he was Moses and God was a light bulb. Larry had shouted through the door to ask if he was 'OK?' He'd heard a queer howling sound before Sonny burst out, running into the garden where he rolled on the lawn in a patch of overgrown ivy ripping at the leaves.

Larry guessed he probably wasn't OK.

Red had remained hunched over his guitar but the only music was in his face, an erratic tempo of twitching muscles and gurning lips. He stayed that way for eight hours.

Elvis concluded it would be best to wait before rapping his own knuckles on the Door of Perception. But that was before he'd been crucified by John for crimes against rock 'n' roll.

It was now Christmas 1965. The Sixties were halfway over.

It was time.

Elvis dropped acid at home in Graceland, sat around a table in the upstairs office. Larry, young Jerry and big Lamar dropped it with him. So did Priscilla, willing to try anything her man tried in the hope it might bring them closer and make sense of the otherwise insensible clockwork of his mind. Sonny, once bitten, was there as the bad trip insurance salesman on standby to see none of them wound up howling in the ivy.

Larry wound up just being Larry.

Jerry wound up giggling in a clothes closet.

Big Lamar wound up running into the garden and throwing his arms around a tree.

Priscilla wound up in the Ninth Circle of Hell, wailing through mascara showers that Elvis didn't love her before slumping beside a fish tank on the upstairs landing.

Elvis wound up hungry.

Sonny rang out for pizza which the rest of them ate tripping in front of the television. It was like eating an electronic mosaic, pointillist particles of red, white and yellow neon that glowed in their mouths like a toffee-apple bite of the sun.

As Elvis chewed his pizza, the TV screen chewed Elvis. It was *The Time Machine* with Rod Taylor, based on the sci-fi novel by H.G. Wells. This was where his search for satori would end: out of his gourd in the fourth dimension as a 19th century scientist fighting Morlocks with a mouthful of dough and tomato sauce.

One week later it was 1966. The week after that Elvis turned 31. His birthday present from God – another joint number one in America's single and album charts for his old pals, the Beatles.

TWELVE SCENES OF '66

— 1 —

The Colonel was having another of his sleepless nights. He was restless as a snake-oil salesman on a midsummer's eve, the smell of warm tar in the downwind breeze, the earth shaking with the distant stampede of townsfolk weighed down with rope and feathers. A sixth sense of foreboding doom.

Though he held a good hand of picture deals to keep the boy busy for the next year or two – one for United Artists, four more for MGM – his luck at the Hollywood gaming table was on the wane. It scared him to admit it but lately he wasn't snowing so good. Either he'd lost his High Potentate's touch or his opponents had begun to see through the cigar smoke – even Hal Wallis. The Colonel had managed to squeeze one more film out of him but Wallis had made the deal seem like Paramount's idea of a charitable donation. The Colonel suspected he'd never be able to snow Wallis for an Elvis film again. He suspected right.

The problem wasn't the Colonel. It was the peaches. Cans of Elvis weren't selling like they used to.

The films still made the studios money but the profit margins were shrinking. Their biggest cost was Elvis and the Colonel's budget-sapping fee: the loose change paid for the rest, and it showed on screen like a maître d' lifting his cloche on a salver of

Bazooka Joes. Elvis films were cheap and too many: three every year. It had worked when one of those films was *Blue Hawaii* and the year was 1961. In 1961 audiences hadn't yet experienced the Beatles in *Help!*, *The T.A.M.I. Show*, James Bond, *What's New Pussycat?* or the Man With No Name. Now they had and nobody was queuing to see Elvis in a helicopter singing *'I need a dog's life'* to four pooches.

The old arithmetic – Elvis + lots of girls + lots of songs = box-office hit + number one soundtrack album – no longer added up. The albums had stopped reaching the top ten and sooner than his label's pessimism could cope with they'd struggle to even reach the top 40.

The past year had borne only one hit single, the grimly sentimental 'Crying In The Chapel'. It was a five-year-old outtake from his 1960 gospel album which Elvis shelved first time around because he didn't think it was good enough. By 1965, old substandard Elvis was all the peach-canners had to play with. With God on its side the song reached number three in Billy Graham's America and snuck to number one in a Britain not yet in full Sixties swing. But it was a freak peak in a sales chart tipping like a fat kid on a see-saw.

These were the chirps of doubt louder than the desert crickets that kept the Colonel awake, frowning at his moonlit blue bedroom wallpaper in his Palm Springs hideaway. Something had to change. He couldn't change the boy. Elvis was Elvis. Ken® was Ken®. But he could change the players at the gaming table. Find new pockets to empty, new faces to blow smoke in, new suckers for his Snowmen's League of America. He'd cashed his chips at most every film studio, but there was still gold to be had in them thar Hollywood hills. Hidden in the crevices of Culver City, along Fountain, down in La Brea, possibly even beyond the ridge in the panning shallows of Burbank. Wherever it was, he would find it.

Or so the Colonel tried to convince himself as the crickets of desert and doubt chirped on under the pale blue moon.

— 2 —

A hundred or more miles away in Bel-Air, the same moon shone down on a one-storey ranch house with a swimming pool surrounded by stone urns recently painted an electric Dexamyl blue by its new tenant.

Elvis moved into 10550 Rocca Place, further up into the hills from Perugia Way, shortly after his acid Christmas when he came back to Hollywood to start his twenty-second feature film. In this one, called *Spinout*, he played a racing driver, again, called 'Mike', again, and had to sing a song called 'Smorgasbord' likening the female species to the hors d'oeuvres of a Scandinavian buffet.

Each night, as this night, after another day of backlot human puppetry Elvis would sit at the piano in Rocca Place and sing. Sometimes alone, other times accompanied by his two musical Angels, Red and Charlie: singing sad songs, sacred songs, even songs without words.

There were no words to Beethoven's 'Moonlight Sonata'. The melody spoke its own sorrow. The title wasn't Beethoven's but added after his death so the public could distinguish his 'Piano Sonata No. 14 in C# Minor' from his other sonatas. The accompanying fiction was that the German maestro, not yet deaf, had composed it for a blind girl to describe, in notes, the melancholic beauty of moonlight.

It was one of Elvis' favourite pieces of music, but when he played it he always sang it, and when he sang it all the misery in the living world found its echo chamber. Not words, just low, deep, rib-rattling *basso profundo*. The sound of the soul of Elvis Presley: as pained and lonely as the groan of the son dying upon the cross.

'Oooo-ooooh, wooo-aaah, waaa-aaaaaah'
Eli, Eli, lama sabachthani in C# minor.

— 3 —

Five thousand miles away, the last man to crucify Elvis sat in his mock Tudor mansion in the Surrey countryside talking to a reporter called Maureen from London's *Evening Standard*.

'Jesus was all right,' said John, 'but his disciples were thick and ordinary.'

He'd given Maureen a tour of his house, showing her his suit of armour called 'Sydney', his gorilla costume, his fruit machine, his toy cars, his five televisions, his Rolls Royce, his Ferrari, his Mini-Cooper, his swimming pool, his wine cellar, his antique Catholic-looking crucifix and his collection of books including an enormous Bible and the works of Aldous Huxley. Lately, he told her, he'd been reading 'extensively' about different religions.

'Christianity will go. It will vanish and shrink,' John continued. 'I needn't argue about that. I'm right and I will be proved right. We're more popular than Jesus now.'

— 4 —

As John's all but unnoticed ripple in English newsprint began its five-month crossing of the Atlantic, over on the other side in New York City, Bob Dylan walked into the slow service elevator of a former cold storage warehouse on East 47th Street with a filmmaker called Barbara. She'd invited Bob there to meet an artist friend of hers who had his studio on the fourth floor. Despite it being a dull March afternoon, Bob wore sunglasses. So did the artist, Andy Warhol.

Andy asked Bob if he'd mind sitting for a couple of what he called 'stillies': short silent screen tests requiring he merely look into a 16mm film camera for one reel and just be himself. Bob obliged and sat for two: one with sunglasses on, the other off.

When the filming was finished, Bob pointed to a large canvas leaning against the studio wall. He told Andy he really liked it and wondered if it would be OK if he took it as payment for his stillies. Andy said he could. Bob was delighted.

It was a double silver screen-print of a young man in western dress with a holster belt and a drawn gun in his right hand.

Bob's prize, a portrait of his hero: Elvis Presley.

— 5 —

As Elvis Presley was being newly hung on Bob Dylan's wall, Bob Dylan was bouncing off the walls of Elvis Presley. Along with the nightly moans of Beethoven it was becoming a familiar sound in Rocca Place. Not Bob himself, but an LP of his songs by the woman Dr Martin Luther King Jr. hailed as 'the Queen of American Folk Music', known only by her first name, Odetta. Elvis' favourite was called 'Tomorrow Is A Long Time', a song Bob himself hadn't gotten round to releasing yet. It opened with Odetta's sonorous rumbles, swooping to a high controlled vibrato, somewhere between blues and opera, over a hypnotically unhurried country guitar.

'I can't speak the sounds that show no pain.'

Elvis played the song over and over, harmonising with Odetta, his timbre taking Bob's loneliness out into the cosmos in a sound to fill the solitude between the stars. The same interstellar otherness he'd been reading about lately in a book alleging to be the transcribed telepathic communications of an extra-terrestrial from Jupiter called 'J.W.'

The Changing Conditions Of Your World.

— 6 —

Back in the world of J.W. Lennon, conditions were changing exactly as he'd planned. The exact same conditions Elvis had planned a year earlier, sat watching Red on the couch in Perugia Way: a guitar, a tab of acid and a copy of Timothy Leary's *The Psychedelic Experience*.

Elvis hadn't had any success cajoling Red to translate his trip into a song. But then Red wasn't a Beatle. John started by recording himself reading Leary's book aloud on a reel-to-reel tape machine so he could play it back once he'd dropped acid. As he started to fly, he started to write, less a song than a blowback in sound which he christened 'The Void'; a tune so strangely original most people who first heard it would have believed, had they been told, that it was the musically transcribed telepathic communications of an extra-terrestrial from Jupiter.

The Beatles recorded the song in early April, since renamed 'Tomorrow Never Knows', so turning rock 'n' roll and *The Psychedelic Experience* into a singularity; and succeeding where Elvis Presley had failed.

—7 —

While the Beatles were finishing their overdubs on 'Tomorrow Never Knows', Elvis was driving back towards Memphis in his customised Greyhound listening to his favourite tapes of gospel music and the greatest hits of Roy Orbison; a singer he admired because he had the vocal range of four galaxies and focussed it in sweet despair like a comet streaking orbits through every one of them.

He arrived at Graceland late Saturday evening where several dozen fans were waiting outside, including a couple of girls in homemade sweaters with his name stitched across their breasts, and the local Lewis family with a 'Welcome Home Elvis' banner. Then the gates closed behind him and the city once more readjusted its social clockwork to his vampiric needs.

Midnights at the Memphian he drowned his eyeballs in God, sex and stupidity: humbled by *The Ten Commandments*, lusting for Bardot in *Viva Maria!*, and snorting like an infant through *The Ghost And Mr Chicken*. The next five or six hours he'd normally spend knocking the images out of his head with black beauties and bumper cars. Except for one night when after four hours on the dodgems an electrical storm cut the power. When it passed and the supply returned, he resumed slamming his Angels until sun up. But in that short lull, as zigzags marbled the dawn sky and the rain hissed upon the ground, as the thunder rolled and the universe displayed its power, another lightning struck Elvis' body.

It sparked and fizzed inside him for almost a month until blasting out of his mouth, brilliant as a searchlight from the tallest tower in Heaven, scorching its intensity onto quarter-inch master tape. When it was done, for a few seconds Elvis looked momentarily dead, as if the life spirit had been sucked from his body, or some indescribably holy static energy now transferred back out into the atmosphere. Like ions after a Tennessee thunder storm.

The light had poured out of him one May night in Nashville where, thanks to his peach-canners' crisis of available material and plummeting soundtrack sales, he'd been allowed his first non-film session in over two years. It was the first time, in all that time, that Elvis had been allowed a chance to sing what he wanted. And what he mostly wanted to sing was songs about God.

He'd selected enough material for a second gospel album and by 4 am that first night had four songs taped, including the one with the light, 'How Great Thou Art', destined to become its title track. But after six hours singing in the pulpit, it suddenly hit him: the enormity of his freedom. He didn't have to stick to gospel. He had a studio, he had a band and he had a microphone: he could sing *anything*.

And so he sang 'Down In The Alley', a thrust of knee-trembling R&B by his old favourites the Clovers. Only after he'd squeezed its sinful euphemisms of their last sticky drop did he appreciate the scale of his victory. He'd made a rock 'n' roll record again.

He still had one more in him before sunrise. It, too, glowed like the first rays of dawn, or equally the last of dusk. It was five minutes long but took him only three takes. He'd already practised it plenty baying at the Pacific moon high above Rocca Place.

'I can't speak the sounds that show no pain.'

It was the Odetta song, 'Tomorrow Is A Long Time'. He sang it as if a satellite drifting through the lonely orbit of Orbison; as if he felt every syllable; as if he finally belonged in the 1960s.

The words of Bob Dylan, kissed by Elvis Presley.

— 8 —

The day Elvis recorded what Bob would later call his favourite cover version of any of his songs, Bob played the first of two nights at London's Royal Albert Hall.

After being booed by mothballed wretches for daring to play electric rock 'n' roll, he spent the rest of the night with his new friend John, who that day had been in the studio with the Beatles cutting some wearisome nonsense about a coloured submarine; considerably less of a rock 'n' roll record than the one about the joys of back-alley sex hammered out in Nashville less than 24 hours earlier.

Bob travelled to John's mansion in the Surrey countryside with its gorilla costume, five televisions and the suit of armour called Sydney. There they took too many drugs and exchanged gibberish until the morning when both shared a limousine back to Bob's hotel in Mayfair. The first thing Bob did when he got to his room was vomit.

Ten hours later he was back on stage at the Albert Hall being booed by more mothballs.

— 9 —

Four thousand miles away in Nashville, Elvis was still in the studio singing about God. The album, *How Great Thou Art*, was turning out better than he could have hoped, much of it thanks to his new producer Felton Jarvis who'd followed his instructions to lend the recordings a modern contemporary feel.

As Elvis had asked him, 'like the Beatles.'

— 10 —

The ripple became a tidal wave, breaking that July in a teenage magazine called *Datebook*. The issue had Paul from the Beatles on the cover next to a list of content quotes.

At the top, PAUL McCARTNEY: *'It's a lousy country where anyone black is a dirty nigger!'*

Further down, BOB DYLAN: *'Message songs are a drag!'*

Further down still, TIM LEARY: *'Turn on, tune in, drop out!'*

But it was the quote just below Paul's that did it.

JOHN LENNON: *'I don't know which will go first — rock 'n' roll or Christianity!'*

It was the same interview with Maureen from London's *Evening Standard* published back in March. The one where John said the Beatles had become more popular than Jesus. A tsunami of foaming blasphemy crashing down upon the shores of God-blessed America.

Two weeks later the Beatles landed in Chicago to start their next American tour. John tried to clarify what he'd meant. 'I wasn't saying the Beatles are better than Jesus or God or Christianity,' he told the press. 'I could have said TV, or cinema, or anything else that's popular. Or "motorcars are bigger than Jesus." But I just said "Beatles" because, you know, that's the easiest one for me.'

Paul was also pressed to explain what he'd meant by calling America 'lousy'.

'There are bound to be extremist people who'll think that we're wrong for saying that coloured people are the same as white people. But I honestly believe that.'

That night in the lousy South, where men calling themselves 'grand wizards' dressed in pointy hats and capes and set fire to crosses in the name of white Jesus, crowds gathered to savour the smell of melting plastic and burning cardboard as once-loved copies of *A Hard Day's Night*, *Help!* and *Rubber Soul* were tossed onto a rising pyre.

Two days later, a second public Beatles bonfire took place in Texas, organised by a radio station in Longview where the local newspaper had called for the group to be 'fumigated and deported'. As pictures of four young Englishmen perished in the flames, hundreds of Texas teenagers watched grooves of *'yeah! yeah! yeah!'* and *'shake it up, baby'* turn to ashes as they hollered their favourite hits of Elvis Presley.

The frightened white men in capes and pointy hats were there waiting when the Beatles reached Elvis' home town of Memphis. They sent their pointiest jackass to be interviewed by local television outside the Mid-South Coliseum where the group were scheduled to play. After misquoting John as having claimed the Beatles were 'more better' than Jesus, the clown from the Klan proudly called himself a member of 'a terror organisation' and promised that he and his pointy brethren had 'ways and means' to stop the concert.

They stopped nothing. The main local protest was a peaceful 'Memphis Christian Youth Rally' held across town at Ellis Auditorium while over at the Coliseum the Beatles' sold-out evening show went ahead – not quite without incident. During the third song a noise cut above the screeching crowd and their own muffled amplified din clear as a gunshot. It turned out to be a cherry-bomb firecracker lobbed from the balcony by a would-be saboteur. The Beatles played on and finished their half hour set as planned. Only afterwards did they reflect on how scared they'd been and how, when they heard a loud bang, they'd all turned to where John was stood.

Just for a second, they thought he'd been assassinated.

— 11 —

Elvis never saw the Beatles play Memphis. At the time he was in Los Angeles. When they later played Los Angeles, he still never saw them. He never would. They finished their tour in San Francisco's Candlestick Park. It would be their last concert; partly because they never could forget the bang of that Memphis cherry-bomb.

The last Tuesday in August, as the Beatles flew home to London from Los Angeles, in Los Angeles Elvis spent his last day chained to the set of another film. His final scene was on the back of a pick-up truck loaded with chicken coops beside his 17-year-old English co-star, Annette Day. The producer had discovered her on a visit to London working in her mum's antiques shop. Annette had no previous acting experience and acted as if she had no previous speaking experience. Elvis needed stiff coaching from his blue felt box to finish the scene, not because of Annette but because of the waking agony of the song they were making him sing to her. A rewrite of the old nursery rhyme, 'Old MacDonald', given a carnivorous twist where everything that clucked, mooed and oinked was turned into fricassee, burgers and pork 'n' beans.

Three months ago he was siphoning the soul of Bob Dylan. Now he was sat next to poultry whining *'ee-i-ee-i-o'*.

The film's working title was *You're Killing Me*.

— 12 —

In Palm Springs, the Colonel still wasn't sleeping.

OH, WHAT'LL YOU DO NOW, MY BLUE-EYED SON?

Nothing had changed.

With *You're Killing Me*, which was released in America as *Double Trouble* and elsewhere as *Songs And Confusions*, Elvis' films ceased attacking the intellect and shifted all focus of assault to the basic workings of the optic nerve. He didn't think Hollywood could drag him any lower than 'Old MacDonald', until his next where he found himself in an exercise class wearing a black leotard singing 'Yoga Is As Yoga Does' as he tied himself in knots. It was a horror film even before they gave the role of his instructor to the woman from *Bride Of Frankenstein*. It was released in America as *Easy Come, Easy Go* and elsewhere as *Pirates In Bikinis*. Nothing had changed.

Nothing had changed on film, nor on record. His latest album was the soundtrack to *Spinout*. Since the film only featured eight songs the peach-canners padded it out with spare tracks from his recent Nashville session, deaf to the jewels they were chucking away with the rest of the trash. The biggest and brightest being 'Tomorrow Is A Long Time', cursed to share the same side of vinyl as 'Smorgasbord', as if the miracle of Elvis Presley singing Bob Dylan had never actually happened. As far as the Sixties were now concerned, it hadn't.

He still had the gospel album, *How Great Thou Art*, scheduled for the new year, but the sound of God would never compete with the sound of the Beatles, the Rolling Stones, the Supremes, the Four Tops, the Monkees, Simon & Garfunkel, Herb Alpert & Tijuana Brass, the Mamas & the Papas or even *The Sound Of Music*. Nothing had changed.

Nothing had changed in Rocca Place. He'd rekindled a love of marijuana, now prone to bursting into stoned sermons in front of his Angels, leaping on tables and yelling jargonised Bible stories spiked with 'sonofabitch' and 'motherfucker' until he couldn't preach for laughing. But he still howled Beethoven at his piano, still practised tiger's claw, dragon's head and other karate punches, and still read books about finding God, Indian yogis and extra-terrestrials. He still confided in Larry and still studied the night sky for flying saucers and other signals from Jupiter and beyond. He still ate more than he should, and still took more pills than he should to compensate. He still read the *Physician's Desk Reference* looking for new habit-forming warnings to ignore. He still thought about Rusty and wondered what he should do about Priscilla. Nothing had changed.

Nothing had changed in Memphis, apart from his bedroom which had been redecorated with two pillow-angled television sets imbedded into a new green leatherette ceiling. He still spent most nights at the Memphian. That Christmas of '66 he watched a film about bikers who just wanted to be free to do what they wanted to do, to ride their machines without being hassled by The Man, to get loaded and have a good time. He watched another about a middle-aged man who hates his existence so accepts the offer from a clandestine company to undergo surgery for a new face, a new body and a new life. He thought about both long after the houselights had risen.

Gary Pepper still loved Elvis more than anyone loved Elvis and had campaigned, unsuccessfully, to have the local Mid-South Coliseum where the Beatles had played renamed the Elvis Presley Coliseum. The week before Christmas, Gary Pepper wheeled to his front door to find Elvis stood in his porch. He was shocked but thrilled, inviting him into his bedroom, its walls postered floor to ceiling with Elvis' face and a few of their shared sex goddess, Brigitte Bardot. They spoke a while about 'cute chicks' and Elvis told him about his upcoming gospel album. Then he handed him a set of car keys.

'Gary, this is your Christmas present.'

The keys were to Elvis' yellow and black Chevrolet Impala parked outside. Gary Pepper was much too disabled to drive it. But that had nothing to do with the tears that were still bubbling down his chin in January.

Elvis gave away several cars that Christmas, including a Cadillac to his friend George Klein, 'G.K. the D.J.', a disc jockey at Memphis's WHBQ. It was a thank you for helping Elvis on his recent drive home. He'd been listening to the station at the wheel of his bus when G.K. played a new disc by one of Elvis' favourite new singers, Tom Jones. It was a modern country song about old sweethearts, oak trees and death row called 'Green, Green Grass Of Home'. Just 50 miles from Graceland, it was also enough to tip Elvis into a maudlin abyss.

'And there to meet me is my Mama and Papa.'

He pulled over at the nearest roadside phone-booth and had one of his Angels ring up G.K. and ask to play it again, 'just this once for Elvis.'

G.K. did and as Tom repeated his hopes of sweet smiles and reaching arms Elvis could barely see the road for sobbing.

Just this once for Elvis became just this twice, and then again thrice. And so the journey continued, the Angels stopping and ringing, Tom Jones singing, Elvis crying, all the way to Memphis in their Greyhound of gloom while every other listener to WHBQ grew ever more tired of Mary's golden hair and lips like cherries.

When he finally arrived in the old home town around 9.30 pm Elvis looked as if his heart had been kicked all 8000 miles to the Rhondda Valley and back. He stepped down from the bus, as if from Tom's train, walked into the hall and plummeted to his knees. Then came a grizzling scream.

'I saw my mama!'

The homesick boyo atom-blast of Tom Jones, four grey walls and the sad old padre had conjured his mother's ghost. It had been eight years and Elvis still wasn't over her death.

Nothing had changed.

Then, without warning, like a violent collapse of gravity, it did.

Last Christmas it had been slot-cars. This year it was horses. Once he started buying them he couldn't stop and by New Year's Eve he had nine.

One horse, black with a white 'stocking', was for Priscilla. She named it Domino. It was one of her two main Christmas presents.

The other was a three-and-a-half-carat diamond ring and a machete through the heart of every woman who'd ever emptied ink, tears, lipstick and X-rated lust into the thousands of fresh fan letters still bombarding Graceland each week.

Elvis was getting married.

THE COWBOY

It was decided. She'd be the One. He didn't so much ask her as tell her. 'We're going to be married.' And he didn't so much decide as concede.

Priscilla's wasn't the only hand twisting the vice of matrimony, though since turning 21 the previous May she considered herself ripe as she'd ever be for a white silk chiffon dress and a tulle veil. She'd been living with Elvis in ungodly sin for over three years. The public had so far been spared the scandal of the unwed King and his live-in concubine, but it was only a matter of time before questions were asked, presses rolled and disgrace rained heavily upon the Gomorrah of Graceland. Her father, Captain Beaulieu – a married man – his father, Vernon – a twice-married man – and the Colonel – a married psychopath – were in moral conspiracy that Elvis could no longer avoid the issue of Priscilla, his intentions and their future. In this, all three were united. Only their motives differed.

The Beaulieus wanted him to marry Priscilla so their daughter would be legally bound to the fortune of Elvis Presley.

Vernon wanted him to marry Priscilla in the hope that once shackled to a wife his son would have to put an end to his reckless spending and the Angels' bankroll.

The Colonel wanted him to marry Priscilla so he could sell the respectable image of Elvis The Ideal Husband to a public who might otherwise start to wonder why, at the age of 32, the world's most eligible bachelor hadn't settled down.

Priscilla just wanted to be Mrs Elvis Presley.

Elvis just wanted everyone to stop breaking his balls. And so he bought her a ring, and a horse.

She loved the ring.

Elvis preferred the horse.

The impulsive horse buying that had started at Christmas with Priscilla's Domino and a palomino for himself that he named Rising Sun continued into '67. By the end of January he had 17. To accommodate them all he razed a seven-room house at the rear of Graceland to build a stable barn: Elvis even drove the bulldozer, making fast and amphetimous work of demolition.

The new barn he named 'The House of "Rising Sun"' and painted the title above the door. There he stabled his and Priscilla's horses, his dad's Colonel Midnight, one for Red called Keno, a horse punningly named after the local Memphis mayor, Mare Ingram, and others called Buckshot, Sundown, Traveller, Thundercloud, Scout, Flaming Star, Golden Sun, Beauty, Lady and El Poco. He even named a horse after his favourite new TV show: Star Trek.

Elvis liked *Star Trek* because it was about life on other planets and sexy women. These days he liked to think about such things more than he did life on his own planet and his own woman. But mostly he just thought about horses.

Every day at Graceland he now dressed saddle-ready in boots, riding chaps and a brick-crown hat. Even when eating. Even when sat watching *Star Trek*. And so, somewhere between sanity and fantasy, between terra firma and outer space, between uppers and opiates, between the manacle of engagement and the lock-pick of escape, between reading Larry's books and nights at the

Memphian watching westerns about horse thieves, Elvis had an epiphany.

God wanted him to be a cowboy.

He was sure of this even before he saw The Sign and after The Sign he was left in no doubt.

The Sign was a 60-foot-high white illuminated cross, 15 minutes' drive from Graceland just over the Mississippi border. The cross loomed down over 160 acres of former cotton land surrounded by a high cyclone chain-link fence called Twinkletown Farm. The farm was up for sale at $437,000 dollars. The Sign, obviously, meant God wanted Elvis to buy it and to the despair of his father, already sweating over the mounting costs of the stable barn with all its horse feed, riding clothes, equipment and trucks, he did.

Rising Sun and the rest of his stud were transported from Graceland out to Twinkletown Farm which Elvis renamed 'Circle G'. Circle was a standard ranch prefix. He told people the G stood for Graceland, as well as his mother Gladys. But it was God by any other initial.

He called it his ranch but it was more a retreat, a landlocked ark to fill with friends and horses away from the flood of unbearable reality. Wherever Elvis went his Angels came too, and since the existing farmhouse wasn't big enough he bought mobile trailer homes for each of them and their families. Once he started buying trailers he couldn't stop; the same way lately he couldn't stop compulsively eating white hot dog buns, stuffing them into his mouth one after the other until his oral cavity was a cement mixer of half-chewed bread so when he tried to speak, as he often did, every word was 'hggnggn'. Similarly he carried on buying trailers for all the painters and electricians he'd hired to renovate the farmhouse and surrounding land. When there was no one left to buy trailers for, Elvis bought a trailer for the trailer salesman. It was retail 'hggnggn'.

Such was the bankruptcy-baiting price of the happiness Elvis found home on the range at Circle G. The happiness of a life lived in capsuled widescreen, coloured by Seconal reds, Demerol pinks and Percodan yellows, adrift in his Wild West sanctuary, riding the plains, shaking his spurs, watching the sun vanish below the horizon astride his beast as a cool zephyr gently ruffled its mane. Free from all that lay beyond the chain-link perimeter fence. His failing records. His never-ending on-screen disgrace. His betrothal. His Rusty and what might have been.

'Aw, *Rusty*... '

In one of his last visits to the Memphian he'd tortured himself by running Rusty's latest film, a remake of the old John Ford western, *Stagecoach*. Rusty played Dallas, the dancehall prostitute with a corset-buoyed cleavage any pistol-packing cowpoke would readily grab holsters for. It made Elvis wonder what she'd think of his new ranch: how she'd look saddled up beside him in tight chaps and a gaucho hat, her fiery hair tumbling out down her nape and the soft bounce of her breasts beneath pink gingham in rhythm to the jog of her chestnut mare.

Elvis wondered a lot about Rusty as he cantered around Circle G. Wondering and wandering, riding and pill-popping, dreaming and yearning, until it hurt too much to wonder any more.

He never wanted to leave Circle G but his Hollywood peach-canners demanded he must and so for the first time in his life, Elvis refused. If they were asking him to choose between the life of a cowboy or a movie star, he chose the cowboy. The Colonel had to plead with the studio to postpone production for another month, allowing him enough time to drag Elvis away from his ranch and back to California. He succeeded, in body. But the boy's heart and mind remained in the saddle, drifting in eternal sunset on the high plains of oblivion.

Oblivion was the safest place for Elvis to be in the spring of 1967. Safer than remembering he'd agreed to be married but hadn't set a date, that Rusty and he would now never be, or that for contractual need of money he was slumped against the wall of a recording studio honking, *Who needs money? Not me!*

Oblivion tucked him into bed each night at Rocca Place in dreams of horses, spaceships and *Dr Strangelove*. And oblivion awoke him there again each morning with the same swaddling semi-consciousness of who, where and what he was.

'Gotta get outta ma bed…'

'Set code prefix.'

'… Goddamn left foot forward…'

'Lock code prefix.'

'… Goddamn right foot forward…'

'Code prefix locked.'

'Walk Attack, Plan R!'

'Mein Führer, I can walk!'

'Ha ha ha ha ha ha ha ha…'

… SMACK!

THE HEADBANGER

The Colonel stood by the door watching the limp body of Elvis Presley slumped in his bed as two men prodded at his head and fussed with a clunky piece of machinery. One was Elvis' regular Hollywood physician, the other a radiologist and the clunky piece of machinery his portable X-ray machine. All three men had arrived at Rocca Place within an hour of the call from Diamond Joe. Joe rang the Colonel first, the doctor second. The doctor rang the radiologist third.

Joe had told the Colonel as much as he knew about what had happened. The Angels had been in the den waiting for Elvis to wake up. There was Joe and his new fellow foreman Marty, otherwise known as 'Moon', alongside Charlie, Cousin Billy and young Jerry. Larry was also there to style Elvis' hair for the new film he was supposed to start shooting that morning. Elvis was late rising but when he finally appeared he moved like he'd been eight hours guzzling hooch, one hand rubbing the back of his head. He mumbled something about going to the bathroom, tripping on a loose television cord and blacking out. His speech was groggy and the whites of his half-shut eyes glistened as if set in aspic. The Angels took turns to run their fingers over his skull, whistling through their teeth as their tips found the knuckle of tender flesh poking up near his crown. That's when Joe rang the Colonel.

The X-rays revealed Elvis had suffered nothing more than a mild concussion. The Colonel was told there was no need for surgery, only a recuperation period of two weeks before it was safe for him to return to work. The new film, a ragged scrap of beach 'n' bikini flotsam called *Clambake*, already postponed by a month, would have to wait.

The doctor and the radiologist left the Colonel in the bedroom. He stood there a while longer, staring at Elvis. His client, a dazed man of 32, chubby around the jaw, stupefied by medication, the doctor's on top of his own. The Colonel's thanks for 12 years of toil turning a Huck Finn into a Jay Gatsby; a stack of bills amounting to $650,000, Elvis' fee for *Clambake*, now disintegrating in a woof of flames.

'Dumb bastard!'

Then it hit him, hard as his own head smacking on a bathroom floor. *Hossana!*

The Colonel looked again at Elvis, insensible in bed, and saw something else. Something that looked like five feet eleven of sitting duck and the cure for nigh on two years of sleepless nights. He pulled a fresh stogie from his pocket and clamped it in his teeth.

'Got you, you sonofabitch!'

When he returned a day later to inspect the patient's progress he was carrying a briefcase. Except for Joe, who lived somewhere between the stuffed billfold and German cigars the Colonel kept in his pocket, the Angels kept out of his way. Ever since the accident they'd skulked around Rocca Place on tiptoe, sometimes whispering aloud whether it had been the equivalent of a 1-A draftee hurling themselves down a staircase in the hope of breaking their back to avoid the next transport carrier to Da Nang: Elvis' Da Nang being possibly *Clambake*, possibly matrimony, possibly both. Whatever the truth, they'd all read the bump on Elvis' head like braille spelling imminent doom. And between them they knew it was only a matter of time before the Colonel delivered it.

Elvis was lying in bed, propped up on his pillows, awake but not necessarily alive, gazing through a fog of painkillers at the large dark shape pulling up a chair beside his bed.

The shape patted his arm and spoke to him. It said it had business to discuss. Elvis blinked and tried to focus on the shape but in the dim light of his room he saw only a fat fuzzy blob. The shape kept on talking about 'present liability' and the 'future security of both parties'. Then Elvis felt something small, shiny and hard placed in his right hand.

The Colonel had no idea if Elvis understood what he'd been saying. Nor did he care. Only that Elvis didn't flinch when he told him he'd now be taking half of his income, not just for his films, which was already the case, but everything else, straight down the middle, 'fifty-fifty', and that the boy wasn't so doped that he couldn't move a pen across a dotted line when placed under his nose.

The Colonel put the pen back in his pocket and the contract back in his briefcase. He patted Elvis' arm and told him he'd be back again in a few days to discuss more business.

Elvis watched the shape walk out of the room as it slowly started to spin. He slurred what sounded to nobody listening like 'fivdee-fivdee.' A second later he was unconscious.

True to his psychopathic word, the Colonel came back the following week. He was glad to see Elvis' father and Priscilla had arrived. They'd both been 1800 miles away in Memphis the day Elvis fell – even if Priscilla would later remember otherwise – but had since flown out to California to be by his side.

The Colonel assured them that he'd be 'making changes' and flicked his eyes to the den where the Angels were sat brooding. Vernon flickered approval. The Colonel then told Priscilla the good news that he, personally, would begin making plans for her wedding, to take place as soon as Elvis had completed the new film. The size of her smile showed she'd fully understood what he meant. They agreed to carve Elvis up between them. The Colonel would take his wallet and his will-power: Priscilla could have his balls, Vernon the scraps.

All that remained was to decapitate some Angels, and for that he needed Joe to collect any rolling heads in a wicker basket.

The Colonel summoned them to their execution around Elvis' bedside. Moon, Cousin Billy, Charlie, Jerry and Larry took their places on the stand while the Colonel, with Joe, oiled Madame Guillotine.

Elvis was conscious, though his eyes never left the sheets covering his lap, like a dummy waiting for a ventriloquist to shove a hand up its back. The Colonel did all his talking. He began by telling them they were all responsible for Elvis' accident. He said nothing about medication. They'd been stressing Elvis, burdening him with money and personal woes, distracting him from his professional responsibilities. That's why the Colonel had decided to appoint Joe as sole official foreman. From now on, any problems, they spoke to Joe. Elvis was to be left alone.

The dummy in the bed didn't stir. The Colonel continued.

There'd be a review of the payroll. There were too many of them doing too little. There'd be wage cuts, he warned, maybe even redundancies. Then he turned his blowpipe eyes on Larry.

'And I don't want him reading him any more *books*!'

The poison dart struck.

'They clutter up his mind.'

Larry looked at the lifeless body in bed: Elvis didn't appear to have any mind left to clutter.

The meeting dismissed, the Colonel stayed by the bedside with Joe. The Angels left, gloomy mutes in Indian file.

Larry carried on walking out of the bedroom, down the hall, out of the front door and into his Volkswagen, driving away from Rocca Place for what he correctly suspected would be the last time. The following week, when filming finally began on *Clambake*, Larry was allowed back on set to style Elvis' hair. But Joe and the other Angels had been warned against leaving the pair of them alone again to speak in spiritual tongues. The days of Teacher and Student were over.

By the summer, Larry was gone. Nobody ever mentioned his name. Nobody gave any indication they missed him. Priscilla least of all.

The first chance she had, one evening at Graceland she gathered together all the books of Larry's she could find. Books written by yogis, theologians and philosophers containing universal love, God, satori, nirvana, a higher state of consciousness and, just maybe, the secret to the purpose of human existence. Books which she piled into a box, took out into the garden, doused with gasoline and burned. She made Elvis watch with her as the pages blackened, turning to specks of ash fluttering up into the night. An inferno of human dreams and heavenly wonder. She smiled to the very last ember.

Elvis gazed into the flames, flickering all Nembutal yellow and Amytal white. He didn't think it necessary to dampen Priscilla's glee by pointing out the many survivors of her holocaust still on his shelves that had escaped her attention. The same way he never told her there were still times when a certain twilight caught his eye and he'd feel the urge to tear himself away and sit alone, looking up at the clouds. Searching the skies for another face of Stalin.

THE HUSBAND

They married in Las Vegas. It was a Las Vegas kind of marriage.

The ceremony took place in a suite at the Aladdin Hotel, a new renovation on the Strip with an Arabian Nights theme. It lasted eight minutes.

Elvis wore a black paisley silk brocade tuxedo with a white carnation, bowtie, diamond cufflinks and cowboy boots. Priscilla wore a veiled white gown with a beaded neckline and pearled sleeves, a rhinestone tiara, false eyelashes and a bandit mask of mascara. The best men were Diamond Joe and Moon. Priscilla's maid of honour was her younger sister, Michelle. The cake was six tiers of yellow sponge, apricot marmalade, kirsch cream and fondant icing, decorated with over a thousand marzipan roses.

The wedding was arranged at short notice. The press were first informed that morning with only a select number of newsmen and photographers invited by the Colonel to attend the ceremony, though enough to ensure that, aside from the best men, the congregation wouldn't be big enough to include the Angels. Elvis didn't argue but it was left to Moon to tell Red, Sonny, Hog Ears and the others that they and their wives would only be able to attend the breakfast reception. It leant the buffet of fried chicken and Oysters Rockefeller a bitter aftertaste.

In their first act as man and wife, Mr and Mrs Presley held a press conference in the hotel ballroom. Someone asked why he'd waited so long to marry.

'I just thought the life I was living was… too difficult,' said Elvis. 'I decided it would be best if I waited till I… I really knew for sure. And now I'm really sure.'

After the reception they changed clothes and flew on to the honeymoon home Elvis had recently leased in Palm Springs shaped, as was his architectural preference, a bit like a flying saucer. They spent their wedding night lost in deep space of procreation.

When they awoke the next morning, Priscilla was pregnant.

The rest of the world awoke to the shock news that Elvis Presley was no longer a bachelor with tears, hysterics and heavy footfall towards the nearest nunnery. None were more stunned than Rusty, who made immediate plans to elope with her actor boyfriend, Roger Smith. One week later they too were married in Las Vegas. Mrs Smith cried through the entire ceremony.

When Mr and Mrs Presley came home to Graceland they organised a second wedding reception for their friends in Memphis. It was a Memphis kind of reception.

They held it in the room next to the pool that only a year earlier had been shrine to his passing slot-car obsession. The Colonel wasn't there, nor the press.

The couple made their entrance just before 9 pm as an accordionist played 'Love Me Tender'. They wore the same outfits they'd worn in Vegas and stopped to pose beneath a floral arch as their guests cheered and applauded. Diamond Joe formally announced them.

'In case no one knows it, that's Mr and Mrs Elvis Presley!'

The buffet included champagne, stuffed lobster, sliced ham, turkey, meatballs, shrimp, sausage, hot dogs, potato salad, cheese and a second, smaller, wedding cake with only three tiers to the six they'd had in Vegas. Elvis picked up the knife to cut it, then hesitated and turned it point first towards Priscilla. There was a strange look in his eyes.

'Maybe I'll just stab you.'

Priscilla grimaced. The guests laughed nervously.

Someone yelled out, 'feed him some cake!' Priscilla took the knife from his hand, chopped a creamy sliver onto a tea-plate and handed it to Elvis. He screwed his face, seized back the knife and hacked himself another wedge big enough to choke a horse.

'Now, *that's* a goddamn piece of cake.'

Elvis stuffed it in his face to more uncertain giggles as Priscilla smiled her ever-straining smile.

When the reception was over, Elvis changed out of his clothes and invited everyone to join him at the Memphian to watch a new western, *The War Wagon*. His wife sat beside him and squeezed his hand but took no notice of what John Wayne and Kirk Douglas were doing on screen. She thought only of the man she'd just married four weeks ago. Wondering why, after his accident at Rocca Place, he still took those pills? And whether, if pushed, he really had it in him to stab her? And why, after a special night like tonight, he'd rather be sat in a cinema watching westerns than in his conjugal bed with her?

She kept on wondering and clutching his hand as the Duke tossed another saddlebag to Kirk Douglas. And as the embryo she didn't know she had inside her wriggled ever slowly towards life.

NANCY

The Summer of Love never shined on Elvis Presley. He remained imprisoned in the shade as its pollen filled the airwaves with skipping the light fandango, setting the night on fire, lonely hearts club bands, beautiful balloons, girls called Windy, ten-feet-tall Alice and pleasant valley Sundays. It shone warm and golden upon Haight Ashbury, the Kings Road and all latitudes between where the hair was long and threaded with flowers, the faces painted, the beads swished, flesh was bared and the air pungent with the smells of Asia. But it shined not on the MGM backlot in Culver City where, as the Beatles were in a London studio chanting *'Love! Love! Love!'* and Bob Dylan in a West Saugerties basement wailing *'I shall be released'*, the newlywed Elvis, needing more than love and beyond hope of release, was being costume fitted as a stock-car driver for his next Technicolor treadmill.

This one was called *Speedway* and amidst the usual Elvis-by-numbers agony of rally races and vacuous songs sung to vacuous kids it at least had two things going for it.

One was a song, its only good song if still one more than in any of his last half dozen films, called 'Let Yourself Go': a funky aphrodisiac blues screamed straight from the pelvis that, for once, he didn't have to pretend to enjoy on screen.

The other was his co-star – Nancy Sinatra.

Seven years earlier Nancy had been there at Fort Dix to welcome him home from Germany: a decorous daddy's girl with short brown hair and modest make-up dressed like a Fifth Avenue secretary. Now she was the Summer of Love's Pussy Galore: a platinum-blonde sex kitten purring sly putdowns in wicked winged eyeliner and dominatrix boots.

Nancy's records were currently outselling his. She'd had four top ten hits in the last 18 months, including two number ones: in the same period Elvis had had none. Her last film had been *The Wild Angels*, the one Elvis loved about bikers getting loaded and having a good time. It was one of the year's 20 top grossing films at the US box office: Elvis' highest, *Paradise, Hawaiian Style*, had only reached number 40. More recently her foxy footwear had trodden in the green grass of Tom Jones to record the theme to the new James Bond film, *You Only Live Twice*: it was exactly the kind of glory that Elvis, a devoted Bond fan who'd have wrung gold-tonsils of any John Barry tune, should have been grabbing were he not at the mercy of his own malevolent Blofeld.

Their film would be trailed to the public as 'the King of Rock meets the Queen of Pop' yet by the Summer of Love Elvis was king of nothing and by the following summer, when it was finally released, king of even less. *Speedway* needed Nancy more than Nancy needed *Speedway*. The peach-canners didn't even try to hide it. They allowed her to perform a solo song, 'Your Groovy Self', both on screen and the accompanying soundtrack: the first time a guest artist had ever featured on an Elvis Presley album. But not even Nancy's groovy tune, and groovier boots, could salvage a clodhopping comedy about back taxes owed to the Inland Revenue Service.

Surprisingly, or perhaps not, Elvis actually enjoyed *Speedway* in as much as he enjoyed Nancy, as much as she'd allow him. At first she tried to maintain a brother-sisterly relationship. It only whetted his appetite for incest. That he'd been married for 50 days when he started the film didn't stop him chasing their family viewing G-certificate romance of 'Steve' and 'Susan' off the page and onto the dressing room floor. They stopped dangerously shy of an R-rating. The clothes stayed on but in the heavy frottage their groins chafed with the friction of two primitives trying to make fire with zipper and fabric, a one-to-one theatrical trailer of what each was missing by keeping their buttons fastened. Elvis ached to see the main feature but Nancy's was the will that cooled the projector. It was enough that he was married. But it was too much that he turned up on set one morning and announced to everyone in the cast and crew that he was going to be a father.

Reporters were invited to the studio so Elvis could share the news of Priscilla's pregnancy with the outside world. He told them he was speechless with joy.

'This is the greatest thing that has ever happened to me.'

But then he never did go the full feature with Nancy Sinatra.

PSYCHOMAS

The pale grey smoke ring drifted through the air like a ghostly lasso, past the stuffed Snowman, above the telephone, breaking in a silent splash on the desk calendar reminding the Colonel it was the middle of December 1967. In a couple of weeks it would be 1968. As business stood, neither he nor Elvis had a lot to look forward to.

Every time the Colonel flicked through a copy of *Billboard* these days the top ten read like hieroglyphics: Vanilla Fudge, the Jimi Hendrix Experience, the Doors, *Sgt Pepper*. Elvis' latest album, the soundtrack to *Clambake*, had made its debut on the chart that month at 188, outsold by yet more hieroglyphics: something called 'Velvet Underground and Nico'.

Elvis had two films left in his contract with MGM, but like Wallis and Paramount before them, the studio was no longer prepared to renew or extend their deal. The reels of Ken® were running out. The Colonel had thrashed around in Hollywood's smaller fish ponds, managing to bag one more film deal with a new production company, National General Pictures, for $850,000. Beyond that, they had nothing.

It was Christmas, but in the Snowman's world there wasn't any snow. The Colonel's singular festive scam had been selling a coil of old rope to radio syndication for $60,000. The idea was even older than the rope. An Elvis 'Christmas Special': 30 minutes of seasonal and sacred songs, most of them from the Christmas album he recorded ten years earlier in 1957. The show's one exclusive was a special greeting by Elvis wishing listeners a merry Christmas and a wonderful new year. It lasted four seconds.

The old songs, and the new message, were sent to stations on tape along with the Colonel's 'script' for local disc jockeys to read between each track; a series of hawking instructions, each subtle as a door-to-door vacuum salesman.

'Speaking of nice things, a friend gave our family the Elvis Christmas album as a gift and we have had *so* much pleasure playing it!'

The Colonel convinced over two thousand stations to air it, twice, on consecutive Sundays in December. But it was only radio, it was only $60,000 and it wasn't going to fill the crater of a gambling debt he'd been digging for the past few years across the tables of Vegas.

Another smoke ring swirled across the office, wobbling into thin air before it could reach the wall of smiling Elvises staring back at him. The smile of a $1 million movie star that no movie studio would pay beans for any more.

'My boy,' he sighed.

The Colonel was down to his last chips: one last spin of the wheel for one last number on the cloth. Red or Black. Passe or Manque. All or Nothing.

As the New Year loomed there was only one number left he could think of playing. He'd been cagily circling it for some time with the West Coast vice president for NBC television over the hill in Burbank, Tom Sarnoff. The Colonel had given Sarnoff his usual smoke-blowing Snowman shtick, offering the network the unique privilege of bankrolling their very own Elvis Presley picture. His bargain price: the standard $1 million.

To his surprise, Sarnoff had tentatively agreed. But there was one caveat.

The Colonel would get his million and NBC would fund a new Elvis film. But as part of the deal they also wanted Elvis back on television. Not as a guest spot on one of their existing variety shows, but his own show. A one-hour TV special, similar to the one Nancy Sinatra had just done for them for Christmas '67, to be shown, like hers, around the same time of year.

Sarnoff's offer caught the Colonel off guard. For seven years he'd deliberately kept Elvis off television to fuel his Hollywood star power. To suddenly allow him back on the small screen, for a whole hour, sounded like an act of flag-waving surrender. But a million dollars was a million dollars.

The Colonel rocked in his office chair, sucking hard on his cigar, the smoke swirling in his throat, slow and steady as the deliberating cogs in his head.

Elvis on television at Christmas time?

It was true he'd just done something similar on radio. Maybe he could do the same again: *exactly* the same. The same radio show, with pictures. 'Silent Night', fake snow and carol singers. Elvis in the glow of a hearth, hanging a bauble on a branch, smiling at the camera and wishing viewers a wonderful New Year. One hour of old rope. Goddamit, for a million dollars if they wanted he'd make the boy wear a Santa suit and a cotton wool beard.

His next smoke ring was a perfect zero-shaped circle. The Colonel smiled, picturing six in a row, and picked up his telephone.

'Sarnoff? It's the Colonel. We need to talk...'

DECEMBER 31, 1967

Elvis was upstairs in Graceland, standing before his dressing mirror, adjusting the collar of his shirt. It was blue, same as the turtle neck sweater he wore underneath it, same as his eyes, only his eyes were no longer truest blue lasers. They were the blue of dreamless moons and lonely Christmases. The blue of bodies he'd seen on his impromptu midnight visits to the National Funeral Home on Union Avenue where the morticians, too surprised to refuse such a famous guest, would satisfy his curiosity about preserving corpses and embalming techniques. His eyes were the same colour he'd seen in the open caskets. Dead blue.

In another mirror Priscilla was checking the sequined neck and sleeves of her black chiffon maternity dress. She was nearly eight months due. The conversion of one of Graceland's upstairs bedrooms into a nursery was already underway. She'd also persuaded Elvis to invest in a second marital home in Los Angeles: a French regency-style mansion in Beverly Hills' exclusive Trousdale Estates with heated swimming pool and panoramic views of downtown. It would be *their* home out West. The days of the Angels, of Rocca Place, Perugia Way and Bellagio Road, of two-way mirrors, sex-crazed chimps and shooting flashbulbs, were gone. She smoothed the dress over her bump and smiled at her reflection. Elvis had been a husband eight months and soon he'd be a father. *Her* husband, *their* baby. Elvis was all hers now. Hers and nobody else's. Hers and nothing more.

Elvis was no longer a cowboy. His ranch, Circle G, had gone the way of his slot-car room: an abandoned, 160-acre money pit of horses with no one to ride them, and trailers with no one to inhabit them. The horses were moved back to Graceland while Vernon sold what trucks, trailers and equipment he could to recoup his son's losses. Before they eventually found a buyer for the land, Elvis spent his last days there playing target practice with his growing arsenal of firearms; finding what little happiness he could in a warm gun.

Elvis was no longer a singer. He'd given it one last try in Nashville that September with his favourite new producer, Felton Jarvis. They'd brought in RCA's new country signing Jerry Reed to lend his magic guitar pickin' to a couple of songs, starting with Elvis' version of Reed's own 'Guitar Man': a rattlin' rags-to-riches comic strip about a roving musician trying to find his place in the world. It wasn't Elvis' story, but its lyrics mentioned Memphis and were close enough in spirit for him to growl as if the smell of its hobo jungles still clung to his nostrils: his life in song with the potential to become the song of his life. Sensing as much, Felton encouraged Elvis to 'sing the living stuff out of it.' By take ten he was shaking so loose he broke breathlessly into Ray Charles' 'What'd I Say?', the song he and Rusty had sung together in *Viva Las Vegas*. She haunted him still.

But the potential song of his life was strangled at birth. 'Guitar Man' was buried as album filler in the pauper's grave of the *Clambake* soundtrack. When, all too late, his peach-canners tried to make amends and release it as a single it disintegrated at number 43. A similar fate had already befallen the other track he recorded with Jerry Reed, a mean employee blues by his Chicago namesake Jimmy Reed, 'Big Boss Man', fizzling out at 38. It was just as he'd written years ago in the margin of a copy of his old favourite *The Prophet* by Khalil Gibran, paraphrasing Gibran's passage about teaching and music in his own block capitals and bad grammar.

'A SINGER CAN SING HIS SONGS BUT THEY MUST HAVE A EAR TO RECEIVE THE SONG.'

The world was no longer listening to Elvis Presley. And so, with no ear to receive him, Elvis Presley was no longer a singer.

The world was no longer watching him either. The routine dismissal of the latest Elvis Presley film wasn't even worth the column space in the *New York Times* who'd stopped reviewing them as policy. The last picture he'd shot that year, a comedy western called *Stay Away, Joe*, had him once again singing *'moo, moo'*. It was a song about a bull called 'Dominick' and would be the last thing he recorded in 1967. The year of *Sgt Pepper*, the Summer of Love and Monterey Pop. The year that consigned him to the cold grave of history.

He had one hour left. One last hour of 1967 and then it would be over, and he no more. Forever buried beside it in the irretrievable past. Forgotten. Erased. Extinct.

Elvis, in blue, spent it with Priscilla, in black, at a private New Year party in Memphis' Thunderbird Lounge. The bill of local live music included soul band Flash & the Board of Directors, R&B singer Denise Stark covering the hits of Aretha Franklin, and rock 'n' roll from the Avantis and former Sun rockabilly star Billy Lee Riley. But Elvis heard none of it for the thunder of blood in his ears.

Eleven fifty-eight. The skies were darkening, the crows were circling.

'Eli… Eli…'

Eleven fifty-nine.

'Lama…'

He felt Priscilla's arms embrace him in the middle of the dancefloor. The touch of her lips.

'… *Sabachthani?*'

Then the light faded.

'Happy New Year!'

It was 1968. Elvis Presley was dead.

ACT II

JAMES

It was people like James who made some people think all people are born either good or bad. James wasn't born bad. He was born into bad. He had crime in his genes the way others have red hair or high cheekbones. His family tree was a gnarly, twisted shrub bearing generation after generation of rotten fruit; thieves, bootleggers, forgers, liars, drunkards and rapists. None of it any excuse for who he was and what he did, but some explanation as to why: because he was born a Ray, the dirt-water in his blood drawn from their same ne'er-do-well, making his veins bulge and his tongue spit whenever he saw black skin. James was a Ray to the mean nigger-loathing marrow.

As an American teenager in wartime he cheered for the opposition. Hitler was his first crush. He loved the Nazis the way other kids loved the St Louis Cardinals, sharing fantasies with his similarly cursed siblings of a United States one day being saved by its own apple-pie Adolf: a President who wouldn't cower like Roosevelt − weak and worried about public opinion − but be strong enough to stand up for the besieged Caucasian, unafraid to kick out the blacks, the Jews and anyone else with suspicious skin and a strange religion. A fifty-state Führer to Make America White Again.

Only after the war, as a U.S. soldier posted to ally-occupied Germany, seeing for himself the destitution of the fallen

Fatherland, did his naive reveries of the Reich collapse. Alcohol and amphetamines numbed his disillusionment until, whilst in their grip, the military police arrested him for going AWOL. He was punished with demotion, severed pay and a month's hard labour before being shipped home and discharged without ceremony.

James was 20 years old with no money, little prospects and a savage heart pumping with the bad blood of his ancestry. Unable to ignore their fateful rhythm, he followed its beat into felony.

He served his first civilian prison sentence for burglary in Los Angeles. They let him out after 90 days. He was back inside two years later, this time in Illinois for holding-up a taxi driver and the attempted theft of his cab. When they released him after 22 months he was arrested again, twice, for petty theft and vagrancy. He was bailed both times but skipped town before either case came to trial.

The law eventually caught up with him after two weeks chasing a trail of forged money orders he'd stolen from a post office. Convicted of fraud, they sent him to Kansas' notoriously tough Leavenworth, a racially segregated penitentiary where he refused the offer of an easy work detail in the prison farm since it meant mixing with black inmates. He entered Leavenworth in July 1955 the week Bill Haley's 'Rock Around The Clock' reached number one. He walked out three years later to find a black group, the Platters, at the top of the charts. The outside world was changing in ways he didn't like. James had no desire to keep pace.

By the spring of 1960 he was back behind bars after a series of armed supermarket robberies. The penalty was 20 years in Missouri State Penitentiary. He endured seven before managing to escape, hiding in a bread truck on its daily run between the prison and its farm and jumping out unseen at a stoplight.

The date was April 23, 1967. James was 39 years old, a wanted but free man in a land already brightening in the first blossoms of the Summer of Love. Its warmth would never touch him.

That July, as *Sgt Pepper* spent its third week atop America's album charts, James and one of his brothers succeeded in a masked robbery of a bank in St Louis, escaping without being identified. He spent some of his share on a new car, a Plymouth, driving it alone to Canada where he robbed a brothel in Montreal. After failing to gain a legitimate Canadian passport using an alias, he returned to the States, changing his car to a pale Mustang, bouncing from Alabama to Mexico before settling in Los Angeles. There he lay low, took dance classes, enrolled at bartender school, changed his nose with rhinoplasty, heard the bells ring in 1968 and, between their tolls, decided his future.

His teenage dreams of an American Hitler had been newly resuscitated by George Wallace, the pro-segregationist Governor of Alabama running on the presidential ticket for his own newly formed American Independent Party under the campaign slogan 'Stand Up For America'. At some point, somewhere, from someone during his nine months on the run, he also learned of the underground bounties put up by two rich Wallace ticket supporters in St Louis, Missouri, where his own brother and sister ran a pro-Wallace and Klan-friendly bar. The first was for up to $30,000. The second was for $50,000. Two prices on the one head for anyone willing to take out 'the Big Nigger'.

It was late March 1968 when James left Los Angeles, heading cross country down his destiny's Interstate to the 'Big Nigger's' hometown of Atlanta, Georgia. The airwaves during his 2000 mile drive would have been blacker than his jutting jailbird ears would have been able to bear: Otis, Aretha, Dionne, Smokey, Diana, Jimi and Sly. America was sittin' on the dock of the bay, dancing to the music and singing *'baby, baby, sweet baby'* with the First Lady of Soul. Except in the $10 room he took in an Atlanta flophouse where he sat silently on his bed drawing circles on a city map of possible locations where he could claim his prize negro scalp. He waited a week before travelling to Birmingham, Alabama, returning with a new pump-action .30-06 rifle. But before he could hear its sweet fire ricochet in the streets of Atlanta he was forced to a sudden change of plan. The 'Big Nigger' announced he'd be appearing at a public rally that week in Memphis. The hunter had no choice but to follow his game to Tennessee.

He spent his last night in Atlanta on Tuesday April 2, alone in his $10 room with only a single bed, a dresser, a washstand but no television. It was perhaps just as well. Had James Earl Ray been near one that evening, he really wouldn't have liked what he saw.

HARRY

It would never get on television. That's what the man from Plymouth motors had said. 'Over my dead body.' But it did: a black man and a white woman together singing side by side, gazing into one another's tearful eyes when, suddenly, she clutched his arm, her fingers on his elbow, her head on his shoulder: her whiteness touching his blackness.

The man was Harry Belafonte. Ten years earlier, he'd been the Fifties 'King of Calypso' bellowing about daybreak and the sometime star of Hollywood dramas. But times had changed.

Harry still made records but by 1968 he'd long since stopped acting to dedicate his time, energy and wealth to black America's ongoing struggle for civil rights. The start of that year, he'd been asked by Johnny Carson to fill his host's chair of NBC's *The Tonight Show* for a week. The highest-rating programme in its late-night time slot, Harry seized it as a platform to interview political allies including Senator Bobby Kennedy, then undecided whether to risk honouring his dead brother's legacy by entering that year's presidential race, and Dr Martin Luther King Jr.

Martin was a close friend: Harry had fund-raised legal fees on his behalf and personally rallied fellow celebrities to attend the March on Washington in the dream-speech August of '63. So was Bobby: Harry had taught him to dance the Twist. Both men, on separate shows, used their interviews with Harry to discuss social inequality, with Martin calling for an urgent response to the country's poverty crisis and Bobby quoting statistics about New York's rat-ridden slums and his pessimism for the outcome in Vietnam. Harry was equally transparent in his opposition to the war, as was Martin, and in his final edition made polite apology to any viewers 'offended by the politics aired on the show this week'.

That was in early February. And yet two months later, here he was back on the same network being squeezed by a weepy English rose, singing what was clearly an anti-war song.

More politics. More offence.

The woman doing the squeezing was Petula Clark. 'That girl from England who sings "Downtown"' as she'd jokingly surmise the extent of her fame. Or as she simply preferred to be called, 'Pet'.

Pet had topped the U.S. charts twice, an otherwise unlikely beneficiary of the Beatles-led 'British Invasion'; prim as a croquet hoop, proper as a crustless cucumber sandwich, a lone Mary Poppins in the age of Mary Quant. Her starchy manner had somehow weathered the Summer of Love, tiptoeing into its top five with the Beach Boys-meets-Broadway curtsey of 'Don't Sleep In The Subway'. Now she'd been hired as the face of Plymouth motors for a new ad campaign and, with their sponsorship, had been granted her first one-hour TV special, *Petula*.

Pet had been another of Harry's guests during his week hosting *The Tonight Show*. Returning the favour, Harry agreed to be her one guest star – something of a coup at a time when he'd turned his back on variety television, more likely to be seen on screen talking about not wishing his son to die in a rice paddy in a foreign land for a meaningless flag than he was singing and dancing.

In gratitude, the show's producers scripted him his own ten-minute solo spot. The staging was minimal: just Harry, surrounded by a few Giacometti-style figures in Perspex cases and joined by dancers for a specially written soul tune dripping with the sweat of freedom marches, 'If A Better Time's Comin''. He also riffed on the old African tribal rhyme 'Hambone' with the teenage son of singer O.C. Smith, and delivered a heart-stopping ballad about love, loss and meteorology from a relatively unknown Canadian folk singer named Joni Mitchell.

Pet was to reappear on camera for Harry's final song, a duet of one she'd co-written and first recorded in French, telling the story of old soldiers escaping into the countryside every Sunday to drink themselves horizontal at their favourite spot, 'The Hill Of Whisky'. Retitled 'On The Path Of Glory', its new English lyrics were a more explicit, much more timely condemnation of war over the same sentimental melody: a soft shudder on the decade's Richter scale of protest songs but enough to make the sponsors, Plymouth, nervous. At a time when U.S. troops in Vietnam were either dying at a rate of over 500 a week or raping, massacring and mutilating as many innocent Vietnamese, the song's lament for young men of all creeds *'red or yellow, white or brown'*, sent to die *'for you and me, amid the pungent smell of death'* seemed a direct rebuttal of the Johnson administration. As Harry, Pet and the show's director had conspired, that was the point. But, as they argued in its defence, the lyrics didn't actually name 'Vietnam', nor specify any war. Nor did the TV staging include flags, guns or military props of any kind. Unable to find just cause to stop it, reluctantly Plymouth consented.

The duet had been choreographed for camera so Harry would stand in the foreground while Pet remained a step or two behind. The first few takes were awkward. The way they were standing looked unnatural and stagey. It was the director who suggested it might work better if Pet walked up to Harry's spot so they were physically stood beside one another. 'To give it more of an emotional connection.'

It worked. The next take they finally bonded, their voices rinsing the pathos from every line, Pet's head at Harry's chest height, instinctively leaning in closer and closer. And then she did it. As the song reached its climax, she reached across and held tight to his left arm. A reassuring squeeze of comfort. An innocent, unscripted, spontaneous impulse. Except in the cross-burning eyes of the man from Plymouth.

His name was Doyle Lott. He'd been watching it live on a monitor in a green room just down the corridor from the Burbank soundstage as it was being taped. When he saw Pet touch Harry, he didn't see the subtlest of embraces between black and white, man and woman, united as one against the unbearable horror of war. He saw only his own head on a chopping block and the ignominious end to a glorious career in motor advertising. He saw shame upon his former military record, a stain on his Silver Star and his war hero's plot in Arlington cemetery forsaken. He saw scandal, outrage and a televised heart attack in the breast of the millions of fine upstanding white folks like himself the length of God-blessed America. He saw much the same as James Earl Ray would have seen.

He bolted from the green room chased by men whose faces were the pallor of salaried compliance and whose suits were a similar shade of pensioned despair.

'She *touched* him!'

He crashed onto the studio floor, hands rubbing his crimson forehead, screaming at no one in particular.

'She touched him,' he repeated. 'A *black* man! She *touched* him!'

For a second, Pet thought it was a joke. Then she looked again at Lott's face. It was a punch, not a punchline, aiming straight at the director.

'There is *no way* that will ever get shown!'

Lott demanded an immediate reshoot. 'With no touching!' If they didn't, he foamed, they'd have to use one of the earlier non-touching takes. 'I'll lose my job. We'll *all* lose our jobs!'

The director refused.

Lott thundered back down the corridor, the suits flapping after him. 'I'm getting straight on the phone to Detroit,' he yelled, meaning his bosses at Chrysler, Plymouth's parent company. 'And shutting this thing down!'

The director puffed his cheeks and strolled over to Harry and Pet, shaking his head. The three of them huddled together to consider their options. Harry spoke first. It wasn't in his nature to concede to such blatant bigotry. But, he added, Pet was only starting to make a name for herself in America. Her first Hollywood musical, *Finian's Rainbow*, was scheduled for release later that year. Something like this could easily harm her career.

'Perhaps we should pick a fight another day,' sighed Harry. 'At least while your best interests are at stake.'

'Forget my best interests,' said Pet. 'What would you do?'

The director looked at Harry, the same question in his eyes.

Harry smiled. 'I'd nail the bastard.'

Had Lott not been too busy bawling into a telephone receiver away from the studio floor he might have spotted the unusual flurry of activity in the gallery. He might have seen the director grab the videotapes and skulk out of the door. Then he might have been able to block his way to the editing room in the basement, stopping him from ordering a nervous tape-op to erase all earlier takes of Harry and Pet's duet. That way he could have wiped the smug grin off the director's face. The one that met him when he finally came off the phone to be told the only take of 'On The Path Of Glory' available for broadcast was the last one.

'The one with the touch.'

They'd nailed the bastard.

It was only the beginning. With the help of his contacts in the press, Harry hammered harder, publicly naming and shaming Lott's failed attempts at censorship as 'the most outrageous case of racism I have ever seen in this business.' In his defence, Lott feebly told the same papers he'd been 'tired' and had merely 'overreacted to the staging, not to any feeling of discrimination.' Hoping to quell the uproar, he meekly rang Harry to offer an apology. Harry didn't accept.

'Apologies in these situations mean nothing,' he later explained. 'They change neither that man's heart nor my skin. Inside, he feels the same way because of how I look on the outside. He can apologise for the balance of his life but it won't alter the attitude he has today. And a man with such an attitude has to be exposed.'

The negative publicity embarrassed the general manager of Chrysler into issuing a statement distancing itself from Plymouth's ad manager. 'It resulted solely from the reaction of a single individual and by no means represents the Plymouth Division's attitude or policy on such matters.' By the time the *Petula* special was broadcast four weeks later, Lott had been 'relieved of his post' at Plymouth and moved elsewhere in the company.

America finally got to see what all the fuss had been about at around 8.40 pm on Tuesday April 2, when the white hand of Petula Clark touched the black arm of Harry Belafonte on primetime television. The whisper of a Caribbean storm in the thimble of an English tea cup.

Two days later, a review in *The Hollywood Reporter* hit newsstands. Its critic praised the show but couldn't help mock the controversy, referring to the disgraced Lott as 'an agency rep who must have been thinking of the white-sheet crowd in the South'.

HARRY

That day, of all days, the white-sheet crowd in the South wouldn't have cared. On April 4, 1968, they had more important things to celebrate.

MARTIN

He didn't come to Memphis to ride the Zippin Pippin. Nor to pop the whip at the Rainbow Rollerdrome, or to try Vanucci's famous meatball sandwich, or take in a midnight movie at the Memphian, or even to sightsee along Highway 51 South, stopping for a photograph at the gates with its wrought iron figure with a guitar and sideburns.

He came for the garbage men. The sanitation workers, mostly black, low paid and denied union recognition by City Hall, like the two who'd taken shelter from the rain, riding in the back of their truck when a freak malfunction crushed them to death. The white Mayor, Henry Loeb, who seven years earlier had been sat scooping crème de menthe parfait beside the man of the hour at the charity luncheon for 'Elvis Presley Day', refused to compensate the dead garbage men's families. So the sanitation union called a strike, organising a peaceful march through the streets of Memphis, many workers carrying signs declaring in block capitals: 'I AM A MAN.' Loeb sent in the police with tear gas and truncheons. 'This is not New York,' he steamed. 'Nobody can break the law. You are putting my back against the wall and I am not going to budge.'

Loeb's stance only calcified the anger and determination of the city's black community. That's when they rang Atlanta and asked for help: for the garbage men demanding better pay and basic workers' rights; for the downtrodden poor; for everyone suffering from the cold heart and plantation soul of its medieval Mayor.

That's why Dr Martin Luther King Jr. came to Memphis.

He came because he felt he must, because he was a man of his word and one word from Martin was worth all four-and-a-half thousand of the U.S. Constitution. A few weeks ago millions had watched him on NBC telling Harry Belafonte about his agenda for the Spring of '68. 'I feel that we are in the midst of a most critical period in our nation,' he began in his slow Southern purr as if carefully conjuring each word before his eyes, letter by letter. 'We are confronting a major depression in the poor community. And I think the time has come to bring to bear the power of the direct action movement on the basic economic conditions that we face all over the country.'

The plight of the Memphis sanitation workers was a chance for Martin to put that direct action into practice, announcing that he and the SCLC – his civil rights organisation, the Southern Christian Leadership Conference – would lead strikers on a rally through the city on Friday, March 22.

The local radio station WHBQ, where 'G.K. the D.J.' once filled the airwaves with Tom Jones' 'Green, Green Grass Of Home' on repeat as a favour for a friend, received an anonymous call warning Martin would die on the streets of Memphis if he went ahead with the march. This wasn't unusual. By 1968 he'd been threatened with assassination over 50 times. Only once did somebody nearly succeed, ten years earlier in 1958 when a woman in a Harlem department store stabbed him with a letter opener as he was signing copies of his first book. The blade had entered so close to his heart that, as the doctors later told him, had he sneezed he would have died. The woman was arrested, certified insane and committed to an asylum. She was also black.

Come the morning of March 22, Memphis awoke in a snow blizzard. Had Martin been destined to die that day, the weather had saved his life. The rally was rescheduled to the following Thursday when nobody shot at Martin. Only at the crowd.

What had been planned as a peaceful demonstration became a riot when a disaffected gang of young men calling themselves 'the Invaders' carrying 'Black Power' banners began smashing windows. The police opened fire. Sixty people were injured and a teenage boy killed. The day ended with Loeb calling in the National Guard to enforce a curfew. Martin, taken to safety in a local Holiday Inn, watched the violence unfold on television, distraught but defiant. The next day before flying back to Atlanta he vowed he'd return to Memphis the following week, the first in April, and try again, only better prepared and better organised.

On Tuesday April 2, he rested at home with his wife, Coretta, and their four children as NBC televised his friend Harry singing with Petula Clark. The next morning Xernona Clayton, a local TV presenter who worked for the SCLC, drove Martin to the airport for his flight to Memphis. The scheduled take off was delayed. There'd been another threat on Martin's life, this time a bomb scare. The pilot reassured the passengers that the aircraft had been guarded all night but they'd had to recheck the hold luggage purely as a precaution. Martin joked to his travelling companion, SCLC co-founder and fellow pastor Ralph Abernathy, at least 'they' weren't going to kill him on this flight. Ralph did his best to bolster him. '*Nobody's* going to kill you, Martin.'

He landed in Memphis early afternoon ahead of more bad weather. Dusk fell with thunder, fierce winds and rain spattering the balcony windows of his room at the downtown Lorraine Motel, a few blocks east of the Mississippi river. He was supposed to speak at a welcoming meeting that night at Mason Temple, the church where two weeks earlier he'd urged all local black employees and students to boycott work and school for the first failed rally. But as the storm howled outside Room 306, so did his depression within. The second march, scheduled for that Friday, April 5, had been slapped with a restraining order by a district court judge. With the night's weather forecast warning of tornados, he didn't believe enough people would risk venturing out to see him. He apologised to Ralph but told him he'd have to go to the Temple without him.

Martin was already in his pyjamas when the phone in his room rang around half past eight. It was Ralph, calling from the Temple. He'd underestimated Memphis. There were around 2000 people waiting to hear him speak, as well as newsmen and television cameras. 'The people want to hear *you*, not me,' Ralph coaxed him. 'This is *your* crowd.'

An hour later, Martin was in his suit at the pulpit of Mason Temple. 'Thank you very kindly, my friends.'

He spoke to the crowd, *his* crowd, about God and faith, about the sanitation workers' struggle and the coming rally, about slavery and the Road to Jericho. Then he reminisced about the time he'd been stabbed ten years ago and how, if he'd sneezed, he could have died. He told them about a letter he'd received while recuperating in hospital from a white schoolgirl. 'She said… "I read in the paper of your misfortune and of your suffering. And I read that if you had sneezed, you would have died. And I'm simply writing to say that I'm so happy that you didn't sneeze."'

The crowd laughed, cheered and clapped.

'And I want to say tonight,' Martin added, 'that I, too, am happy that I didn't sneeze…'

All right!

'Because if I had sneezed I wouldn't have been around here in 1960 when students all over the South started sitting-in at lunch counters…'

Yes sir!

'If I had sneezed, I wouldn't have been around here in 1961, when we decided to take a ride for freedom and ended segregation in interstate travel...'

All right!

'If I had sneezed, I wouldn't have been here in 1963, when the black people of Birmingham, Alabama, aroused the conscience of this nation and brought into being the Civil Rights Bill.'

ALL RIGHT!

'If I had sneezed, I wouldn't have had a chance later that year, in August, to try to tell America about a dream that I had had...'

YEEEAH!

'If I had sneezed, I wouldn't have been in Memphis to see a community rally around those brothers and sisters who are suffering...'

YESSIR!

'I'm so happy that I didn't sneeze.'

After 40 minutes on his feet, his face sparkling with sweat, his shirt clinging to his body, he finished by sharing the story of that day's bomb scare and the other threats he'd received from 'some of our sick white brothers'. He swore it no longer mattered to him. Then, in a voice wild as a once-trapped thunderbolt suddenly uncaged, he explained why.

'Because I've been to the mountaintop... And I've looked over, and I've *SEEN* the Promised Land. I may not get there with you. But I want you to know tonight, that *WE*, as a people, will *GET* to the Promised Land! So I'm happy tonight. I'm not *WORRIED* about *ANYTHING!* I'm not fearing *ANY* man! *MINE EYES HAVE SEEN THE GLORY OF THE COMING OF THE LORD!*'

Martin was taken back to his motel in the white Cadillac his driver had loaned from a local funeral home. He was spiritually replenished but physically spent, sleeping until mid-morning when Ralph had to shake him from his bed for more meetings about the march. The decision was made to reschedule again for the following Monday, April 8, allowing enough time to overturn the legal injunction. When that afternoon a local judge ruled in their favour, it seemed his luck in Memphis had finally changed for the better.

That Thursday evening he'd been invited to dinner at the home of local pastor Reverend Billy Kyles. Around 5.30 pm, Martin was in his room with Ralph, dressed and ready to leave, when Billy knocked to collect them. At the last moment Ralph said he had to go to the bathroom and put some aftershave on. Martin told him he and Billy would wait on the balcony and grab some air.

He stepped out into the cool Tennessee evening, the sky starting to darken above. He was in fine humour, thinking of the prime rib, chitterlings, pig's feet, greens and blackeyed peas he'd been promised for supper, chatting over the railing down to his friends in the car park a storey below. At about 6 pm, Billy turned to join them downstairs and walked back inside.

Leaving 39-year-old Dr Martin Luther King Jr. alone on the balcony of Room 306 of the Lorraine Motel, Memphis, just long enough for a single metal-jacketed .30-06 bullet to shatter his jaw, slice his jugular vein and sever his spinal cord.

They found the rifle in a blanket dropped outside a boarding house the other side of Mulberry Street where the rear bathroom offered an uninterrupted view of the motel. Its discovery coincided with the disappearance of one of its guests, 'John Willard', last seen pulling away minutes after the shooting in a pale Ford Mustang with Alabama license plates. A lot like the one James Earl Ray had been driving since dumping his old Plymouth.

BOBBY

They pronounced him dead at 7.05 pm, Memphis time. It was 8.05 in Indianapolis where an oblivious crowd of over 2000 had gathered at a park in the heart of its black inner city. They'd come, as the leaflets had promised, to 'See, Hear and Meet Robert F. Kennedy at 17th and N. Broadway, Thursday Evening, April 4, 1968 – All Welcome, Rain Or Shine.' But the presidential candidate was late, it was cold and the crowd were already restless when the fear and confusion prompted by unconfirmed reports about Martin passed from one shaking head to another. Some heard he'd been shot, others that he was in hospital. Nobody knew if he were dead, or if any of it were true.

Bobby knew. He was told about the shooting by a *New York Times* reporter as he boarded his campaign plane at Muncie. When he landed in Indianapolis 40 minutes later he learned Martin was dead. Not just dead but assassinated, the same as his brother. The brother whose tweed topcoat he still wore, and was wearing that night when he was greeted by the local chief of police who pleaded with him not to go ahead with his rally. With King dead, they couldn't guarantee the safety of a white politician before so large a black crowd. The risk of a riot was too severe.

But there was a strange, detached look in Bobby's eyes, as if tuned to the loneliest of cosmic wavelengths; beaming that night direct to his brain and the newly snapped heart of Mrs Coretta

Scott King but received nowhere else. 'I'm going to go there,' he insisted. 'And that's it.'

When Bobby arrived at the park after 9 pm, climbing onto a flatbed truck for his stage, his dead brother's upturned collar shielding his neck from the chill, the crowd still didn't know for sure what had happened in Memphis.

'I have bad news for you,' said Bobby, stepping to the microphone. 'For all our fellow citizens, and people who love peace all over the world. And that is that Martin Luther King was shot and killed tonight.'

The air jolted like time being punched. Gasps, cries, sobs and shrieks of 'no!' A bomb drop of grief.

Bobby had felt its blast before. He knew every wave of its horror, pain and anger and recognised its ripples in the thousands of black faces stretching back from the truck all the way to the tenements across the park.

'I feel in my own heart the same kind of feeling,' he told them. 'I had a member of my family killed, but he was killed by a white man.'

The air jolted again. Bobby had never said it before. Not in public, not in the four-and-a-half years since his brother was murdered on the worst day in America's living memory. Until this day, standing before the crowd in Indianapolis, no longer a candidate, no longer a man but the ghost of November '63. Not once did he gaze down at the piece of paper in his hand, notes he'd scribbled during the short ride from the airport after refusing to take those of his advisers. Instead, he quoted by heart his favourite Greek poet, Aeschylus, with the slow and steady voice of one who truly understood what wisdom lies beyond the threshold of a night of such despair.

'What we need in the United States is not division,' said Bobby. 'What we need in the United States is not hatred. What we need in the United States is not violence or lawlessness, but love and wisdom and compassion toward one another, and a feeling of justice towards those who still suffer within our country, whether they be white or whether they be black.'

That night across the USA, coast to coast, city to city, the bullets flew and the blood ran. Riots in New York, Washington D.C., Chicago, Baltimore, Detroit, Minneapolis and a hundred others. Thirty-nine deaths. Over two-thousand injured. Fifty-thousand National Guardsmen deployed. Division. Hatred. Violence. Lawlessness. But not in Indianapolis.

Five hundred miles south in Atlanta, in her first night of widowhood Coretta was home watching news reruns of Martin's speeches on TV in a pink nightgown. The telephone had been ringing constantly with condolences from senators, congressmen and President Johnson. All offered their help. None suggested any. Most were fielded by Xernona, the woman who'd last driven Martin to the airport. Then, around 2 am, Bobby rang.

Bobby told Xernona he'd been trying to get hold of Coretta for hours and she obviously needed more phone lines: he'd booked a telephone engineer who'd be with her shortly to fix just that. He also knew Mrs King had to get to Memphis as soon as possible to retrieve her husband's body. He told her there'd be a private plane waiting for Coretta at the airport the next morning. 'My family,' he added, 'has experience in dealing with this kind of thing.' The murdered corpse of Dr Martin Luther King Jr. was brought home to Atlanta on an aircraft chartered by Bobby Kennedy.

That Friday, Harry Belafonte flew in from New York to assist Coretta with the funeral arrangements. He offered to cover the cost of her widow weeds – in any case, the white salesman at the department store respectfully supplied them free of charge – and was one of the few beside her when she saw first saw her husband's open casket at Spelman College, a black women's school in Atlanta

University, lying in state in the very chapel where eight years ago that week Martin had spoken to staff and students about moving mountains and the Promised Land, and where she herself had given a scripture reading.

The mortician had made a crude attempt to plug the bullet wound in the jaw with clay. Xernona improvised a quick fix, borrowing Coretta's dark face powder then mixing a shade with some from Harry's white wife, Julie, blending them together to better disguise the wound. Harry placed a handkerchief under Martin's neck so no make-up stained the coffin lining. When Xernona was done, he placed it back in his pocket. 'This,' said Harry, 'is a piece of history.'

The last thing Harry did before the public were admitted in to grieve was straighten Martin's tie. Sixty-thousand people queued to see the body that weekend.

On the Monday, the march Martin had planned in support of the sanitation workers took place in Memphis. Coretta and Harry walked at the head of the sombre crowd. It felt less like a protest march than a dress rehearsal for the next day's funeral procession.

Later that night, Bobby arrived in Atlanta. He was one of the last to see Martin in the chapel, just after 1 am on Tuesday April 9, the day of the burial. He walked up to the casket, crossed himself, then left in total silence.

The main funeral service was held at Martin's own church, the Ebenezer Baptist. Beside Harry and Bobby, the congregation included Motown boss Berry Gordy, the Supremes, Aretha Franklin, Sammy Davis Jr., Sidney Poitier, Eartha Kitt, Marlon Brando, Paul Newman and Bobby's sister-in-law, Jackie Kennedy.

In symbolic honour of his dying wish of a Poor People's Campaign, the coffin was taken the four miles to a second service at Martin's old college on a farmer's cart drawn by two mules. Bobby was among the thousands following the procession.

At the Morehouse campus, Mahalia Jackson, the one who'd prompted Martin at the Lincoln Memorial to 'tell 'em about the dream', sang his favourite gospel song, 'Take My Hand, Precious Lord', before the crowd joined hands for a communal 'We Shall Overcome'.

It had been a rare clear and sunny day after a week of unremitting rain and storms. But the weather stayed fine into the early evening, as Martin's coffin, now in a hearse, was driven to its journey's end at South View Cemetery. It was a week to the day Harry had been seen on television clutched by Petula Clark. Now he was clutching the arm of Martin's widow as she watched his coffin slip inside its tomb. An epitaph had been temporarily stencilled onto the white marble to be permanently engraved later. Lines from an old negro spiritual that Martin often quoted, including the day he shared his dream.

'Free at last, Free at last, Thank God Almighty I'm Free at last.'

As Bobby and the rest of the mourners drifted away, the heavens opened and a hard rain fell.

STEVE

It didn't rain in Los Angeles. It rarely did. Presidents and Nobel Peace Prize winners could be slain in broad American daylight but the skies above Hollywood stayed blue as its matte paintings of paradise. The blue of happiness. The blue of I-don't-want-to-hear-about-your-unhappiness. A sunglasses blue that refused to turn umbrella grey even on the day they buried Martin.

It was still blue when the telephone rang in Suite 410 at 8833 Sunset Boulevard, a glass-fronted office block on the wilder west of the Strip, one block from the Whisky A Go Go, opposite what used to be comedian Jerry Lewis' club, Jerry's, serving 'American and Hebrew viands'. Only now it served 'the biggest topless show in the West' under new management as a strip joint, the Classic Cat, where Jim Morrison from the Doors came to shoot pool and director Russ Meyer to talent-scout amongst its top-heavy 'Kittens'.

Across the street, looking down at the Cat's neon-lettered façade, behind the glass in Suite 410 where the telephone rang, was the office of a new music television company, Binder-Howe Productions. Binder was the television, Howe the music.

At the age of 35, Dayton 'Bones' Howe had been making records for over a decade. Tall and lean with a face the same aspect carrying thick-rimmed glasses and even thicker sideburns, Bones started in '56 as assistant engineer at Radio Recorders on Santa

Monica Boulevard, bridging the decades overseeing everything from rock 'n' roll, easy listening and surf to his first love, modern jazz. His Midas touch didn't properly shine until later in the Sixties, first as engineer of Barry McGuire's 'Eve Of Destruction' and the Mamas & the Papas hits, including 'California Dreamin'', then as weatherman to the Summer of Love with the 5th Dimension's 'Up, Up And Away' and the Association's 'Windy', his first number one as producer. Sixties pop had a pulse and Bones, much like his *Star Trek* doc namesake, had proven he knew where to find it.

To see Bones' new partner's name on a rolodex anyone might easily pronounce it 'Bine-der', like a ring binder, when it ought to rhyme with cinder or Linda: 'Bin-der'.

Steve Binder was Los Angeles born and bred. You could see it in his beige skin, wavy hair, stubby sideburns, twinkling eyes and causally hip clothes. He understood the city, its tempo, its lonely depths and crowded shallows, its codes of conduct, its money, its greed and desperation, its rewards for artifice and penalties for reality, its stock exchange of wealth and vanity, its industry and its people, where they kept their knives and how best to not to wake up with one in his back.

The same age as Bones, Steve started in TV directing Soupy Sales, a kids' slapstick comic rarely recognised without a shaving-foam pie dripping off his face. He found his television mentor in Steve Allen, the producer and host who once famously made his star guest sing to a basset hound, and under Allen's wing began specialising in music, directing the series *Jazz Scene USA*.

He switched to rock 'n' roll for his first documentary feature film, the 1964 *T.A.M.I. Show* concert at Santa Monica Civic Auditorium headlined by James Brown's twitchy hips and Mick Jagger's twitchier lips. Its success took Steve to New York to direct a new youth show for NBC, *Hullabaloo*, launched as a rival to

ABC's weekly pop showcase *Shindig!*. Roughly the same format, where *Shindig!* stuck acts on a plain stage before a screaming audience, on *Hullabaloo* each performer was given their own specially tailored set, dressed with props, fashion models or dancers in go-go cages. Every song its own miniature theatre production caught on videotape. The kind of thing that could even catch on someday.

After one season, Steve returned West. Much as he enjoyed *Hullabaloo*, he'd become concerned music television was still too preoccupied with how it looked rather than how it sounded, and so began searching for someone from the recording side of the business to start a new partnership. He found Bones through his shared management with Lou Adler, Dunhill Records boss and producer of the Mamas & the Papas. Since Bones had already been contracted by Atlantic Records to produce Leslie Uggams, the African-American star of Broadway's *Hallelujah, Baby!*, Uggams was chosen as the subject of Binder-Howe's first one-hour TV special commissioned by ABC in late '67.

They followed it in early '68 with another for NBC starring Petula Clark. The one with Harry Belafonte, sponsored by Plymouth.

Steve had been the director.

Because of it, his name had made the papers, though the papers didn't know the half of what had gone on between himself and Plymouth's Doyle Lott; the phone calls, the threats, the summit meeting in Detroit where he had to convince the president of Chrysler to let Harry stay in the show as Lott fumed across the table. But it had been worth the fight. The Uggams special had yet to be broadcast so *Petula* brought Steve and Bones their first joint good reviews. 'Stylish', 'sophisticated', 'contemporary', 'a prizewinner' with 'the finest in camera work and a brilliant sound system'. And, with 'the touch', they'd struck a small if significant victory for racial equality. Or so it seemed for all of 48 hours until the news came through from the Lorraine Motel in Memphis.

Hollywood stopped. Shoots were cancelled as stars were sent home to grieve. The Academy Awards, scheduled for the following Monday, were postponed. Rat Packer Joey Bishop threw out the script of that night's live ABC show to pay tribute with impromptu guests such as Kirk Douglas, coming straight from his film set to recite Martin's 'I Have A Dream' speech before the cameras. Marlon Brando, who only three weeks ago had played host to Martin at a special anti-war assembly in his Beverly Hills home, was moved to quit acting altogether to devote himself to the civil rights effort. 'I felt I'd better go find out where it is,' Brando told the press, 'what it is to be black in this country.'

Downtown, the City of Angels didn't burn like other cities burned that night, nor as it had burned years earlier in Watts. Few had heard Martin's last speech at Brando's, about taking 'the inchoate rage of the ghetto' and transforming it 'into a constructive and creative force', but Los Angeles instinctively reacted in kind, with church services overflowing into the streets and a mass public memorial at the Coliseum. But the heavens never did open and no hard rain fell. The skies stretched blue on blue, from Hollywood and Vine to the far west of the Strip. Where, in Suite 410, the telephone rang.

The secretary, Ann, answered then patched the call through to Steve's office.

'Bob Finkel,' she told him, 'from NBC.'

Steve knew the name. Bob Finkel wasn't just from NBC: Bob Finkel *was* NBC. Eighteen years in the game and just turned 50, he'd been one of their top variety producers for years with a trio of Emmys to show for it. He'd won all three for *The Andy Williams Show*. That was Finkel in a nutshell: primetime, dinner jackets, bowties, 'Moon River' and 'tonight's guest – Phyllis Diller!' Steve couldn't think why a guy like Finkel would be calling the guy from *Hullabaloo*.

'Hello? Yes. Hi Bob, this is Steve.'

In his own office next door, Bones was listening to a new album by a young New York singer, Laura Nyro. She was managed by a friend of theirs, David Geffen. It was Steve who'd first told Geffen about Laura over dinner. One track in particular, 'Stoned Soul Picnic', Bones was sure would be perfect for his next 5th Dimension record. *'Red yellow honey, sassafras and moonshine.'* He decided to solicit Steve's opinion on it.

The door to Steve's office was ajar. Bones had one foot in the room before he realised he was busy on the phone. He heard Steve say 'thanks', then 'um' and a triplet of 'uh-huh's. Then Bones heard a name which made him freeze.

Steve kept talking, telling whoever was on the other end of the line that he had too many projects coming up, one in particular, a movie deal with veteran producer Walter Wanger. Steve was already working on the script and they planned to start shooting by the end of the year. Bones heard him say 'sorry', then several 'thanks', then saw his hand place the receiver back in its cradle.

'Did I hear right?'

Only then did Steve notice Bones was stood there.

'I did, didn't I?' There was an odd disbelief in Bones' eyes. 'Are you fucking *crazy*?'

'Ah,' smiled Steve. 'You mean…'

'Man!' laughed Bones, rolling his head back. 'Do you realise you just turned down *Elvis Presley*?'

BONES

It was the first of September. The day after an angry white mob attacked and overturned a car full of blacks in Tennessee. The day after a similar white mob, many of them children, blockaded a newly desegregated school in Texas, stringing up a negro effigy above the entrance and daubing their vehicles with 'Dead coons are the best.' A new day when a Florida town awoke to leaflets for that night's Klan meeting inviting 'all white people who are interested in white supremacy'. A Saturday like any other in the Disunited States of 1956. Jackie Gleason on the TV. Marilyn Monroe at the cinema. Elvis Presley at number one. Blue skies at lunchtime above Santa Monica Boulevard.

It was a working Saturday for 23-year-old Bones Howe, five months into his apprenticeship at Radio Recorders. He arrived before noon, caffeine in his blood and the Picasso paradiddles of Shelly Manne never very far away from his head. He walked in, past the guard checking off his name and the sign 'No Vistors Allowed', neither of which had been there the day before. But neither had Elvis Presley.

Bones was more curious than excited. He was a jazz cat and his stack didn't blow for some shaky country hick whooping and wriggling like he had a box of firecrackers down his pants. He'd seen his silly whizzbangs earlier that year on stage at a movie theatre in Sarasota. Elvis broke a string and a girl in the audience ran to the nearest music store for a replacement. Elvis shook his legs and people screamed. Bones hated it. He hated his records too. He'd started at Radio Recorders as 'Heartbreak Hotel' hit number one. All these weeks later Elvis was still there, this time with the double knockout of 'Hound Dog' and 'Don't Be Cruel'. Bones didn't get it. But for a paycheque of $72 a week, he'd bear it.

He greeted his boss, Thorne Nogar, the studio's head engineer, grabbed them both coffees from the machine down the corridor and began arranging the microphone stands. 'Thorny' told him it would be a fairly simple set-up: drums, piano, a bass, one guitar, backing vocals and a lead mic for Elvis. The band were already there waiting. So was a confederacy of suits from the record label, busy talking to Thorny in the control booth as the unmistakeable bulk and bluster of Colonel Tom Parker strolled purposefully through the door. Behind him were two younger men with black oily hair and sideburns. The skinnier one, with a face that might have just swam from Alcatraz, grabbed a folding chair from against the wall and sat himself in a corner. The other was unmistakably Elvis Presley.

He was *gorgeous*. Did Bones' brain just say that? Yes. Gorgeous. He hadn't thought so watching him in Sarasota, but then he hadn't been mere inches from his face. He was gorgeous from his yellow socks to his red shirt and the puckering perfection above. The perfection said 'hi' to Bones. Gorgeous, and polite.

The skinny one was Elvis' cousin and mute shadow, Gene. He'd brought him along as company since Elvis didn't know the studio. He'd never recorded out West before. His eyes flickered around the room like a bird of prey surveying unknown territory. They fixed on the piano. A moment later he was sat down, his hands on the keys, eyes closed, cooing *'Blue moon, I saw you standing alone...'*

A Rodgers and Hart standard. And – *Jesus!* – the kid plays piano.

In a stroke of ivory Elvis switched into 'Hound Dog'. He didn't seem to be singing for Gene, for his band, for Bones, for Thorny, for anyone other than himself. Not because he wanted to, but because he *had* to, his flesh and bones slave to the master of his voice.

With the mics set up, Bones took his place in the control room behind Thorny at the desk. The Colonel and the suits from the record label were staring through the glass. Bones thought they'd come to direct the session. They did nothing. Just sat there, watching Elvis at the piano lead the band through the first song like they were watching a movie. It was a ballad, 'Playing For Keeps'. It went to 18 takes. Not because Thorny or the Colonel or the suits told him to. It was Elvis, primed for the perfect echo in his Shake Rag soul who kept on pushing. That's when it hit Bones like a bass drum pedal thump in his face.

Elvis was *running the show*.

He ran it for the next three days, deciding what songs they'd play, throwing away those that didn't work, changing what he wanted to be changed, telling the band what he liked and what he didn't until he was convinced everyone had given it their best, him most of all. When he listened to each playback it was with his whole body, like he was breathing in the music, circulating it around his lungs and through his veins, either exhaling in satisfaction or spluttering to try again, even if for the twenty-seventh take. By Monday evening they had 13 songs. Bones engineered and Thorny mixed. But the real producer, both of them knew, was Elvis.

Bones had been completely wrong about Elvis. The kid had that magic every musician dreams of possessing and every engineer dreams of recording.

'*Feel*,' he told Steve.

He and Thorny worked on many more Elvis sessions over the next few years. It never mattered if it was rock 'n' roll, Christmas songs or his latest soundtrack, Elvis was always the one in charge whipping the storm and trapping the lightning.

'I don't *know* Elvis,' said Bones, 'but I know how he works, and with him it's all about the music.'

'Yeah, but those *movies*,' said Steve. 'C'mon? They're a *joke*.'

'Sure.' Bones tumbled his eyes. 'But they're not the Elvis I saw. If I ever had the chance to work with him again – not one of his goofy movies, I mean something *proper*. To work with that voice with today's sounds, today's musicians. You kidding? Man, I'd jump at it.'

Steve listened, nodding softly, rubbing his chin, a smile creeping across his face. His eyes glanced back to the still-warm telephone on his desk. He tapped a pencil.

Elvis Presley, huh?

What the hell.

ANDREAS

The psychopath Andreas Cornelis van Kuijk in his masterful disguise as Colonel Thomas Andrew Parker sat back in his chair with a gentle creak, savouring his first cigar of the working day. It wasn't yet 7 am but the Colonel was an early bird with worms to catch and they'd be due any minute. He'd been sent them by Finkel at NBC: a Mr Binder and his associate, a Mr Howe. Finkel told the Colonel they were the right team for the television special he'd signed for at the start of the year as part of his two-for-one deal with Tom Sarnoff. One movie, one TV show. The Colonel didn't care much about either but he appreciated the $1 million it would wedge in his billfold and the sight of his name back where it belonged in black type on the front page of *Variety*. Everything else was snow.

Two men were sat on lunch stools at a counter on the other side of the office, an A&R agent from RCA and the Colonel's long-serving dogsbody, Tom. The Colonel used to summon Tom by squeezing a cuddly hound dog that let out a barking noise. Whenever Tom heard the bark, he had to run to the Colonel. The Colonel was that sort of boss and Tom, still here, was that sort of employee.

Tom and the man from RCA had been called there early as witnesses to a special early morning matinee performance by the First High Potentate Snower: the maestro of flim and the shaman of flam who, before their very eyes, would shortly unleash his supernatural gifts of gab and grab on a couple of young suckers from TV land. The griddle was on and the Colonel was ready for a new day stuffing foot-long buns with slaw and onions. *Come an' get 'em, suckers! Roll up, roll up!*

They rolled up bang on 7 in a canary-yellow '57 Ford convertible.

It was early May, weeks after Finkel first rang Steve in his office. Bones had convinced him to ring Finkel back. A few days later Finkel met them both for lunch at the Brown Derby on Hollywood and Vine. Finkel had his own production company, Teram, named after his kids, Terry and Pam. As he told Steve and Bones, Sarnoff had given his Teram the job of producing the Elvis Presley special for NBC. He'd had preliminary meetings with the Colonel, and Elvis, but they were nowhere nearer finalising the specifics. He told them Elvis had called him 'Mr Finkel' throughout, never 'Bob', which worried him. Finkel knew the show needed somebody younger, somebody roughly Elvis' own age. That's why he'd come to Steve and Bones. He'd seen the *Petula* show and read all about the Belafonte brouhaha. Steve obviously wasn't afraid to stand his ground and that's precisely what Finkel needed.

'I don't think it'll be easy,' Finkel told them. 'But it could be great.'

The sponsor would be Singer, the sewing machine people owned by General Electric who also had their own national chain of stores selling household electrical goods including TVs and record players. Singer had already sponsored a high-rating Herb Alpert & Tijuana Brass special for CBS. Neither they nor the ad agency, J. Walter Thompson, nor the network were Finkel's problem. The obstacle was the Colonel. Because it was scheduled to air that December he was set on it being a Christmas show complete with carols, children and chestnuts roasting on an open fire.

'Which is not what we want,' said Finkel.

Steve asked what Elvis wanted.

'I don't think Elvis wants to do TV, full stop.' Finkel lay down his fork. 'Look, I'll be honest with you. As things are, I don't even know if there'll even *be* a special. This thing's been stalling for weeks. What I really need is someone who can help push this thing along. This needs someone who understands the record business and someone who understands television. And I'm looking at both.'

Bones brought up his past history with Elvis. Maybe he and Steve could talk to him?

'You don't just *meet* Elvis,' Finkel smiled. 'You'd need to speak to the Colonel first. If you really want to do this then I can call him and set up a meeting, tell him you're the men for the job. If he agrees, then we go ahead. But it's up to him.'

And so Steve and Bones found themselves on the MGM lot in Culver City at 7 am on a Friday morning knocking on the door of Elvis Exploitations.

The Colonel enjoyed seeing the momentary doubt in their eyes when they saw the oilcloth table surrounded by wooden chairs, unsure whether they'd taken the wrong turn into the wrong room until the familiar face of Elvis Presley smiling from the walls reassured them that this, indeed, was the place. They saw the smoke before they saw the Colonel who appeared from behind it like the sudden sight of land through a misty sea. He wore his best casino smile and his worst shirt with the tails flapping loose over his waist. He balanced on a cane, a recent necessity after one too many heart scares, which only made his gait that bit more sinister.

He spoke without removing the cigar from his mouth, like the Penguin from *Batman*: Steve thought his voice not too dissimilar.

'Mr Binder, Mr Howe, sit down, boys, sit down.'

The younger men pulled up a chair each at the main table, the Colonel joining them at its head. 'So you boys know NBC paid *one million dollars* for Elvis?' he quacked. 'One million dollars,' he repeated, smiling. 'And I didn't even have to switch the label on my suit.'

He started telling them the story of how he held Hal Wallis to ransom with the fake suit label routine, how he squeezed more millions from United Artists and MGM, and how he'd made a record sum from Elvis' appearances on Ed Sullivan back in the Fifties.

'And do you know how much Sinatra paid for Elvis? Twice what he paid himself.' The Colonel glugged on his cigar, giving birth to another fat smoke ring.

'I suppose you boys have heard people say the Colonel's just an old carnie?' he continued. 'Yessir, I was born on the midway.'

The Colonel was gearing up for his greatest hits.

'Touring fun fair, West Virginia. Orphaned as a child. Raised by my uncle on his Great Pony Circus...'

Steve and Bones wore polite masks of fake interest.

'Made my way selling hot dogs. Then I came up with the Foot-Long Hot Dog...'

He told them about the buns, the slaw, the onions and the pre-placed sausage in the dirt.

'But that was before the chickens.'

He told them about Tom Parker's Dancing Chickens. The hotplate, the straw, starting the week with six chickens, ending it with one.

'Well, a fella's gotta eat.'

They waited for the Colonel to glug to a standstill like an outboard motor.

'So,' he puffed. 'Finkel tells me you're the boys to do this here special for Elvis?'

Steve said they were.

'This is going to be the best special on the air because we won't let it be bad,' the Colonel oinked. 'And we're not going to tell you what to do, so long as you don't get out of line.'

They nodded.

'We don't care what material you submit for the show. If Mr Presley likes it, Mr Presley will do it. However, Mr Presley must be the publisher of the material, or else we'll communicate with the publisher and arrangements must be made.'

They nodded again.

'And here's something that may help.' The Colonel stood up and waltzed with his cane to a filing cabinet, pulling out a large square-shaped box. 'This,' he smiled, placing it on the table in front of Steve, 'is your TV show.'

The box had a picture of Elvis on the front beside the words 'Season's Greetings'. Inside was a tape reel of the 1967 radio show made up of old Christmas and gospel songs and a copy of the DJ's script. 'We broadcast this last Christmas to over 4000 radio stations coast to coast. Heard by millions.' The words pumped through his stogie in Injun smoke signals. 'We just want the same thing,' he blew, 'with pictures.'

Steve and Bones exchanged glances.

The Colonel smiled greasier than a short order cook's apron. 'I can promise you boys are going to have a million dollar experience.'

The canary-yellow Ford drove back to Sunset Strip with a backseat strewn with pocket Elvis calendars, badges and two stuffed Hound Dog toys.

Back in his office, Steve opened the tape box and flicked through the radio script with a heavy sigh. '"What better way to ring in the season than with the King?"' He dropped it on his desk with a miserable thud.

Bones was leaning against the door. 'Well?'

'Well that was a waste of time,' sighed Steve. 'This is Perry Como shit. We can't put our names to this. Maybe I should call Finkel now and tell him the deal's off.'

At that same moment the phone rang. Steve answered.

'Bob?'

It was Finkel.

'Uh-huh,' Steve nodded. 'Wow... OK... Sure... Got it. Four o'clock. Yes... Thank you. I will... Yes... Yes, thank you, Bob... Bye.'

Steve put the receiver down. He turned to Bones.

'You're not going to believe this. That was Finkel.' He shook his head, half laughing. 'He said we must have sure charmed the Colonel because he just rang him to say we're in. He wants another meeting. Today at 4 o'clock.'

'At his place again?'

'No. The Colonel wants to meet here,' said Steve. His eyes seemed to be somersaulting. 'With Elvis.'

4.00 PM, SUITE 410

The wall clock said 3.54 pm.

Bones had met him before. He had no need to be nervous but his stomach mocked him in can–cans and jitterbugs. So did Steve's. It was like waiting to meet Superman or Dracula, a thing from film and fiction, not a man of flesh and blood. 'Elvis Presley.' When his name was first written on an index card in Sam Phillips' Sun Studios back in 1954, somebody laughed that he sounded 'like something outta science fiction.' That's how Steve and Bones felt at that moment. About to make contact with the man from Mars.

3.55 pm. A long black Lincoln Continental with Tennessee licence plates rolled in to the building's underground garage. Steve and Bones kept their eyes on the clock.

3.56 pm. Their eyes turned to the elevator doors down the corridor outside their reception, ears pricking for the faintest sound of bells and whirring cables.

3.57 pm. Tense, deafening, nothing.

3.58 pm. Something. A low humming noise. The elevator shaft mechanically inhaling. A pulse in the chain of lights above the metal doors.

3.59 pm. The humming stopped. Deep breaths. A bell chimed.

4.00 pm. The elevator doors slid open…

ACT III

DADDY

Eyelids closed. Darkness. Dry mouth. Deep breathing.

Eyelids open. *'Fuck!'*

He was still alive. It was 1968, and he was still alive.

He awoke from his barbiturate swamp late on New Year's Day, under monogrammed golden sheets in his remote-controlled black leather bed, his pregnant wife beside him. He could just about make out a reflection in the angled television screens in the ceiling above. When he moved his head, the reflection moved with him. As he'd feared. He wasn't dead and gone to Heaven. He was alive and still in Graceland.

He stumbled to his bathroom and switched on the light. The same maroon tiles. The same barber chair. The same bottles of Old Spice and Brut. The same towels, monogrammed like his bed covers to remind him who he was. 'E.P.' Cursed to live another year on God's earth as Elvis Presley. The man from yesterday trapped in a today of tomorrows.

Seven days later he turned 33. Record speed age. There'd been many birthdays before when he was number one in the album charts. This wasn't one of them. The Beatles, yet again, had seen to that. Elvis had one record in the Top 100 that week: *Clambake* at number 50. This was his punishment for the crime of being Elvis Presley in 1968. Rock 'n' roll mummification.

'He who in the 20th century shall dare evoke me beware, for neither by fire, nor water, nor force, nor anything by man created can I be destroyed!'

He spent the night of his birthday at the Memphian with Priscilla as she rubbed her tummy to her baby's kicks, along with his Angels, Gary Pepper and other fans. The film was about a crazy museum worker who resurrects an ancient Jewish Golem to commit murder.

'He who will find the secret of my life at his feet, him will I serve until beyond time!'

It was the early hours of Tuesday morning when they returned to Graceland. Priscilla went straight to bed. Elvis stayed up a while with Pauline the cook who fixed him some bacon, biscuit and omelette. It vanished in a few snuffling forkfuls. Pauline made up a second plate which he took up to his room. Priscilla was sleeping. He ate most of what was on the plate, washed down with orange juice and a couple of red devils. He thought about the film, the Golem, old powers once thought dead suddenly brought back to life, his eyelids sinking.

'WHO in the 20th century shall dare evoke me?'

And was a wraith once more.

He no longer dreamed: he no longer cared. The blues, pinks, reds, yellows, whites, greens and blacks managed his troubles for him. In their employ, work was a means to an end with no meaning. A punchline without a joke, as his first session of the year in Nashville proved. He tumbled in with eyes like opium dens and a mouth like a Tijuana Bible. For two nights he sonofabitched and motherfuckered through two film songs, a Chuck Berry cover and, the saving grace, a 2 am spontaneous skip through another tune by 'Guitar Man's Jerry Reed, 'U.S. Male'. Its spoof macho lyrics sent Elvis raving into a sulphate giggle about *'cornholing'* the Man in the Moon with *'the balls of a big hairy coon.'* It was a Southern spit 'n' sawdust parody of a sentimental country ballad, 'The Prisoner's

Song'. Elvis couldn't finish for laughing. After four hours of retake cabin fever his band could only laugh with him. Elvis' own prison had finally sent its singer insane.

It was the insanity of helpless repetition. His diary for 1968 was no different from 1967, or 1966, or 1965. He'd been contracted to make three more films that year, and whatever soundtracks they entailed. He had just a handful of records scheduled – the cleanest usable take of 'U.S. Male' for his next single, another gospel single for Easter, and one album, the shabby soundtrack to *Speedway* – but neither he nor his weary peach-canners predicted a miracle reprise. They predicted correctly: 'U.S. Male' took over two months to stagger to 28, the gospel single went nowhere and *Speedway* would be his worst-selling soundtrack of all time.

The only change was some other TV thing. 'A Christmas special,' as the Colonel had told him. That was all Elvis knew, and that it was with NBC, home to some of his favourite shows: *Star Trek*, the spy comedy *Get Smart* and *Laugh-In*, a wacky new satire hosted by Dan Rowan and Dick Martin which flat killed him, especially when they brought on a ukulele oddball called Tiny Tim who sang in a shrill spinster falsetto.

NBC had also broadcast the Nancy Sinatra special that Christmas. Elvis had watched it with Priscilla while visiting her parents, now living on an air base in California. They only had a black and white set so Elvis bought them a new one so he could enjoy Nancy in colour. She gave him his money's worth and a jig in his pants that his in-laws still felt sat on a separate sofa. Nancy even made her sponsor's adverts look sexy – Royal Crown Cola, 'the one with the mad, mad taste!' She'd been lucky: for a while, until her ad agency chose otherwise, she was nearly sponsored by Plymouth motors.

It reminded Elvis how Nancy had been there the last time he'd appeared on TV. Her dad's show live at the Fontainebleau, Miami

Beach. She looked a lot different then. So did he. No sideburns and sergeant stripes, straight out of the army, 1960. Eight years ago. *Eight years.* He thought about how terrified he'd been backstage. He could still feel it like the murmur of an old wound, deep in his gut. The cameras, the lights in his eyes, the noise of the audience. *The fear.* He tried not to think about it. The blues, the pinks, the yellows and the reds saw that he didn't. Not much. Though he still thought about Nancy.

And Rusty. *Always*, Rusty.

And God, Stalin and outer space. And Golems, monsters and cowboys. And anyone and anything that stopped him thinking about the one thing becoming ever harder for him to ignore with each new day he woke up sweating under golden sheets beside his wife's swollen belly. Until the moment came when *it* came. And Elvis became 'Daddy'.

It happened at one minute past five in the evening of February 1, on the fifth floor of the East Wing of Memphis Baptist Memorial Hospital. After six hours in labour Priscilla gave birth to a girl weighing six pounds and 15 ounces, with dark blue eyes, brown hair, Priscilla's nose and Elvis' mouth, chin and forehead. They named her Lisa Marie.

The new nuclear family came home to Graceland four days later: Elvis in blue, Priscilla in pink, Lisa Marie in swaddling white. Awaiting them was a Krakatoa of fan mail erupting in cards and baby gifts. Elvis' favourite was a bottle of holy water from the River Jordan. Among the first well-wishers over the threshold was Gary Pepper who gave them a baby stroller. Gary had read in the papers about the upcoming TV special and told Elvis he should sing to his daughter on camera. It tickled him so much that when the next day a fan waiting outside the gates asked if Priscilla would be joining him on the show Elvis told them, 'No, but Lisa Marie is.'

The cutest thing about Lisa Marie, everyone agreed, was her eyes. The way they locked on her Daddy at all times, following him around the room, wherever he moved. A baby girl only a few days old, already transfixed by Elvis Presley.

At one month old they changed her surroundings but Lisa Marie, eyeballs on Daddy, didn't notice. She was taken out West to her parents' new four-bedroom mansion on Hillcrest Drive, Beverly Hills. A marital home, though they weren't alone. Its one Angel in residence was Charlie, there to unzip the pecker of Elvis' shadow every time it needed a piss. Elvis' double first cousin Patsy also moved in with her husband Marvin, nicknamed 'Gee Gee', soon an honorary Angel in his own right.

It meant Elvis and Priscilla rarely had privacy, for all the difference it made. Now she was the mother of his child, he could no longer bear to touch her. But his hands wouldn't waste too much time finding someone else.

PLIANT LIPS

Her name was Susan. She was a crippled mermaid. Or so she appeared when he met her on location of his new film, in a wheelchair being pushed by a member of the crew. She had eyes of Mediterranean blue, toffee skin and long luminous blonde hair that had been combed over her shoulders and stuck to her bare breasts with pasties. He couldn't see her legs because they were hidden in a flesh-pink fishtail, the reason she was unable to walk and being wheeled around the set. Elvis smiled at her. She smiled back and her insides gurgled. Their horizontal destiny was thus decided.

Susan Henning was a California Girl from pedicured toe to pearl white teeth. She started modelling at the age of six. At 11 she was acting with Bette Davis in an episode of *Wagon Train*. At 14 she was cast as Hayley Mills' uncredited twin double in Disney's *The Parent Trap*. At 18 she was crowned 'Miss Teen USA' and engaged to '77 *Sunset Strip* actor Robert Logan. At 19 she was married with a child. At 20, she realised she'd made a terrible mistake. At 21 she was living alone with her daughter, in the process of getting divorced and on the books of the Bill Cunningham modelling agency. That's when they found her a small role in the new Elvis film, a romantic comedy called *Kiss My Firm But Pliant Lips*. Elvis played a fashion photographer. Susan had one brief scene as one of his models. She had to sit on a diving board dressed as a mermaid while a killer whale leapt out of the pool to snap a lunch roll out of her hand. The foil-wrapped roll contained raw fish so the whale would jump as trained.

The scene was filmed at Marineland amusement park on the Californian coast, famed for its giant Sky Tower allowing panoramic views over the Pacific Palos Verdes coastline. After the shoot was done, Susan was wheeled back to her trailer to change out of her mermaid suit when there was a knock on the door. It was Diamond Joe. He'd come on behalf of his boss to ask if she'd like to go 'up the tower' with Elvis. Susan said yes, she very much would.

Elvis waited until their elevator reached the top, 414 feet above sea level staring out over the sea, before he asked if she'd like to 'go out' with him. Susan wobbled. It wasn't the altitude but the ring on her finger. She'd just gotten engaged again. But she was still only 21. More to the point, she was a woman and he was Elvis Presley. She gave him her number.

Back at ground level, Elvis kissed her cheek and promised he'd call her soon. Then he climbed into his Lincoln so Joe could drive him back home to the wife he no longer slept with and the child whose eyes followed his every move.

His dinner was waiting at 6 on the dot. Meatloaf, mashed potatoes, peas and gravy. If he wouldn't let her please him in the bedroom Priscilla was determined not to disappoint in the kitchen. Elvis cleaned his plate then spent the rest of the evening watching TV. Priscilla sometimes snuggled beside him with Lisa Marie in her arms. But tonight it was just him and Charlie, his chosen smokes, thin Villiger Kiel cigars, and his Friday favourite, *Star Trek*. In this episode the crew of the Enterprise found themselves on a planet modelled on ancient Rome. Captain Kirk was tended on by a gorgeous blonde slave girl in a baking foil bikini. 'I'm ordered to please you,' she purred.

Elvis laughed. Charlie echoed him.

'Mah boy, *mah boy*.'

It was their new catchphrase. Something cooked up out of a W.C. Fields impression. They'd begun saying it for no good reason whenever they saw a woman who played their pulses like bongos. Most weeks *Star Trek* brought out the 'mah boy' in Elvis. Just as Susan had.

Susan was his kind of woman. Beautiful and spiritual. Like their lovin'. Afterwards they'd lie in each other's arms and talk about their shared love of God. Sometimes Elvis read passages from the Bible to her. Other times they'd recite memory verses. He liked to hear Susan say 'The Lord's Prayer' but he didn't like it rushed. He wanted each word enunciated carefully with due reverence. Slow and thorough. Like their lovin'.

Elvis had never liked people playing with his hair, but Susan was special. When she crept behind him as he sat on the couch and started running her fingers deep into his scalp, he didn't stop her. It had grown long enough for her to knot a short braid. Elvis saw it in the mirror and laughed. He asked her to do some more. A Beach Boys parting to one side. A waterfall kiss curl down to his nose. The silliest was when she squished up both sides to create one long central fin. Elvis the Mohican. They both howled.

The only thing Susan didn't like about Elvis, and his hair, was the greasy goo he put on it. In every other respect he was the most ideal man she'd ever met. They both loved bananas, and peanut butter, and the Lord, and each other. And they were both parents. Susan sometimes mentioned her daughter, Courtney. Elvis liked to talk about Lisa Marie too. How she was growing every day. The funny faces she pulled. How her eyes followed him everywhere. How much he loved his baby girl.

But not once in her company did Susan ever hear Elvis say the word 'Priscilla'.

WELSH FIRE

Suddenly it wasn't so bad being Elvis Presley in 1968. He had a sexy 21-year-old blonde girlfriend. He had a 22-year-old brunette wife at home with meatloaf and gravy waiting on the table every 6 o'clock. He had a sweet baby girl who couldn't take her eyes off him. He had two Great Danes called Brutus and Snoopy. He had, by the last count, at least half a dozen cars including two Cadillacs and a Rolls Royce. He had a mansion home in Beverly Hills, and another in Memphis with four maids, three guards and two gardeners. He had *Laugh-In* on Mondays, *Ironside* on Thursdays, *Star Trek* on Fridays, *Get Smart* on Saturdays and *Mission: Impossible* on Sundays. He had Charlie to laugh at his jokes and light his cigars and Joe to fetch his pills and chauffeur him to work.

He still had to work.

The new film only had four songs but they weren't so bad either. He taped them all in one day in a new studio, Western Recorders, with a new producer. Elvis knew Billy Strange as a Hollywood session regular who'd played guitar on some of his earlier films including *Viva Las Vegas*. He was now Nancy Sinatra's arranger and conductor, having just overseen the music for her NBC TV special. Strange was more pop than country, more LA than Nashville, more 1968 than anyone Elvis had ever worked with. So were his musicians. Outside of the LA session circuit nobody would have heard the names of Hal Blaine, Al Casey, Larry Knechtel, Chuck Berghofer and Don Randi. But everyone with an AM radio and a working ear canal would have heard their music. 'Be My Baby', 'You've Lost That Lovin' Feelin'', 'California Dreamin'', 'I Got You Babe', 'Good Vibrations', 'These Boots Are Made For Walkin'', 'River Deep – Mountain High', 'Up, Up And Away'. The Sixties pop pit orchestra.

In their precision fingers, and Strange's baton, each of Elvis' new songs was served its own unique flavour. 'Almost In Love' was crushed velvet, red wine and candlelight. 'Wonderful World' was dew, buttercups and Alpine sun. 'Edge Of Reality' was Lewis Carroll, 007 and Haight Ashbury. But Elvis' favourite was the one that tasted of Emma Peel, James Brown and the Whisky A Go Go: 'A Little Less Conversation'. Co-written by Strange, it was mostly the work of a young musician from Texas called Mac Davis who'd imagined its Muscle Shoals swagger ideally suited to Aretha Franklin. *'All this aggravation ain't satisfaction-ing me.'* It demanded full throttle sex and swing. Elvis burned rubber.

The song's corresponding scene in the film paired him with another volcanic 'mah boy!' blonde. So 'mah boy!' she'd already appeared in an episode of *Star Trek*. She had a name like a perfume, Celeste Yarnall, and a body that could knock Racquel Welch's off a freshman's locker door. The script required that Celeste kiss Elvis. They rehearsed more than they needed and not enough as either would have liked. Susan had already filmed her scene and was never on set at the same time. Priscilla was home preparing the meatloaf. Elvis was enjoying being Elvis Presley again and Celeste was only too keen to boldly go where other women had gone before.

They met the first week of April, when the air was sweet with blossom, day kissed night in skies of velvet blue and the tide rolled away to the whistle of Otis Redding. Until silenced by gunfire.

It was Thursday evening in Los Angeles. Elvis arrived home from another day's filming. The table was laid and the steam rising from the gravy boat. The television was echoing from the lounge.

'Martin Luther King Jr…'

Lisa Marie's smiling eyes locked on her Daddy.

'… was killed tonight in Memphis, Tennessee…'

Her Daddy didn't smile back.

'… shot in the face as he stood alone on the balcony of his hotel room.'

Killed in Memphis. It was like a .30-06 bullet through Elvis' own jaw.

Why did it have to happen in Memphis? Why did it have to happen at all?

But, *Memphis.*

He sank into the nearest chair. Martin's face was on the screen. The announcer was reading a brief summary of his life.

'Dr King perhaps was never more eloquent than on that day in August 1963 when he stood before the Lincoln Memorial in Washington and to the tens of thousands there and the millions more at home he spoke of his dream.'

They cut to the black and white clip of Martin.

'I have a dream…'

His voice boomed from the television. It found company.

'That one day,' echoed Elvis, 'this nation will rise up…'

'And live out the true meaning of its creed.'

'We hold these truths to be self-evident…'

Their voices merged. *'That all men are created equal.'*

Elvis had a thing for memorising certain speeches. The way he did with scriptures, or passages from *The Prophet*, or favourite scenes from *Dr Strangelove*, or famous quotes by General MacArthur, even some of President Kennedy's he'd learned off a record. Martin's dream was one of those speeches. And now the dreamer was dead. Murdered one mile from 706 Union Avenue where Elvis' own dream began in Sun Studios: a white kid from the projects singing black blues. Murdered two miles from where Otis had whistled from the dock of the bay in Stax Studios: black soul produced by a white guitar picker. Murdered in the city of music where sound had no colour.

It was to music Elvis fled while the nation grieved. That weekend he took Priscilla to Las Vegas to see Tom Jones in residence at the Flamingo Hotel. Diamond Joe had rung in advance and arranged a table right in front of the stage, close enough to feel the backdraft of his every Welsh thrust. Tom thrust a lot that night. The more he did, the more he reminded Elvis of someone. In his voice he had the power of the Ten Commandments, in his hips all Seven Deadly Sins. He could raise a smile with 'Delilah', a tear with 'Danny Boy' and the roof with 'Land Of 1000 Dances' which had everyone, including Elvis, on their feet. He was both gigolo and preacher, boxer and tenor, sex and opera, heaven and earth, heart and soul. That's when it hit Elvis.

Tom Jones reminded him of him.

Not a mirror reflection but a crystal ball. The him the kid on *The Ed Sullivan Show* could have grown into had the Pentagon and Hollywood not gotten in the way. What an Elvis Presley could look like in 1968. If only someone dare evoke him.

Elvis led a standing ovation at the finale. Later, he joined Tom backstage for a cigar and a glass of champagne. He told him the story about the time on his bus and the radio playing 'Green, Green Grass Of Home' and making G.K. the D.J. repeat it 'four times, till we sat and sobbed our hearts out.' Both men laughed. Then Elvis spoke earnestly. 'Your show out there, man. You really lit a fire in me tonight.'

It smouldered the 300 mile Sunday drive back to Beverly Hills. Until Monday, when doused on return to the set of *Kiss My Firm But Pliant Lips*.

On Tuesday, they buried Martin. Los Angeles was three hours behind Atlanta where the main service had already taken place that morning. It was lunchtime when Elvis turned on the TV in his dressing room to catch the latest on the funeral, by then marching to Morehouse Campus.

Celeste was with him, joining him in his 'studio diet' of plain hamburger and green beans. If they were watching when Mahalia Jackson sang the marrow out of 'Take My Hand, Precious Lord', one of Elvis' favourite hymns which he'd recorded in the Fifties, she never remembered. She'd only remember him wiping the tears from his eyes then bursting into 'Amazing Grace'.

'I once was lost, but now I'm found.'

That month the record industry rushed out tribute albums collecting clips of Martin's most famous speeches. Elvis bought one called *In Search Of Freedom*. It opened with the words *'I got into Memphis'* from his final speech at Mason Temple. It closed with *'Free at last!'* from the March on Washington.

Elvis finished the film in the first week of May, as he and Priscilla attempted to celebrate one year of married life. They held a party at their home in Beverly Hills with a catered buffet. Elvis bought her a giant bouquet of flowers and a watch so she could better count the seconds since they were last as one. She was still counting the next morning. It had been over three months. But he'd promised her an anniversary holiday in Hawaii in a couple of weeks. She could only wait and focus all hopes on whoopee in Waikiki. Until then, the seconds ticked.

Elvis had his own countdown to worry about. His next film wasn't scheduled until July but the Colonel wanted the TV deal out of the way first. The recording dates had just been blocked off with NBC for the end of June, seven weeks away. So far Elvis had been to one meeting with a Mr Finkel, the producer. The Colonel had done all the talking, and most of that about Christmas. Elvis wasn't sure what he wanted to do, only that it wasn't Christmas. But he'd said nothing, just smiled with glazed eyes masking a quart jar blizzard of Martin's casket on a mule-drawn cart and Tom's watusi on a Vegas stage.

He heard no more about the TV show until one Friday when the Colonel rang to tell him Mr Finkel had chosen a director. He wanted Elvis to meet them that afternoon at their production office, less than a mile away on the Strip. The Colonel would join them a little later.

It was around a quarter to four when Elvis climbed in the back of his new black Lincoln Continental Mk II with Charlie, big Lamar and Joe at the wheel. It rolled through the newly installed security gates, out of Hillcrest, snaking downhill, slipping onto the Strip with all its stacked heels, hot pants and ruffled blouses ('mah boy, *mah boy!*'), past 'Exotic Burlesk Revue' at the Largo and 'The Nazz' at the Whisky A Go Go. Then, slowing opposite the Classic Cat at the corner of Larrabee, it turned left, then a quick right, down the ramp and into the basement garage of 8833 Sunset Boulevard.

4.01 PM, SUITE 410

The elevator doors slid open.

They stepped out into the corridor, Diamond Joe and Lamar at the front, Elvis behind with Charlie. Ahead of them, with the reception door open, was Suite 410.

Steve and Bones stood waiting for them. Their first sight was of two stocky men with flabby chins and full bellies. As they came closer they could see another squat figure with combed up hair and sideburns. Beside him, cutting through space and time like a ship's prow through icy sea, came jade hair, bronze skin, topaz eyes and cheeks that belonged in the limestone altars of ancient temples. It was like Prince Charming chaperoned by three Rumpelstiltskins.

'Elvis. Hi, I'm Steve Binder, the director.'

The topaz gleamed.

'Hello, Steve.'

Everyone spent a minute shaking hands and exchanging hellos. Steve led them over to the reception couches where their secretary, Ann, had laid out some soda and potato chips. He motioned to Joe, Charlie and Lamar. 'Please, sit down.' The Angels didn't move.

Steve flushed and tried again. 'Uh, Elvis? We can go and talk in my office with Bones if that's OK with you?'

Elvis' eyes made a cautious sweep of the two strangers. Both men looked to be in their early thirties, close to his age, maybe a little older. Neither of them wore ties. Both dressed casually and both had sideburns. Sideburns were a good sign. The male plumage of conscription to rock 'n' roll.

'It's OK,' he signalled to Joe. 'You wait here. I've gotta go talk some business with these guys. The Colonel'll be along later.'

Joe said 'sure' and the Angels sat down. Lamar's was the first hand in the potato chips.

Elvis followed Steve and Bones down a hall to the office, the door closing behind them. The room was lit by a floor-to-ceiling window looking out down onto the Strip. Elvis took the chair Steve offered him and crossed one twitching leg over the other.

'Do you, uh, mind if I smoke?'

'No, go ahead,' said Steve. Elvis offered him a thin cigar. Steve took it 'for later'. He didn't smoke. Nor did Bones, who did the same. Elvis lit up and drew in a lungful. His leg still twitched.

'You may not remember,' said Bones, clearing his throat, 'but we've met. I used to work at Radio Recorders.'

'Oh, yeah?' Elvis brightened.

'With Thorne Nogar. We did "All Shook Up", "Teddy Bear"...'

'Oh, man!' Elvis nodded. 'Thorny. He was the best. That's really somethin'.'

Elvis' eyes switched back and forth between the two men. He couldn't place Bones, but if he knew Thorny that was good enough.

'That was a *long* time ago, man,' smiled Elvis. 'I was still just an itty bitty kid.' He sat back, curling white smoke to the ceiling. 'So who d'you work with now?'

Bones told him about the Association and the 5th Dimension. Elvis knew of them but he hadn't any of their records. Steve then gave his résumé, about *The T.A.M.I. Show*, with James Brown, which Elvis had seen, and the *Petula* special with Harry Belafonte, which he hadn't. Steve asked him how he felt about doing television again. 'Scared to death,' Elvis smirked, leg jiggling. He told them it had been eight years. 'Not since I did the Sinatra show. I was petrified, I don't mind admittin'.'

'This will be different,' said Steve. 'This is your show. The idea is that the whole thing is built around you.'

'See, I, uh,' Elvis fidgeted. 'I really don't know about TV. It's not my thing. I only know about music, making records.'

'Then that's what we'll do,' said Bones. 'You make a record, with us, and we'll put pictures to it.'

The cigar tip smouldered as he took another drag. *A record with pictures.* 'Hmm,' he hmmed.

They asked him about the Beatles. Elvis said they were OK, but he liked Tom Jones, also Aretha, Otis, Sam & Dave, a lot of the new soul music. He said he thought studios had improved and Bones agreed.

Steve brought up the new Jimmy Webb song recorded by actor Richard Harris, 'MacArthur Park': a seven-minute fit of maudlin Rachmaninov about a rain-sodden cake currently gaining AM airplay despite its demanding length. Elvis wasn't to know Bones had been offered the song first for the Association: to his dismay, they'd turned it down. Just as Bones and Steve weren't to know Elvis had just been in the studio with the same musicians who played on 'MacArthur Park', Hal Blaine, Larry Knetchel and Al Casey.

Steve asked if he could ever see himself singing such a song.

'Yes,' said Elvis. 'Yes, I think I could.'

It was the right answer. Steve was encouraged. 'Elvis, where,' he hesitated. 'Where do you see yourself these days?'

Elvis' eyes narrowed. 'You mean my music?'

He shifted in his seat.

'I, uh, I don't really know. Y'know, I've been doing movies now these past few years, so many of them that I haven't had a lot of time for much else. But I still, y'know, I want to make records still.

My new one, "U.S. Male", that's about the biggest I've had in a while. I mean, uh, it's doing OK."

Steve nodded politely.

'Why?' Elvis blew hard on his cigar. 'Where do you see me?'

He held Steve's gaze through the smoke.

'Well, I…' Steve stopped. 'Honestly?'

'Yeah.' Elvis didn't blink. 'I'd like to know.'

'I think,' Steve paused, gathering his nerve. 'I think your career's in the toilet.'

Time stood still.

Elvis inhaled through his nostrils, his lips tight. His head boiled. *Motherfucker!*

His eyes flashed at Steve like a Bowie knife in the desert sun.

Until a twitch. Then a smile.

Goddamn toilet, sonofabitch!

Then the blade withdrew.

'Man,' he let out a sigh which became a laugh. 'Well, that makes a change, someone talking straight.' He shook his head. 'See, I just don't know, man. There's things I wanna do. I've been thinking about all kinds of stuff lately. Going on stage again. I mean, uh, I'd like to. But I don't know. Audiences, these days. I don't know if they'll even like me.'

'That's how you can use this TV special,' said Bones. 'Remind the audience at home who you are. What you're really about. The music.'

'We can tailor it any way you want,' added Steve.

Elvis smiled. 'You know the Colonel wants Christmas, don't you?'

Steve rolled his eyes. 'Leave that to Andy Williams and Perry Como. That's not you. It's not us either. We want to give them Elvis Presley.'

Elvis rubbed his chin, his head rushing with smoke and the ebb of amphetamine sulphate. *Elvis Presley.* Now, who *was* that fella?

'You tell us,' said Bones. 'Just what is it that you want to do?'

He closed his eyes. The question torpedoed his skull.

Just what is that he wanted to do?

Then exploded in a voice he'd last heard in the dark of the Memphian.

He wanted to be free. Free to do what he wanted to do!

'I...' said Elvis.

Free to ride! Free to ride his machine without being hassled by The Man!

'... I want...'

And he wanted to get loaded! And he wanted to have a good time! And that's what he was gonna do! He was gonna have a good time! He was gonna have a party!

'I want... I want everyone to know *what* I can really do.'

He opened his eyes. Steve and Bones were beaming back at him.

'Then we can put a team together,' said Steve. 'We can pitch you our ideas and you can pick the ones you like. We can get started straight away. It'll be your decision. This is *your* show.'

The Colonel was waiting for them when they walked back down the hall, sat in reception regaling the Angels with an old carnie yarn about midget wrestlers. He stood up, one hand on his cane, the other tipping his hat to Steve and Bones. The Colonel asked Elvis if he was happy with the meeting. Elvis said he was and that he'd given Steve and Bones the go ahead. They'd arranged that he come back after his vacation in Hawaii, leaving them enough time to work up a rough outline.

'If Elvis is happy, then I'm happy,' clucked the Colonel. 'Be seeing you, boys.'

Elvis shook their hands again and walked back towards the elevator, flanked by his Angels in the same formation, the Colonel tapping behind. Their separate chauffeured cars rolled out of the basement a few minutes later, the black Lincoln Continental retracing its route West along the Strip, past the Whisky, the Largo, the stacked heels and the ruffled blouses as Elvis sat in the back with a rascally smile quietly humming what sounded like 'MacArthur Park'.

LEFT: The Shake Rag Defender. The girl below his knee in the light short-sleeved dress with long dark hair (face partly obscured) is Elvis' 'little sister' Pat Parry from Stamford Hill, London.

RIGHT: Couture For A King. The shining leather armour designed by Bill Belew.

BELOW: The Blue Moon Boys of Burbank (left to right): Lance LeGault (head next to guitar), Elvis, Charlie Hodge (from rear), Scotty Moore, Alan 'Hog Ears' Fortas (from rear) and D.J. Fontana.

TOP: 'Mah boyo, mah boyo!' Priscilla is submerged as the River Taff meets the Mississippi backstage in Las Vegas, April 6, 1968.

RIGHT: Shadowplay. 'Guitar Man' Elvis and his scaffold of silhouettes.

BOTTOM: Still in the same jacket and polo neck he wore to see Tom Jones, Elvis sets his phasers to stun Celeste Yarnall in *Live A Little, Love A Little*.

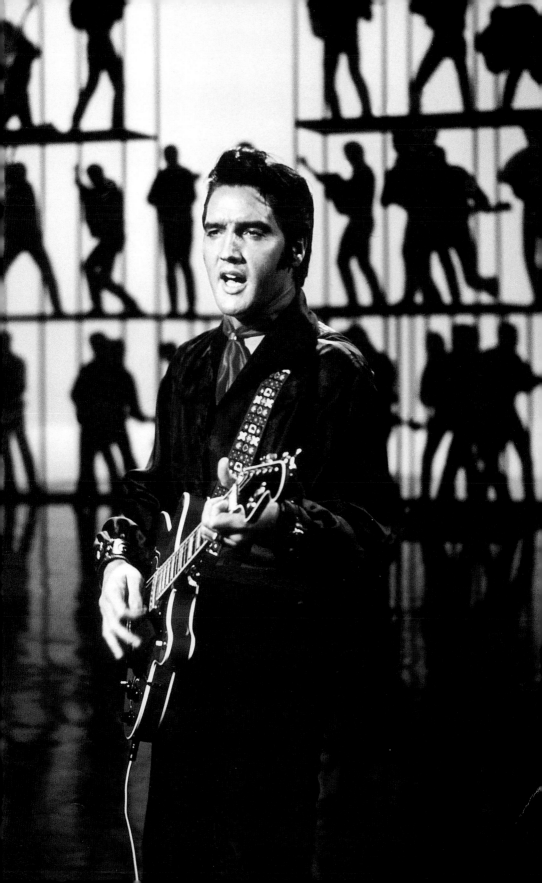

ABOVE: Forbidden Fruit. Elvis nibbles as Susan Henning giggles on the 'bordello' set.

LEFT: 'Saved!' The Reverend Presley hoochie-coos away his demons in Gene McAvoy's art-nouveau church.

RIGHT: Case study in mental undressing

THE PITCH

The silvery white sands of Waikiki shook to the Kohl-streaking scream of 'YOU DON'T LOVE ME ANY MORE!' Priscilla's watch kept ticking by the bedside. It was the only rhythm the room had seen all week. It was meant to be their wedding anniversary holiday. Just Elvis, Priscilla and three-month-old Lisa Marie. And Diamond Joe and his wife, Charlie, cousin Patsy and Gee Gee. A cosy romantic getaway for eight.

Elvis' idea of making up to Priscilla was to take her to a martial arts tournament in Honolulu. Priscilla took one cried-out eyeful of a young karate champ named Mike Stone and made up ideas of her own. They flew home still Mr and Mrs Presley, but no more than names on a plane ticket.

Los Angeles hadn't changed. Only the billboards on the Strip and the name above the Whisky A Go Go. And the five new faces waiting to meet him in Steve's office, all drinking in the mirage of the thing called Elvis Presley like a child's first giddying sip of alcohol. Nearly all were veterans of the *Petula* show who'd spent three weeks spinballing ideas over coffee cups and wastebaskets for the rough script they now had to present for his approval.

'Elvis,' began Steve, 'this is Gene McAvoy, our set designer.'

Gene had studied to be an architect but swapped reinforced concrete for painted plywood on Broadway before moving into television. He first met Steve in New York as the set designer on

Hullabaloo, following him back to LA where they worked again on the Lesley Uggams show, then *Petula*, which sent Gene on reconnaissance to San Francisco for its hippy dance sequence. He came back with sketches for a playground in the shape of a peace sign but no better understanding of kids he considered barber-shy garden thieves. By his own admission, Gene was 'a bit of a stiff'. He didn't like Elvis either. 'A blight on society,' he'd grumble in private.

Elvis smiled at Gene and offered a hand.

'Pleased to meet you, sir.'

And Gene fell in love with Elvis Presley.

Next in the line-up was Earl Brown. 'He'll be helping with vocal arrangements and any special material.' Earl had been a member of white harmony group the Skylarks – all smiles, bowties and 'Singin' In The Rain' – going on to form his own Earl Brown Singers, TV regulars of *The Danny Kaye Show*. But as a songwriter he could be surprisingly modern, supplying Harry with the protest funk 'If A Better Time's Comin'' in the *Petula* show. Steve secretly hoped Earl might be able to concoct something equally unique for Elvis.

'And this is Bill Belew, our costume designer.'

Bill was a sweet boy from Virginia who'd been drafted straight out of art school. He was an army secretary in a medical unit in Korea when Josephine Baker, the great Black Pearl of the Folies Bergère, banana-danced into town. After Bill helped repair some of her stage clothes Josephine suggested he go into show business: from a woman who made a living singing *'Oh, mister, don't touch me tomatoes!'*, it seemed more than sensible advice. Returning to America, Bill found work as a dresser in the costume department at NBC, busying his thimble for Hollywood fashion master Ray Aghayan and his partner, Cher's wardrobe designer Bob Mackie. Frocking Petula had been his first big TV gig.

'Nice to meet you, Bill.'

Bill's eyes made a quick inventory of his inside leg. 'And you, Elvis.'

'These are our writers,' said Steve. 'Allan Blye...'

Allan was a Jewish comedian and singer from Winnipeg who started his career in Canadian children's TV, now scripting for ABC's riotous satirical variety show *The Smothers Brothers Comedy Hour*. Until recently he'd been one half of its chief writing duo, 'the Cowboy and the Cantor'. Allan was the Cantor. The Cowboy was Mason Williams, an Oklahoman comic and guitar maestro whose life was about to change thanks to an instrumental he'd written called 'Classical Gas', recorded with the same musicians who'd landscaped 'MacArthur Park' and destined for similar chart success. Allan and Mason wrote the *Petula* show, but with Mason gone Allan was now paired with an old friend from Canada.

'... And Chris Bearde.'

Chris had come to Canadian TV via England, where he was born, and Australia, where he was raised. He'd been in LA less than a year as a writer on NBC's *Laugh-In*, Elvis' favourite new hippy vaudeville of 'Sock it to me!', 'Here come da judge!', the stringed wibbles of Tiny Tim and Chris' 'Gladys and Tyrone' sketches about a dirty old man and a handbag-thwacking spinster. Chris was a born gag man for whom the sun rose chuckling each morning in anticipation of another knock-knock or the sight of a chicken crossing the road. If today wasn't funny, it would be by the time he told it tomorrow. Chris would never let the truth stop the swing of a good punchline.

Elvis settled in a chair and lit up a cigar. 'So, what've ya got?'

'I think the best way is if Allan and Chris talk through where we're at so far with the script,' said Steve.

Allan and Chris took their centre stage in the middle of the office carpet.

'Shoot!' grinned Elvis.

'OK,' began Allan, looking down at his sheet of paper. '*Just Elvis!* That's the title. We start off with a big production number. One hundred and one Elvises! You and a hundred dancing lookalikes.'

Elvis twinkled softly.

'You sing and they all dance to "Guitar Man"...'

Two weeks earlier, Allan and Chris had ransacked the biggest record store in Hollywood, Wallichs Music City, for every Elvis disc they had, spending days hot-housed in an office along the corridor from Steve and Bones, forking through the vinyl haystack – the electric wails and sedated moans, the bottled lightning and the dull embers, the heroic infantry and the cannon fodder, the holy and the banal, the deafening heartbeats and the flatlined murmurs – searching for the needle strong enough to fashion as a hook to hang the show's storyline. They found it on side one of *Clambake*. Jerry Reed's 'Guitar Man'. It was already a movie in miniature: the young carwash picker quitting his job to follow his dream; his perilous road to fame; the poverty, the hardship, until, finally, the happy ending. Reed had already plotted the dots of a story. All Allan and Chris had to do was join them.

'Then we have a concert section,' said Chris, 'Elvis and a giant orchestra. You bow to the conductor...'

At first they'd fantasised doing something with Elvis and *West Side Story*, or a conversation between Elvis and its composer Leonard Bernstein. They settled instead on the idea of 'symphonic Elvis', Steve suggesting they revive an in-the-round setting similar to that they'd used for the finale of their *Petula* show.

'Big orchestral sounds and a small band playing all the old hits,' explained Allan. '"Heartbreak Hotel", "Blue Suede Shoes"...'

'*You ain't a-nuthin' burra howndawg!*' clowned Chris.

Elvis smirked.

'Then we have what we call the sentimental part,' said Allan. 'You talk and joke about your career, some of your old haircuts and clothes, the silly movie songs. Maybe something like "Cotton Candy Land"…'

'Or, this one,' winked Chris, *'A-how would you like to be, a little kangaroo?'*

Elvis looked at them curiously, the corners of his mouth twitching.

'Then a gospel section,' said Allan. 'Something with a rockin' negro feel. Clapping hands, stomping feet. *Hallelujah!*' He waved both hands in the air like a preacher. Elvis chuckled.

'It'd be a medley of sacred songs. "How Great Thou Art" or something.'

'Then what we call the mean chunk,' said Allan.

'Mean and *evil!*' hissed Chris.

'We go back to "Guitar Man" again. We use that as a frame to tell a story with a whole bunch of mean songs. Elvis in a series of nightclubs. *"If you're lookin' for trouble?"* Dah-dah-dah dah-dah!

Elvis nodded, rocking a leg.

'Part of it will be a karate dance number. Sort of *Slaughter On Tenth Avenue*. This is big, bad, *mean* Elvis. Like a rock 'n' roll crime opera. Real dirty. "Let Yourself Go", "Big Boss Man", "Little Sister", "Wheels On My Heels", coming back to "Guitar Man".'

'Then, the last number,' said Chris. 'We end on a Christmas song.'

It was Steve's insurance policy to placate the Colonel.

'Elvis says goodnight to the audience.'

'Roll credits!'

Allan and Chris stood there sharing the same beseeching grin. Elvis whistled. 'Boy!' He rubbed his chin, still smiling. 'You two guys kill me, man.'

'It's still only a rough,' said Steve. 'We can work up the script properly this week. Anything you want us to do, anything you don't like, we can change.'

'No, man.' Elvis drew on his cigar just enough so its grey eye blinked orange in the ash.

'I like it.'

Smoke spiralled towards heaven like sacred incense. The ceremony of a power evoked.

'I like it all.'

THERE'S A GUY STOOD ON THE SIDEWALK SWEARS HE'S ELVIS

Every day that week the black Lincoln Continental parked in the basement garage of 8833 Sunset Boulevard. Every day Elvis rode the service elevator to the third floor with Diamond Joe, Charlie and Lamar. Every day he sat in Suite 410 with Pepsis and cigars discussing the show with Steve, Bones and the rest of the team. And every day, Steve noticed, Elvis would wander to the window and gaze down at the Strip below. He watched it the way he watched television. A faraway fantasy hidden behind a magic screen, the window pane a safety curtain between his universe and theirs. It made Steve wonder what Elvis wondered. Then one day, he asked.

'What do you think would happen?'

Elvis turned round.

'If you went out there now?' said Steve.

Elvis snuffled a laugh. 'You kidding?'

'No. I'm serious.'

Elvis shook his head. 'I'd probably be killed, man.' He tugged the front of his shirt. 'They'd claw this right offa me.'

'I don't think they would,' said Steve. 'I don't think anyone out there would know who you are.'

Elvis stared back down at the Strip. 'You *are* kidding, man.'

'Ten, five years ago, sure,' said Steve. 'But nowadays, I don't know.'

'Get outta here, man,' Elvis laughed.

'I mean it,' said Steve. 'Let's do it now.'

'Go out there?'

'Out there. Just you and me. We'll just stand by the door. If I'm wrong, if it gets crazy, we'll run straight back in. C'mon? What do you say?'

Elvis peered down at the Strip again. It was late afternoon, not yet rush hour. The sun high, its white reflection streaking the rooves of the thin passing traffic. The sidewalks were quiet. Hippy kids wandering nowhere slowly in suede boots. A woman with thick arms joined in a forklift of grocery bags. A negro bum laughing at nothing. Nobodies in cheesecloth and denim thinking they're somebodies. Then his own face staring back at him in the glass, floating above the awning of the Classic Cat like a disembodied ghost. A somebody. Or maybe a nobody.

He turned back to Steve.

'OK.' Elvis stiffened. 'Let's go.'

Joe, Charlie and Lamar were on the couches in reception when they saw him approaching down the hall and automatically stood up.

'I'm going outside for a minute with Steve,' said Elvis. 'You guys stay here.'

'Outside?' asked Joe.

'Just out on the Strip,' said Steve. 'A few minutes.'

Joe frowned. 'I'll come with you.'

'It's OK,' said Elvis, calm but firm. 'Just me and Steve. You can watch us from the window. We're not gonna be long.'

Charlie and Lamar exchanged confused glances. Joe's frown compressed. 'The Colonel won't like this.'

'The Colonel ain't here. Don't worry, man.' Elvis patted Joe's shoulder. 'This is between me and Steve.'

The three Angels stayed on their feet, six anxious eyes following Elvis as Steve led him to the main street elevator. Not the one Elvis normally took from the parking lot, but one of two on the front of the building, made of glass, its passengers visible to any passers-by like specimens in a jar, which is exactly how Elvis felt the moment he stepped in and it sank to street level. The doors opened. One small step for man. One giant leap for Elvis Presley.

Terra firma, West Sunset Boulevard. Fresh air, exhaust fumes, afternoon heat. In front of them, the Classic Cat. Over to their right, the Melody Room, a jazz bar once popular with the Mob, long past its best. Over to their left, Muntz Stereo & CB Center. Westbound traffic to Beverly Hills and Bel-Air. Eastbound traffic to Ben Frank's Coffee Shop and the Chateau Marmont. Sedans, coupes, jeeps. Mustangs, Chevys, Plymouths. None of them stopping. Just one man on the sidewalk opposite, stumbling out of the Classic Cat. He adjusted his tie, looked over at Elvis, then looked away again without breaking his stride. Elvis chuckled.

'You wait and see,' he said, eyes flicking side to side like a burglar on the lookout.

Another minute passed. No shouts, no beeps, no screams. Elvis straightened his spine, his chin up, hands on hips, legs apart. He could have been cast in bronze.

Steve laughed to himself. *Jesus.* He's *trying* to be seen.

A hippy couple were heading towards them on their side, his arm around her shoulders, his fringe in his eyes and what he hoped to pass for a moustache drooping down in thin strands around his lips. Her hair was long, black and parted like Joan Baez, a peace symbol on a leather thong bouncing on her small chest with each step. Elvis eyeballed them as they drew closer. They looked right back at him. And kept on walking.

Elvis whistled through his teeth. 'Well, I'll be a doggone...'

The gaps in the traffic were shortening. Rush hour was yawning to life. A redhead in a GTO coming up on the lane right next to him. He waved and called. 'Hey there, honey.'

Nothing.

A pink and white VW van. Window stickers. 'Have A Nice Day.' 'Kennedy.' 'Make Love Not War.' Long blonde hair blowing bubbles in the passenger seat. The windows down, the radio fuzzing. *'Yummy, yummy, yummy, I've got love in my tummy.'* Elvis tried again. 'OK there, baby,' he waved. The blonde looked at him, chewing steadily, then looked away. The van rolled on.

Elvis dropped his chin to his chest, laughing to his feet.

'Mah boy, *mah boy!*'

He looked over his shoulder to see Steve, arms folded, leaning against the building.

'Bet you think this is kinda funny, don't you?'

Steve smiled, shrugged, quickly throwing his eyes up to his office floor. 'Think they saw?'

Elvis looked up. He could just about make out Lamar squashed against the glass, Joe and Charlie peeping either side of him.

'Sonsabitches,' laughed Elvis. 'Damn right they saw.'

He looked both ways again. More cars, more chicks. If they saw him at all they saw only some sorry asshole trying to look like Elvis Presley. 'OK, OK. Let's go back up.'

They rode the glass elevator in silence, Elvis still watching the world that no longer knew him with eyes the helium blue of cool rage. Steve felt their chill. He was glad. He needed Elvis to show those bastards who he was and what he was made of. Now, Steve knew, he would.

But more than that, Steve was relieved. His gamble had paid off. The hippy couple, the redhead, the blonde in the van. Steve knew they'd all seen Elvis. They just weren't programmed to believe it. Passing glances of shock killed in a split second of reason. Elvis, alone, scuffing his heels on the corner of Sunset and Larrabee in the afternoon sun. A vision too improbable for the laws of time and space. Not real, just a dream. The sort that strikes a girl at 5 am when she wakes with a start, chest pounding, skin damp, eyes like a developing polaroid of the fuck-times-a-thousand caramel God who'd waved at her late last afternoon. 'That... couldn't?... wasn't?... no? *Shit!*'

The thing called Elvis Presley. The ghost of Sunset Strip.

THE DARK

Priscilla had stopped making meatloaf. Elvis was never there to eat it. Every afternoon, once he'd risen and breakfasted, he'd ride down to Steve's office, staying gone midnight, coming home to bed in the early hours to do the same thing all over again tomorrow. When she did see him she sensed a strange new speed about him that wasn't all Smith, Kline & French. An alien energy like all his colours had been turned up. It wasn't just that he'd been burnished by the Hawaiian sun but some other inner heat making him glow with toxic urgency.

The Colonel had seen just as little of Elvis. He knew he was neither needed nor wanted at Steve's office. He'd tried charming Steve into his inside pocket by granting him membership of his Snowmen's League but, as he was quickly realising, the slick young smart-ass director was the kind that ripped the lining.

The tear came when the Colonel found out Steve had sacked Elvis' chosen arranger, Billy Strange. Elvis was so taken with Strange at the 'A Little Less Conversation' session that he'd personally recommended him to Steve. Strange had agreed to arrange the special, just as he had Nancy's, but overestimated his workload. When he failed to deliver the first week's lead sheets on time, jeopardising the already tight schedule, Steve sought Finkel's go-ahead to replace him.

The Colonel spat lava. Without Strange, the special was off. 'Elvis won't do it!'

But Elvis did. It made the Colonel look foolish. The Colonel wasn't the kind of psychopath who took easily to looking foolish.

Steve's new musical arranger was another *Petula* veteran and another Billy, Billy Goldenberg. Son of the esteemed New York percussionist Morris 'Mo' Goldenberg who also worked for NBC, Billy was a pianist, composer and Broadway veteran at the age of 32. He also hated Elvis Presley. He hated the music, he hated the man. A punk straight off the pages of *In Cold Blood*. But as a favour to Steve, and against his better judgement, he took up his own room at Suite 410 with a piano where he waited with a heavy heart to have his grimmest preconceptions confirmed.

Elvis greeted him with the same good grace as he had the rest of the team and, to Billy's surprise, instinctively sat at the piano without blowing gum or reaching for a switchblade. As they spoke, Elvis' hands swept the keys and, before Billy knew which way up his world had been turned, settled on a tune that was neither rock 'n' roll, nor pop, nor even gospel. A tune Billy knew inside out and back-to-front though it took him longer than normal to realise, not expecting to ever hear it flow from the fingers of a Charles Starkweather. *Adagio sostenuto.* C sharp minor. *Jesus!* Billy smiled.

It was Beethoven. 'Moonlight Sonata'.

The moon was particularly bright that Tuesday night, the heavens' headlamp lighting Los Angeles' way into Wednesday morning. Elvis was with Steve, Bones, Billy and Earl around the piano in the music room. Allan and Chris were in their writers' office next door, a black and white television buzzing in the corner. A few minutes past midnight. Outside their windows the city was alive, writhing in hot flesh, exotic smoke and stiff alcohol.

And dollar tips, red lights and car horns. And cheers, screams and the smell of gunfire.

'It's not possible… it's not possible…'

The buzz from the television became a rattle. Loud enough that Elvis and the others next door in the music room stopped what they were doing and came through.

'Oh my God… Senator Kennedy…'

They'd shot Bobby.

Sixty-three days after they'd shot Martin, they'd shot Bobby. Four years, six months and 15 days after they'd shot his brother, they'd shot Bobby. Five miles southeast from where Elvis had been leaning on a piano with Billy at the keys, there in Los Angeles, they'd shot Bobby. The night Bobby beat his Democrat presidential rival Senator Eugene McCarthy to win the California primary, they'd shot him. In the kitchen of the Ambassador Hotel as he was walking to a victory press conference. Minutes after he'd stood on a podium thanking his supporters, praising America as 'a great country, an unselfish country, a compassionate country'. They'd shot him. They, a young Jordanian, Sirhan Sirhan, shot him in the head with a .22 calibre revolver.

'Senator Kennedy has just been shot!'

Shot. Not yet dead. Not for another 24 hours. But the shaking pictures told their own truth.

They stood impaled by the screen's blue white light.

'I… I don't believe it.'

The voice was Elvis.

'I just don't believe it.'

On a night defying America to speak, Elvis tried to find the words. About sadness and confusion, hope and bloodshed, Shake Rag and Memphis, black and white, brotherhood and freedom, JFK, Martin and, now, Bobby. They all sat and listened, his voice a candle in the darkness. It flickered until the first faint glare of dawn. The cruel blue day that greeted them suddenly seemed to belong to a different world. A broken one needing new songs to heal it.

They buried Bobby three days later. The requiem mass was held in New York's St Patrick's Cathedral. Harry Belafonte was in the congregation. Later that day the coffin was taken by train to Washington D.C. where it was buried in Arlington Cemetery. Andy Williams had sung Bobby's favourite song at the funeral service. They sang it again on the final procession by the Lincoln Memorial where Martin shared his dream. It was 'The Battle Hymn Of The Republic.'

'Glory, glory, Hallelujah!
His truth is marching on…'

Bobby was interred beside his brother. Martin's widow, Coretta, was there to pray by the graveside. A light rain fell as he was lowered into the ground.

A cold and grey ocean away, someone bearing the passports of 'Ramon Sneyd' and 'Ramon Sneya' was spending their first night in a London police cell. They'd been detained trying to pass through Heathrow Airport earlier that morning. A Scotland Yard detective later identified them as an American citizen wanted for 'serious criminal offences'. His real name, James Earl Ray.

The day they buried Bobby, they caught the man who killed Martin.

3000 WEST ALMEDA AVENUE

'Beautiful, downtown Burbank.' It was neither beautiful nor in much of a town to be down. But it was Burbank. Home to NBC and its peacock since the early Fifties. A complex of glass-fronted offices and giant plain white hangars, amphitheatres to *The Dean Martin Show*, *Hollywood Squares* and *Rowan & Martin's Laugh-In*, where Elvis arrived in the third week of June to see for the first time the chosen stage of his hour of reckoning, and so prepare his final steps towards it.

A shooting script had now been finalised by Allan and Chris, sticking closely to the bones of their original pitch: an opening 'Guitar Man' with 100 dancing Elvises; an 'arena' live concert part with band and orchestra playing a selection of hits; an 'informal' section of 'talk and songs'; a gospel medley; a 'mean and evil chunk' using 'Guitar Man' as the basis for a miniature rock 'n' roll operetta including 'Let Yourself Go', 'Trouble' and others; and a closing 'Christmas song'. Most of the music had been selected, apart from the Christmas number which no one could agree on and which Steve wanted to replace with something original by Earl, another 'message song' like the one he'd written for Harry. The visual elements were also near completion, with Gene's set designs making economical use of his tight props budget while Bill had been talking Elvis through his costume ideas.

His task was to dress the body but Bill's aim was to draw the eye towards Elvis' face, framing it with high Napoleonic collars rising to the jawline. As a signature motif, he also suggested small ring-fastened neck scarves which, like the clothes, would be a different colour in every section of the show. Elvis loved Bill's sketches, apart from one: an updated version of the gold lamé Nudie Cohn suit Elvis had worn, briefly, in 1957, later featured on the sleeve of his second greatest hits LP. Elvis told him he'd never liked it, only the jacket which, the few times he did wear, was always offset with black slacks. Bill complied, but knew he still had to create something equally striking, equally iconic. A suit of clothes worthy of amplifying the 20-kiloton sexuality beneath, stitched with Valentino's kiss, Garbo's eyes, Hayworth's hair and the burlesque snap of Gilda's gloves.

Gloves would be the answer.

Just recently, Bill had ordered a pair of opera gloves for one of his designs. The glove maker had recommended a certain type of leather, cordovan: the type that reacts to body heat and moulds to the shape of the wearer. He could do the same with Elvis. Wrap him in leather like a giant opera glove for the public's eyes to unpeel. Not the motorcycle armour of Brando in *The Wild One*, nor the demonic battle dress of Gene Vincent. More sensual than rebellious, tailored the same as a pair of jeans and a Levis jacket, with front seams, buttoned breast pockets and waist band, all replicated in skin-kissing cordovan leather. Glistening like he'd just been dipped naked from the neck down in sticky black tar. Bill showed Elvis his sketches. Elvis agreed to be dipped.

His first day in Burbank, Elvis met the show's two choreographers. Claude Thompson had trained in New York under Alvin Ailey, founder of America's first all-black modern dance company, and had also been part of the *Petula* team. By odd coincidence Claude shared his name with an NBC make-up artist on *Laugh-In* who, confusingly, would also join the Elvis special crew. The other choreographer was Jaime Rogers – his name pronounced 'Hi-me' if cursed by a life of typo corrections as 'Jamie' – the 28-year-old Puerto Rican dancer who'd played Loco the Shark with the headband in Elvis' old Memphian favourite *West Side Story*. Jaime's troupe included another former Shark, Gus Trikonis, the boyfriend of *Laugh-In*'s Goldie Hawn who'd sometimes creep on set for a peek at rehearsals. Elvis teased her about her spiky Vidal Sassoon crop. 'You look like a chicken that's just been hatched!' Goldie clucked bright red. She thought him the handsomest creature she'd ever seen. But so did everyone.

The first time Tanya Lemani met Elvis he had to ask 'can I have my hand back, please?' She'd been shaking it so long poleaxed by his beauty she forgot to let go. Shaking is what Tanya did best, usually her belly. She'd been jingling and jiggling her coin-skirted hips and cork-popping flesh on screen since the age of 19: jangling her joggles in *The Man From U.N.C.L.E.*, jengling her jiggles in *I Dream Of Jeannie*, jongling her jeggles in *Get Smart* and jingling her juggles in *Star Trek,* a galactic outrage for which she was fatally stabbed a dozen times before the opening titles rolled. If ever a script called for a skimpy Nefertiti to wiggle her zills and bobble her bedlah, be it in a night club, a Casbah or on an alien planet, be the character Arabian, Greek or Argelian, Tanya and her quicksilver torso of a thousand and one shimmies usually got the part.

Such a part was required in the big 'Guitar Man' operetta where Elvis sang 'Little Egypt' in a small club with a belly dancer. If he recognised Tanya from *Star Trek* he never said, though he said plenty of other things that made her blush to the soles of her feet. The fantasy was too delicious but Tanya declined reality's bite. She had strict rules about married men, as William Shatner had just learned the hard way. Elvis, likewise, would have to find other limbs to interlace.

The limbs found him during his first dance rehearsal. Elvis was stood at ease, feet apart, when a long, smooth female leg poked through the gap below his groin, a high heel shoe on its slender foot which began wriggling in tight circles. He looked down and laughed. 'Mah boy, *mah boy!*' He spun around to see its mini-skirted owner. He laughed even harder.

'Hi.' It was Susan.

Elvis hadn't seen her for a few weeks, not since before Hawaii. He had no idea she'd been cast in his show too. As she told him, 'playing a virgin hooker'. They had a dance number together. And the next two weeks of rehearsals.

'Mah boy,' smiled Elvis. '*Mah boy!*'

That night, after Joe had driven Elvis back home to Beverly Hills, he told Priscilla that, although it was only six miles away, he found the commute took too long, wasting valuable time he could better use preparing for the special. But as luck would have it, NBC had given him a dressing room that was more like a hotel suite, the same previously used by Dinah Shore and Dean Martin, with its own living room, kitchen, bathroom and back bedroom. That's why he'd decided he'd be better staying there, in Burbank, for the duration of rehearsals. Just a couple of weeks until the special was over. He'd call each day to see how she and Lisa Marie were doing. It wasn't like he'd be out of town, just over the hill.

Priscilla, widow of the empty dining table, timekeeper of tormented chastity, Mrs Presley in deeds but not in deed, told him she understood. The special was the most important thing in his life right now, as anyone could see. It was only two weeks, like he said. She'd miss him, but she had Patsy there to help out. She'd manage.

His energies were clearly needed elsewhere.

LIAR'S POKER

The same week that Elvis moved in to his dressing-room suite, a small broom closet nearby on the studio floor was cleared so it could be furnished with a desk, chair and telephone. Once this was done, two junior staff employed by the William Morris Agency were equipped with the uniforms of royal palace guards, complete with peaked hats, and ordered to stand outside on permanent sentry: there to advertise to the rest of the crew and anyone else who happened to accidentally wander onto NBC Stage 4 that the Colonel had arrived and the Burbank branch of Elvis Exploitations was now open for business. Specifically the business of sport and snow or, failing that, sabotage.

The Colonel had dangerously little to do and dangerously too much time to be doing it. The TV show was taking care of itself without him and his idle paws ripe for Satan's mischief. Elvis was busy every day in rehearsals, sometimes with the choreographers and the moral support of his regular movie stand-in Lance LeGault, the singer he'd first met at the Crossbow Inn back in 1960. Other times he'd be in the music room just off his dressing room, running over Billy's arrangements with the day shift of NBC staff pianist Claude Williamson and drummer Frank DeVito, standing in for his friend Hal Blaine. Frank was another of the LA pop pit orchestra who'd recorded with Sinatra and played on the Beach Boys' 'Surfin USA'; a jazz man at heart but impressed by Elvis'

Southern gentility, Olympian voice and perfectionist's ear. Frank didn't even mind the Angels hanging around for the brief respite of horseplay and karate chops, nor the cigars, even if he didn't smoke, though when offered Frank took one all the same. As he liked to tell the story, 'what kind of mug refuses a cigar from Elvis Presley?'

Which left the Colonel bored as a widow scamster with a box of ratty Bibles and no door to knock on. He'd tried knocking on Steve's but Steve wasn't the kind who opened. None of them were. It was like nobody had taught these young 'uns how to *play*. Not like in the good ol' days. Hal Wallis and Paramount: now *there* was a crew who appreciated a good snow. Like the time the Colonel walked around the set with a microphone, its lead sticking out of a suitcase, interviewing members of the cast for 'a promotional radio interview'. His interviewees assumed the suitcase contained some portable recording device. The microphone jack was stuck in a pineapple. That's what the Colonel missed. The sweet smell of bullshit and tropical fruit. That's why he cleared out the broom closet and made the Morris agents dress up like toy soldiers. It was a psychopathic cry of help for a sparring partner. Steve could see it. So could everyone on set.

So could Bob Finkel. The show's executive producer had already been inducted into his Snowmen's League and, being something of a game gamesman, volunteered himself as decoy to keep the Colonel's cane from poking around the rehearsals where it wasn't wanted.

It was the cane that planted the seed. Finkel made a wager. If he could out-snow and out-prank the Colonel, he'd claim the cane as a scalp of victory.

'Finkels,' beamed the Colonel, 'you're on!'

The next morning, Finkel arrived at his office to find the Colonel's royal guards comically barring his entry.

The morning after that his office was duct-taped shut.

In retaliation, he set up his own 'Finkel's Floating Office' on the studio floor, a small podium with a telephone, monitors and chilled sodas as rival fortress to the Colonel's broom cupboard.

It still didn't get him the cane.

The Colonel invited Finkel out for lunch, treating him to 'a fine champagne' and promised he'd sent him a crateful of the same vintage as a gift. When he did, Finkel held a dinner party at his house where the first cork was popped and out flowed substituted mineral water.

Finkel took the bait of one of the Colonel's favourite games, the dollar bill serial number bluff, liar's poker.

'OK, Finkels. How many sixes?'

'Three?'

'Two.'

Finkels never played with less than Jacksons and the Colonel never won by less than several Benjamins.

The Colonel had a favourite old photo of himself in full Confederate Army regalia. He gave Finkel a glossy 13 x 10 print and wrote on the back, 'This photo not to be sold, not to be shown on TV or any other media without full payment for its use – $5000 deposit. Can only be displayed in Colonel Finkels' office at all times.' A week later Finkel knocked on the Colonel's cupboard and handed him his own portrait: taken in front of an American flag, dressed like Napoleon in a feather-plumed bicorne hat, signed by 'Admiral Bob Finkel'. The Colonel chuckled. It was good – *very* good. But he still wasn't getting the cane.

While the Colonel snowed, Elvis sang, and didn't stop singing even after the day's rehearsals were through. He was too full of music to stop, a shaken up soda bottle of rhyme and rhythm still frothing in his dressing room long gone midnight, a guitar in his lap, Susan at his shoulder, pickin' and hollerin' with Charlie and Lance while Diamond Joe, Lamar and Hog Ears sat tapping, drinking, smoking and yeehawin' him on. God groovin' with his Angels on a timeless cloud nine of pills and licks, just like they used to in Bellagio Road and Perugia Way. Before Priscilla. Before Larry. Before the Beatles. When Elvis was happy to be Elvis Presley and the universe even happier to count him among its stellar riches.

It was a privilege to witness and a sin not to share. That's how Steve felt, sat in the corner, trying to decode the giggling Memphian 'hot dang's and 'mah boy's, his knee keeping pace with the hairpin bends from one song to the next, guitars slip-slidin' in a spontaneous fluid of blues, country and rockabilly. You could never script it, thought Steve. But you *could* film it.

The Colonel hated the idea. He didn't understand why anyone would want to see sloppy Elvis instead of polished Ken®. Most of all he hated the idea because it had come from Steve.

'Bindle', as the Colonel called him, was starting to wear his poker-hand's patience. Yesterday it had been over the agreed closing Christmas song. The Colonel had checked the latest script and noticed on page 88 under the heading 'Christmas Song' it still said 'Song To Come'. He'd summoned Steve with Elvis to his closet office and asked them why. Steve had given him some horseshit about wanting to use 'an original ballad'. The Colonel had reminded Steve that he was working for Elvis 'and Elvis wants a Christmas song.' Elvis acted like he wasn't even in the same room and said nothing. The Colonel added that if Steve couldn't pick a Christmas song he'd pick one for him. The old Frankie Laine tune, 'I Believe'. Elvis had recorded it back in the Fifties. 'My wife always liked that one,' puffed the Colonel, 'and Elvis sings it real nice.' He'd sent Steve on his way like a scalded schoolboy, so he'd thought, but now he was back cluttering up his doorframe, asking about dragging cameras into Elvis' dressing room. The Colonel told him that was a direct violation of Elvis' privacy. It was a fat smoky 'no'.

'What if we take it out of the dressing room?' Steve persevered. 'Recreate the same thing on the soundstage? We could use the same set as the arena section. There'd be no extra props, no extra cost. We've nothing to lose by trying it out.'

The Colonel's eyes shrank to poisoned pinpricks. His reason scrambled for another fat smoky no. 'We film *next* week, Bindle.'

'If it doesn't work out, we won't use it,' said Steve. 'You have my word on that.'

The Colonel's reason cramped and buckled. 'If you really want to waste your time with this crap,' his stogie belched, 'go ahead.'

Steve sloped off with a smile on his face the Colonel already felt stupid for having put there.

He savoured the rest of his cigar thinking how best to remove it.

THE SONG

'Fuck him!'

That's what Elvis told Steve the day they left the Colonel's office when he'd hauled them over his Christmas coals with an earful of 'I Believe'. A grinning 'Fuck him!' with an elbow in the ribs. 'Stick to what you're doing, man. You get me that song.'

The challenge fell on the staves of Earl Brown, already assigned the job of 'special material' and so far having constructed the gospel medley from his new arrangements of existing and traditional sacred songs. For The Song, the one that would cancel Christmas and close the show, Steve's brief was to write something with a social message, much like he'd done for Harry on *Petula*, strong enough to make its point yet not so strong that it wouldn't get past the nervy network censor and even nervier sponsor.

Earl knew exactly what Steve wanted, and what Elvis needed. He'd known the moment Sirhan Sirhan squeezed a trigger in the kitchen of the Ambassador Hotel. He'd been there that night in the office with Elvis. He'd seen the dismay in his eyes and heard the lump stick in his throat as he poured out his sorrow for Bobby, for JFK, and especially for King. Elvis had even recited the 'I Have A Dream' speech. It meant that much to him that he'd learned it by heart. This, now, was Earl's challenge. To write something for Elvis that meant *that* much. A musical 'I Have A Dream'.

Sam Cooke had already done something like it back in 1964 with 'A Change Is Gonna Come'. Cooke had aimed to write a black 'Blowin' In The Wind' only to miraculously distil the hope on Martin's face that day in '63 on the steps of the Lincoln Memorial in a single, stunning philharmonic spiritual. Elvis, a fan of Cooke's, owned a copy, not that Earl would have known when he chose to march in its melodic footsteps, his tune similarly climbing like a gospel hymn, swaying like a soul ballad. His title and lyrics were just as transparent of its ideological source. 'If I Can Dream'.

Earl wrote it in the early hours watching the sun rise over his garden at home in Sherman Oaks, a few miles west of Burbank, taking it straight to NBC that same morning. Steve and Finkel were the first to hear it, Earl singing while Billy, who helped a little with the arrangement, played piano in the rehearsal room. It was everything Steve had asked him. A Black Panther salute in a Christmas bauble. Emotional, memorable and network-and-sponsor-proof. Steve told Earl it was perfect.

'Bindle!'

The door to the office next door was open, suited men on couches peering out past the Colonel and his vapours blocking the gap between.

'What the hell's going on?'

Steve counted slowly in his head then said, 'It's the new song.'

'What new song?'

'For the end of the show.'

'The *Christmas* song?'

'*Instead* of the Christmas song.'

A splutter of ashes. 'Out of the question.' The Colonel had started to turn his back when Steve called after him.

'Well, let's see what Elvis says when he hears it.'

The Colonel swivelled on his cane. 'That's *not* a Christmas song, Bindle.' Smoke, spittle. 'That's not even an Elvis kind of song.'

'I'd like to try it, man.'

Nobody had noticed Elvis walk in the other doorway, just in time to catch the end of the song. 'Let me hear it again.'

A wisp of smoke hung where a second earlier the Colonel had been stood, the office door now pushed ajar.

Billy started playing its ebbing hallelujah chords.

'There must be lights burning brighter somewhere...'

As Earl sang, Elvis leaned on the piano, hanging his head down, barely moving.

The song finished. Elvis raised his head. 'OK. Play it again.' Then dropped it. He didn't smile, nor move so much as a finger. Earl reached the crescendo a second time.

'Riiiight nooow!'

Elvis lifted his chin, letting out a long breath like he'd been holding something in. He looked up at Earl. 'I'll do it,' he nodded. 'I'll sing it.' Then to Steve and Finkel. 'That's it.' Then to the office door. 'That's our song.'

The office door was open again, the Colonel back blocking its light, smoke trickling in front of him like a drunkard's piss down an alley. At first he didn't say anything, just screwed maggoty eyes at Steve as the wispy piss trickled on. Then he took out his stogie and cocked his head to one side. 'Norm,' he barked to the room behind him. 'Get me a new contract.'

Norm was Norman Racusin of RCA Records, the contract two sheaves of pre-prepared paperwork surrendering song publishing to 'Gladys Music', named after Elvis' mother and owned by the Colonel. Norm offered Billy the pen first. He declined. 'It's your song, Earl,' said Billy. 'You wrote it.'

Earl graciously signed on the dotted line. Billy was right. 'If I Can Dream' *was* his song.

At least until the ink dried when half its royalties became Elvis and the Colonel's.

6000 SUNSET BOULEVARD

There were 35 of them. More musicians than Elvis had seen gathered in a single studio his entire life. A few he recognised from the last time he'd stood in Studio 1 of Western Recorders three months earlier to cut the soundtrack to *Kiss My Firm But Pliant Lips*, since renamed *Live A Little, Love A Little*: Al Casey and fellow *Pet Sounds*-men Larry Knechtel, Chuck Berghofer, Don Randi and, leading the charge from the rear, drummer Hal Blaine. The same pop pit orchestra, only this time the *full* orchestra: more guitars, including Tommy Tedesco, who'd twisted endings into the *Twilight Zone* theme, and Mike Deasy, who'd helped Glen Campbell get to Phoenix on time; the ubiquitous Hollywood harmonica of Tommy Morgan; three percussionists including Frank DeVito; a cavalry of strings, brass and woodwind including the French horn of William Hinshaw, the violins of Leonard Malarsky and Sidney Sharp, and the cello of Emmet Sargeant, all of whom had blown and bowed on Sam Cooke's 'A Change Is Gonna Come'; and the backing vocals of Phil Spector's Blossoms featuring the powerhouse of Darlene Love. Enough musicians to paint the Sistine Chapel ceiling in sound. It took Michelangelo four years. It took Elvis four nights.

The sessions were to pre-record the music for the main production numbers. Bones was there as producer, Billy to conduct the arrangements he'd been finessing for the past two weeks, and

Steve to lend whatever moral support was needed. Elvis needed it the moment he registered the size of the orchestra. He told Steve he wasn't used to anything this big. Normally it was just him and a small band, any orchestral parts overdubbed later without him. With so many musicians he was worried about losing his way, and for the first few takes it seemed like he had. Adding to his unease was the complexity of the arrangements. Most were medleys, their component parts to be recorded separately then pieced together, a method second nature to the Beatles but completely alien to Elvis.

The tension showed. He missed a cue and cursed himself.

'*Goddamn it!* Hold it...'

A deep breath, a straightening of the spine, a focus of the mind to rock 'n' roll's every latitude and longitude. Then the seizing of the day.

That first night, as John Lennon scrabbled in Abbey Road splicing up 'Revolution 9', in Western Records Elvis did some splicing of his own, chopping between the individual parts of the big 'Guitar Man' operetta, a 16-minute song suite linked by the Jerry Reed tune. There was one new number, a short two-bit-town blues called 'Nothingville' specially written by Mac Davis and Billy Strange. The rest were all songs Elvis had recorded in the past, each dragged wide-eyed and go-go-hipped into a 1968 of 'Sock it to me!', *Barbarella* and the Pigeon-Toed Orange Peel: a bestial 'Let Yourself Go' spinning its tassels with the kittens of the Classic Cat; a faster, vampier 'Big Boss Man'; a minxish 'Little Egypt'; a growl of 'Trouble'; and a purring 'It Hurts Me', a soul ballad doomed to the scullery of a B-side four years ago, now the fairytale belle of the ball. In between were snatches of a similarly funked-up 'Guitar Man', a kitsch Keystone cop rag and an acid kung fu instrumental. As a piece of music by Elvis Presley, a Revolution, whatever its number.

The second night he moved on to the gospel medley. Darlene Love led 'Sometimes I Feel Like A Motherless Child', clearing the aisle for Elvis' neon preacher, singing the word of the Lord in the light of Las Vegas. It, too, throbbed with the distinct tempo of 1968, sacred music for the Age of Aquarius, making a love-in of Sister Rosetta Tharpe's 'Up Above My Head' and a laugh-in of 'Saved', Leiber and Stoller's rockin' Elmer Gantry satire which he squeezed for every sinful hoochie-coo.

The third night, as four miles away Paul McCartney was spending the evening in the company of Linda Eastman at the Whisky A Go Go, Elvis was back in the hobo jungles of 'Guitar Man'. A second shorter medley with 'Trouble' for the show opener, even less Jerry Reed and more James Bond than last time, its flow ratcheted by the washboard-zipping guitars of Tedesco and Deasy that Bones would pick out as a running motif.

The fourth night, they turned to the two remaining standalone songs. One was another bespoke Mac Davis and Billy Strange chocolate-box of a tune called 'Memories'. The other was Earl's song. *The* Song. 'If I Can Dream'.

The band took it to the mountaintop. The sound at the summit was 'Georgia On My Mind' by Cecil B. DeMille. After five takes there wasn't anywhere higher to go but Elvis wanted to keep climbing. He didn't have to. The plan was to use what they'd recorded as a backing and have Elvis sing the vocal again live for the TV cameras. But once the band had packed up their instruments and gone home, he hung back to run through the tape a few more times.

It was late Sunday evening. The studio was empty save for Steve, Bones and the engineers in the control room and Elvis alone out front. Bones rolled the tape. Elvis sang along to 'If I Can Dream'. The control room bristled with gooseflesh.

When it was over, he asked to run it again. 'I wanna try it with a hand mic.'

Steve understood. All night, Elvis had been singing into a stationary microphone. A handheld one would allow him to move around freely, as he would on TV. It wasn't enough to gauge his vocal. Elvis wanted to gauge his performance.

Bones was about to play the tape when Steve made a suggestion. 'Elvis, you OK if we turn out the main lights?'

Elvis nodded at him through the glass. The engineer flicked the switches. One by one the overhead strip lights vanished in an ever increasing gloom, leaving the studio in near total darkness save for the dim glow of the tape machines and mixing desk like a far-off city in the desert night. Looking through the glass they could just make out the silhouette of Elvis, stood flexing the cable in his right hand. 'OK, Elvis?' asked Bones. The silhouette raised a hand.

The music began. In the pitch black it felt like a phantom orchestra had suddenly appeared just beyond Elvis, out of vision. The first two verses they watched his silhouette sway. They heard his voice from the speakers but it seemed to be coming from elsewhere: from *every*where. Then, in a blink, he plummeted. The silhouette was crouched on the floor, rocking on its knees, but its voice only grew bigger. A voice to exalt every valley, make low every hill and mountain, make plain every rough place, make straight every crooked place. A voice revealing the glory of all flesh together, transforming jangling discords into a beautiful symphony of brotherhood, from the prodigious hilltops of New Hampshire and the mighty mountains of New York to the snowcapped rockies of Colorado and the curvaceous peaks of California; from every hill and molehill of Mississippi, every village and hamlet, every state and city. The song of a King, sung by a King.

When it had finished Elvis lay still, on his knees, in the dark. Darker than the summer night outside in Los Angeles. And in

Tupelo where his brother's bones rested with the worms. And Memphis where his mother's lay beneath a marble Jesus. And in Atlanta, and Arlington where when next it rained it polished the tombs of King and Kennedy like the softest of sad applause.

THE BLUE MOON BOYS

The morning after Elvis recorded 'If I Can Dream', a plane landed in Los Angeles from Memphis carrying a man and his guitar. He took it on as cabin baggage being too precious a cargo to risk in the hold. A Gibson Super 400 CES: Gibson, the make; Super 400, the model; CES, the body design, Cutaway Electric Spanish. More specifically a Florentine with a sharper cutaway curl, in a sunburst finish, the wood pale at the centre darkening outwards to the edges, a masterpiece of Kalamazoo craftsmanship in maple, mahogany, rosewood, pearl, nickel and gold.

He'd bought it five years earlier to record an album called *The Guitar That Changed The World*, though it wasn't so much his instrument that changed the world as the man himself. The actual guitar he used to change it was the same make, Gibson, but a different model, a gold ES 295, the one he plugged in the night of July 5, 1954 at Sam Phillips' Sun Studios in Memphis when a 19-year-old human electric shock with nothing to earth it named Elvis Presley started fooling with a black blues song the way no white kid before had ever fooled with such things. The gold guitar laughed to see such fun and the kid ran away with the tune. 'That's All Right'. Sun Records 209. The name on the original label, 'Elvis Presley, Scotty and Bill.' That's how the guitar of Scotty Moore put a twang in the Big Bang that changed the world.

They became a band. The Blue Moon Boys. Elvis, Scotty and Bill Black on bass. They made their first three records without a drummer before eventually finding Dominic Joseph 'D.J.' Fontana. He looked like one of the Barrow Gang and hit calfskin much like they hit gas stations. D.J.'s was the stick-'em-up snare that heeled 'Blue Suede Shoes' and yanked the leash on 'Hound Dog'. There was no better drummer for Elvis Presley.

The Blue Moon Boys shone their last beam together in 1958. All had weathered the worst of the Colonel's financial insults and ostracisms, but when Elvis returned from the Army only Scotty and D.J. were willing to work for him in a reduced capacity as day-rate session men. Bill was gone.

Too sore over royalties, contracts and the Colonel, he quit to start his own instrumental group, the Bill Black Combo. Their few hits included a remake of 'Don't Be Cruel' substituting the voice of Elvis with the hiccups of a Hammond organ played by the cousin of Jerry Lee Lewis. Then one day in 1965 Bill was admitted to Memphis Baptist Memorial Hospital after complaining of headaches and foggy vision. They discovered a brain tumour. Two surgeries failed to remove it. A third would have risked rendering him a vegetable. Bill made minor recovery but lapsed back into a semi-coma and died. He was 39, a husband and father of three. Elvis didn't attend the funeral for fear of any fans creating too big a disruption, but later made a private visit to Bill's widow. 'This comes as such a shock to me,' he told the press, 'that I can hardly explain how much I loved Bill.'

He'd never have another band like the Blue Moon Boys. He'd never have another band. He'd have great musicians in the studio – jazz jangler Barney Kessel, the ubiquitous Glen Campbell, the Big O's drummer Buddy Harman, even Bob Dylan's Jerry Kennedy and Charlie McCoy from *Blonde On Blonde* – but never the same feeling as when four individuals fuse as one living organism and in shared soul and spirit become the Shake Rag Defenders.

Theirs was the spectre Steve had heard wailing every night in Elvis' dressing room. The old songs. 'I Got A Woman', 'One Night', 'Love Me'. The best songs. The songs Elvis played to remind him who he was after each day rehearsing a TV show designed to remind everyone else the same thing.

'Have you ever thought what it's like to be an Elvis Presley?'

The question was in the script. It was the weakest part, what Allan and Chris had called the 'Informal Talk & Songs' section where Elvis was supposed to sit and joke about his early days and send up some of his goofier movie songs including 'Wooden Heart', 'Cotton Candy Land' and the one about clowns and kangaroos, 'How Would You Like To Be'. They'd written him a monologue, stitching together some of the stories he'd told them in meetings, rendered *Laugh-In* style.

'I said to Ringo, "Are you really Ringo Starr?" He said, "Yeah, baby." I hit him right in the mouth! And Ringo said, "Now I know I really made it!"'

All of this could be scrapped now Steve had the Colonel's begrudging permission to recreate the dressing room jams as part of the show. Essentially it was the same 'Informal Talk & Songs' idea with less contrived talk and better songs. Elvis preferred it too. But then Steve had mentioned 'a live audience' and the old war wound of the Fontainebleau Miami Beach began to throb. It was one thing to mess around on guitars with Charlie and Lance for his Angels in the dressing room. The same thing in a TV studio before cameras and the general public was a catwalk for a naked emperor. He'd already been persuaded to perform before an audience for the 'arena' part of the show, but only with the assurance of singing with a live band and orchestra. If Steve wanted him to busk it in front of a similar audience, he'd need back up. He'd need his Blue Moon Boys.

With Steve's consent, Elvis dialled Memphis. The receiver picked up and a girl's voice said 'hello'.

'Could I speak to Scotty Moore please?'

'He's not here,' said the girl. 'Who's calling?'

'This is... ah... Elvis Presley.'

'OK. *Sure*. And this is Elizabeth Taylor.'

Click. *Brrrrrrr.*

When Scotty came home his new girlfriend, Emily, told him about the prankster. A few hours later, he rang again. This time Scotty answered. When he came off the phone he told Emily to start packing a case as the next day they'd be flying out to California. 'To see Elvis.' Liz Taylor was mortified.

And so Scotty, with his Gibson and his girlfriend beside him, flew to Los Angeles, first rendezvousing with fellow Blue Moon Boy D.J. before heading straight to NBC where Elvis was waiting, his Gibson J200 acoustic already out of its case and in his lap.

The three of them had last been together only five months ago in Nashville, when Scotty and D.J. played on 'U.S. Male' the night Elvis sang his stoned prisoner's song. But the vibe, then, wasn't anything like it had been once upon a lost highway with the Blue Moon Boys. This was. A slingshot back through time to four men, one car, instruments on a roof box with a canvas cover, drug stores, Pepsis, burgers and every town a new set of lipsticked phone numbers on the windscreen. Music of liquid copper and wrangled starlight forged only by his voice and their hands.

Charlie strummed along with them, but only as acoustic understudy to the six-stringed soliloquies of Scotty's hammer-on Hamlet and Elvis' amplified Othello. Even Scotty knew nobody played beastly two-backed blues the way Elvis did.

Without a kit, D.J. used an empty guitar case like a giant tom-tom while Lance acted as metronome with a tambourine. Steve, Allan and Chris took notes, making suggestions of how best to structure it for the cameras. Steve's main worry was that Elvis would keep singing and forget about his dialogue. They'd made a cue sheet of topics for him, everything from his sideburns to his thoughts on the current music scene. Elvis agreed he may need 'something to go off', especially as the Memphis sallies wisecracking the jams to daybreak would be hard to fake without Joe, Lamar or Hog Ears. So it was decided Hog Ears would join them on stage too as a reserve gag pitcher and punchline catcher as Elvis' swing dictated, disguised as an extra percussionist slapping an upturned guitar. Fourteen years after the original trio, they were now six: Elvis, Scotty, D.J., Charlie, Lance, and Hog Ears.

The new Blue Moon Boys of Burbank.

THE PSYCHO SHOW

The ladies and gentlemen of the press, some 50 of them, arrived in beautiful downtown Burbank at the appointed time of 6 pm. Ushers with Elvis badges led them to their seats in Rehearsal Stage 3, placed in rows before a long table six chairs shy of a Last Supper, its underside cloaked in black velour. Behind them, at the back of the room, stood the Colonel overstuffing a blue sports shirt, an Alpine hat pulled down to his eyebrows and a cigar bevelling in the corner of his mouth. He gave a signal and a door to the right of the head table opened. Simultaneously, some 50 pulses quickened.

Elvis entered in dark pants, an electric blue shirt open at the collar, a spotted neckscarf beneath, a thick leather watch strap on his wrist and a Villiger Kiel in his hand. The cigar was smouldering. So was his face, with diamond dust and the smell of warm sugar. The reporters blinked and the air stuttered. Double-fuck. It was *that* Elvis Presley.

Six others entered with him and took their seats. At the far left sat Lamar, then Bones in a smart jacket, shirt and tie. Next to him was Steve, sandwiching Elvis between Finkel, also smoking one of Elvis' cigars, all three wearing similar neckscarves. Steve hated wearing his but it was Elvis' idea, so he did what he must to keep him happy. Diamond Joe and Charlie were sat on Finkel's left, leaving the surplus Hog Ears standing behind them.

The head of publicity at NBC had begged the Colonel to allow the press access to Elvis ahead of the TV show. This was the Colonel's best offer. Fifteen measly minutes.

Why had he decided to do TV again?

'Uh, well, my last television appearance was on Frank Sinatra's show in 1960. We figured it was about time to do another. Besides...' Out of sight Elvis playfully kicked Steve under the table. '... I thought I'd better do it before I got too old.'

A muttering of laughter. A holler from the rear.

'We got a good deal!' the Colonel roostered. 'The offer was so good we couldn't refuse it. Which is the only kind of offer I'm interested in, folks!'

Was he going to wiggle his pelvis like the old days?

'Uh...' Elvis nudged knees again. '... The pelvis was a natural reaction to the music. I can't say just what will happen in the show. I might surprise you with what I do. Everything in the show comes out of the music.'

Did he think his audience had changed?

'They don't move as fast as they used to...'

The knees.

'But, uh, my audience is older now. The girls are in their twenties and have babies.'

Did Elvis feel he'd gotten older too?

'Oh, man. I'm not ancient!'

The room chuckled.

But did Elvis feel he'd changed since his early days?

'Soundwise, yes. I pick my material more carefully. I have to keep up. Sound engineering has improved a lot since those days which means I have to improve. I think we get a better sound now.'

Had marriage changed him?

'Well, everything has to be considered when you're married and have a baby.' He wiggled the cigar in his fingers. 'Though it's got me smoking these things more.'

Was Priscilla expecting another child yet?

'Uh... Not that I've had anything to do with.'

Was the TV Special going to be broadcast in other countries?

'If they make a good deal,' yelped the Colonel.

And how was his relationship with the Colonel?

'Well...' Elvis glanced over at the unblinking toad in the Alpine hat amidst a fog of tobacco. 'The Colonel and I have our areas of disagreement.' Steve felt his knee nearly knock out of its socket. 'But no arguments.'

'OK, folks!' The Colonel's watch had ticked its fifteenth minute. 'No more questions!'

Elvis stayed a few seconds to pose for photographs then swiftly disappeared through the same side door, his Angels tight at his heels. The Colonel took up position by the other main door, passing out photos and badges while ensuring none of the reporters could exit without the finer details of his own life story exhausting their shorthand. They'd come for an eyeful of Elvis and would leave with a padful of the Colonel. The greatest hits: the carny orphan raised on his uncle's pony farm; the foot-long hot dogs; the dancing chickens; and how he made his millions from the thing called Elvis Presley.

'You know Elvis once told me in gratitude, "Colonel, you put a lump in my throat." And I told him, "Elvis, you put a lump in my wallet."'

The Colonel liked to see their curling mouths and busy pencils. Sure they were laughing. Laughing with him. Everybody loved the Colonel, same as they loved Elvis. That was the deal, folks.

Fifty-fifty.

★

The Colonel was 58 when he went to bed that Tuesday night and 59 when he awoke on Wednesday morning. At 5 o'clock the birthday boy tapped his cane to Stage 4 where Elvis was finishing his last day of rehearsals and where a large crowd were waiting to greet him with cake, champagne and confetti cannons. Everyone was there. The Angels, Steve, Finkel and the whole cast and crew from the dancers to the tape-ops.

'Happy birth-day to yooooo!'

The psychopath Andreas Cornelis van Kuijk smiled. Everyone loved the Colonel.

A piano had been wheeled in, Billy taking the stool as Elvis stepped forward, microphone in hand and mischief in face. Billy started to play and Elvis started to sing with the help of painted cue cards. It was a special version of 'It Hurts Me' with new lyrics by Allan, written especially for the Colonel.

'It hurts me to see the budget climb up to the sky...'

Everybody laughed. The Colonel smiled.

'It hurts me when Bindle gives me trouble...'

Elvis struggled to keep a straight face. The whole studio was laughing. The Colonel kept smiling. They were laughing. With him.

'It hurts me the way that Finkel spends my dough...'

Laughing.

'Tell me the truth, is it too much to ask, for one lousy tired ol' Christmas song?'

At him.

Elvis laughed the hardest. Steve was bellyaching. Finkel was juddering, wiping his eyes. The Colonel's teeth glistened like the snarl of a cat. A voice in his head spat *'Klootzakken!'* and the snarl clinched tighter.

So this was Finkel's idea of a snow? A dripping egg in the Colonel's face laid by his very own golden goose. It was clever, certainly, and original, yes. He'd give Finkel that much.

The cunt still wasn't getting the cane.

THE LAST JUDGEMENT

Thursday, June 27, 1968. Elvis awoke knowing today was not like any other day. He'd been weighing upon the earth's crust for over 12,000 of them but the course of his life had been determined by just a few. The day he was born and his twin brother died. The day he first set foot in Shake Rag. The day his family moved to Memphis. The day he walked into Sam Phillips' Sun Studios and told the receptionist he didn't sound like nobody. The day he met the man who was once Andreas Cornelis van Kuijk. The day he cut 'Heartbreak Hotel'. The day he first buckarooed his bones before a television camera. The day he lost his manhood to the United States Army. The day he lost his mother. The day he first lost his mind in a fizz of dextroamphetamines. The day he came home from Germany. The day his lips first tasted Rusty's. The day he said 'I do' in Las Vegas. The day he first held Lisa Marie.

Today was going to be one of *those* days.

He took his first lonely look in the mirror. It was him, and only him. Whatever happened today would be down to him, and only him. The sickness of the champ on the morning of the title fight. It *was* a fight.

In the black leather corner, smelling of Beale Street and hot bedsheets, 'the Memphis flash!', Elvis — the King! And over in the blue Hawaiian corner, smelling of Palookaville and canned peaches, 'the Hollywood goon!', Elvis — the Ken®!

The original Shake Rag defender versus every bloated racing driver, beach boy, chopper pilot and trawler skipper ever to take his perfect body Technicolor hostage. The y'know-I'm-evil good versus the goody-good evil. Just as Chris would swear Elvis told him in their first script meeting. 'I don't wanna be any more goody-good cocksuckin' singing mechanics!' Today was his one and only chance to bury them once and for all. His voice the arsenal, his stage a mass grave for every gormless Tulsa, Chad and Mike to serenade a puppet, pooch or truckful of chickens. All he had to do was open his mouth, aim and fire.

The hour of judgement not scheduled until the evening, that morning the slate clapped on his first scene in front of Steve's cameras. It was a section of the main 'Guitar Man' operetta, Gene's set a comic book amusement pier loosely based on his impressions of Santa Monica, dominated by cardboard neons advertising 'GIRLS', 'SHOOTING' and 'TUNNEL OF LOVE'. Elvis, in powder blue denims, had to face off with the 'Big Boss Man', tubby character actor Buddy Arett as a stogie-chomping gangster, then sing 'It Hurts Me' to his brassy raven-haired moll, occasional Matt Helm 'slaymate' Barbara Burgess, simultaneously making chop suey of Jaime Rogers' gang of chain-wielding thugs in a gymnastic karate fight. It took several takes as Elvis fluffed his lip-synching, ripped his pants and struggled with a prop guitar that failed to smash on cue. The on-set laughter helped ease his nerves but by lunchtime his stomach's morning butterflies had become spiky iron bats.

The afternoon had been set aside for a last rehearsal of the new Blue Moon Boys. The set had been changed over with raised bleachers surrounding a simple red-bordered white square platform, lit from beneath, in the centre acting as the stage. There were no ropes or corner posts but being in the round it looked a bit like a boxing ring. On it, five standard blue-padded NBC chairs were arranged in a loose circle around a low glass table for a jug of water and Elvis' cue sheet. Microphones had been placed on stands by each chair as well as an amplifier: the custom-built Echosonic model Scotty had also flown in from Memphis, the one he'd first used on 'Mystery Train' in 1955, then 'Heartbreak Hotel', 'Hound Dog' and every teenage rampage thereafter. A sacred wood and wire umbilical cord to Elvis' imperial past.

They ran through ten songs, Elvis still in his denims, the band in their stage wear of matching ruby red shirts and bottoms. Elvis laughed little, his eyes twitching with newly born self-doubt.

Steve could see he was nervous, which made Steve nervous, and by then Steve already had enough bats in his own abdominal belfry. They'd been roosting there since the night before when he drove home after their little party for the Colonel. On the way out the guard at the gate had asked him if he wanted 'a ticket to see Elvis?' Steve didn't know what he meant. Then the guard showed him the stack of tickets in his cabin.

They were for the first of Thursday's two live tapings, the one at 6 pm. Specifically, the tickets that the Colonel had asked for. He couldn't sell them — like all TV audiences, they were free admission — but he'd assured Steve and Finkel that if given the entire allocation he would pack the bleachers with Elvis apostles flown in especially from Memphis. 'Real fans,' said the Colonel, 'not your Hollywood phonies.' It seemed a fair gesture. They gave him the tickets. The same tickets that only went as far as the NBC guardhouse, leaving an empty plane without a pilot still standing on a Memphis runway. And the prospect of Elvis playing to an empty TV studio.

'Who wants a free ticket to see Elvis Presley?'

The patrons of Bob's Big Boy, lost in sweet 'n' greasy nirvana of Half Pound Ground O' Rounds and Silver Goblet shakes, looked up at the young runner waving a wedge of paper stubs in the air.

The same look they'd have given somebody who just asked 'Who wants a free unicorn and a sack of magic beans?'

'The King of Rock 'n' Roll live tonight! Just down the road at NBC!'

Bob's Big Boy was less than a mile away, straight along Almeda. As the nearest roadside diner, Steve sent his staff there praying they'd be able to press-gang enough Elvis fans, however casual, inside and out in the parking lot. Those they found, once they realised the tickets were genuine, didn't need hard persuasion.

Bones helped by contacting a couple of local radio stations whose D.J.s sent out APBs for every Elvis fan in Los Angeles to stampede to Burbank for 6 pm. By 5, the queue at the gate was starting to look close to a reasonable audience.

The Colonel said nothing.

Partly because of the ticket fiasco, they were now running late. Steve's bats had flown up from his guts to start flapping in his throat. And then his ears.

'Steve?'

He looked round and saw Joe. A very troubled looking Joe.

'It's Elvis. He needs to see you, right away…'

Elvis was in his dressing room, Bill's black leather melting over his body like an LP on a bonfire, a make-up girl flicking a final brush of powder on his cheeks, staring at his own face in the mirror. His mother's eyes. His father's cheekbones. The man Jesse Garon could've become. His face.

But whose face?

The boy who didn't sound like nobody, the Hillbilly Cat, the Memphis Flash, Elvis the Pelvis, the King of Rock 'n' Roll, Clint Reno, Deke Rivers, Vince Everett, Danny Fisher, middle name 'Mis-er-eee'.

Or Private 53310761, Tulsa McLean, Pacer Burton, Glenn Tyler, Chad Gates, Toby Kwimper, Kid Galahad, Ross Carpenter, Mike Edwards, Mike Windgren, Josh Morgan 'n' Jodie Tatum, Lucky Jackson, Charlie Rogers, Rusty Wells, Lonnie Beale, Johnny Tyrone, Frankie's Johnny, Rick Richards, Mike McCoy, Ted Jackson, Guy Lambert *'with a moo moo here'*, Scott Hayward, Joe Lightcloud, Steve Grayson, Greg Nolan.

Which one of you motherfuckers is it to be?

Or Elvis Presley?

'And darkness was over the face of the deep.'

Eyelids closed. Darkness. White noise. Numbers. Scriptures. Methamphetamine 30. Hydrochloride 20. Genesis 1:3.

'And God said "Let there be light."'

Eyelids open.

'Fuck!'

Five minutes later, Steve had said all he could. He patted Elvis on the shoulder. 'Good luck.' And closed the dressing room door behind him.

On the studio floor disc jockey Robert W. Morgan from LA's KHJ was finishing his warm-up. The Colonel and his dogsbody Tom had shuffled the audience, plucking the youngest, prettiest girls to sit closest on the side of the stage. The red-shirted Blue Moon Boys, Scotty, D.J., Hog Ears and Charlie, were all seated and waiting. Lance, in black, was perched on the edge with his tambourine, Joe beside and Lamar just behind him in the crowd.

Steve was sat in his director's gallery focussed on the main camera monitor, its eye, like all eyes, on the one remaining empty seat on stage. The audience murmured, giggled and gulped. Steve's bats vomited bats eating bats vomiting bats. He closed his eyes for a couple of seconds, exhaled slowly, then opened them.

The chair on the monitor was still empty.

He closed them again. He could hear his heart throbbing in his ears like the theme from *Dragnet*. Then several gasping shrieks.

When his eyes snapped back open the first thing they saw was a screen seeping liquid black leather.

THE SECOND COMING, THE COMING AND THE SECOND SECOND COMING

He walked weightless in a vacuum of hot light and damp noise, past a frieze of faces pelican-jawed, doughnut-eyed, knot-lipped and nail-feeding, finding his spot on the red-trimmed square stage where he stood, laughing, hands on hips, a black-mirrored mainsail in a storm of want. He was still laughing as he sat down, swinging to Scotty's electric strums, D.J.'s waggling finger, Charlie's 'mah boy, mah boy' and the watermelon sweep of Hog Ears' grin, his hand reaching for his acoustic guitar.

He said 'OK.' Then, motioning to leave, 'Well, goodnight.'

In the gallery, Steve died ten deaths in a tenth of a second.

Until the next tenth when Elvis chuckled and the storm chuckled with him.

'Let's see, what do I do now folks?'

He sat stroking his guitar neck, sandwiching his tongue between his lips, a spit-shined moonless night of sweat and leather, guzzling all light and colour with its unquenchable blackness. A scorpion, a stag beetle, a raven's beak, an unplayed record slipped fresh from its sleeve. Wild and *new*. The new of new worlds and new races, the familiarly human yet unknown, like the first pale Pilgrim's sight of tawny Patuxet flesh. It was Elvis, but undiscovered Elvis, an Elvis of another *other*, as if the first Elvis wasn't *other* enough. Nobody could do anything other than look at him and when they looked at him they found they'd forgotten how to breathe.

'He's so *perfect!*'

A girl sat beside him couldn't help tremble it aloud. The tremble of truth. He *was* perfect.

'The guy over here on my left...'

He started introducing his band. He joked that Scotty had been playing with him since 'I first started out in 1912'. The crowd giggled but he was much too blinding a black sun for them to see its red planets.

'The first thing that we recorded...'

His voice was chocolate and their ears licked every syllable.

'... the very first thing was an old rhythm and blues type song...'

Chocolate, chocolate, chocolate.

'... and it went like this...'

The black sun exploded in the black of Sun 209.

'Well, that's all right wi' mama!'

The Big Bang.

'That's all right wi' yooo!'

'That's All Right', his magic 'Shazam!', and the power evoked. The power of a clockless July night in '54 playing music so frighteningly free he feared they'd be 'run out of town!'

'That's all right... c'mere, baby!'

The power of innocence told anew by experience. Elvis pounding, Scotty tickling, D.J. smacking, Lance's tambourine bedspringing, all boots thumping hard as the walls of a Houston whorehouse until they could pound, tickle, smack and thump no more, collapsing as one in a satiated groan.

'Mah boy, mah boy!'

What music. What ecstasy. What *sex*.

Was he God or Devil, or both? A diabolical divinity. Lucifer Christ. An Angel of the Lord tailored by the Marquis de Sade, his whip his guitar.

'Well, since ma baby left me!'

The lash came down with 'Heartbreak Hotel'.

'Oh, yeeeaaah!'

And cracked again with 'Love Me'. Rock 'n' roll his slave, he its master. He growled with pleasure.

'That's dirty, dirty!'

His bloodlust whetted, he swapped whip for machine gun, changing his acoustic guitar for Scotty's electric. The Guitar That Changed The World now in Satan's lap.

DA-DANG, DA-DANG, DA-DANG, DA-DANG!

All hail the High Executioner, come to wreak vengeance on the peach-canned damned. The Tinseltown traitors who'd sold his soul to the cinemascopic hell of Hawaii, Acapulco and Cotton Candy Land. A one-man firing squad with a loaded Gibson Super 400.

'Yeah, baby!'

Every string a trigger and from all six the bullets flew. Claret and bone and flesh and sinew spewing, spurting, splattering forth from fat cheeks, jellied hair, army stripes, racing helmets, turbans, tuxedos, leis, maracas and ukuleles.

'You got me peepin'…'

Oh, sweet violence. A Ken®ocide of Tulsas, Chads, Mikes, Charlies, Guys, Ricks and Johnnys as one by one their crimson corpses fell.

'You got me hidin'…'

And sweeter still sex. The cry of silk sheets, shag carpet and paradise found in Perugia Way. Scoobie and Rusty. It was *Their* Song. The Jimmy Reed blues, 'Baby, What You Want Me To Do'. Elvis plucked and shucked himself back there, peepin' and hidin' over, under, sideways, down with the woman of his dreams, the mating cry of Elvis and Shelvis, forgetting all about the cameras, the audience, the time, the place. And the wife.

'Let me see what I'm supposed to do next here...'

The Shake Rag Don Juan was getting steadily smashed on his own sublimity. He picked up his cue sheet and started reading aloud the list of prompts Steve had prepared for him. About 'shooting from the waist down' and 'not being able to touch hands with body... er, body with hands'. The girls swooned and whinnied at his every chocolate joke.

He spoke about new music and new groups. He mentioned 'the Beatles' and wanted to say 'the Byrds', though it came out 'bee-yurds', which sounded close enough for Chris to spend the rest of his life convincing himself, then others, Elvis had really said 'the Beards' as a nod to his surname.

'Rock 'n' roll music is basically gospel or rhythm and blues...'

The more he talked, the quieter the studio hushed.

'It all boils down to just, uh...'

So quiet it disturbed him.

'I don't know what I'm talkin' about, really, y'know, I'm just mumblin', man...'

The pistol popped and the orgy resumed with 'Blue Suede Shoes', then another roll with Rusty in a second 'Baby, What You Want Me To Do'. He joked about his snarling lip – 'I got news for you baby, I did 29 pictures like that.' (He'd only made 28 but nobody was counting.) D.J. reminded him about Jacksonville in '56 so he told them about the time 'the PTA, the YMCA or somebody' banned him from moving anything except his little finger. Hog Ears prodded him to do the same with the Steve Allen story about 'the li'l old hound dog on stage' but Elvis kicked it away. 'We can't talk about that one.'

'That's one thing about this TV special I'm doing,' he added. 'They're gonna, uh, let me do what I wanna do... which is sit down!'

Chocolate laughter.

'Not really...'

At Scotty's request, he awed and clawed the flesh off 'Lawdy, Miss Clawdy', his body simmering in sweat.

'Man, you talk about somethin' hot, baby, this leather is tough!'

He cooled only slightly with 'Are You Lonesome Tonight', blowtorching back from 'When My Blue Moon Turns To Gold Again' into 'Blue Christmas'. Every part of him seemed to be dripping: his hair, his lips, his jacket, his guitar. A David sculpted from Hershey's syrup and chocolate Jell-O pudding. The slavering slaves licked him with their eyeballs, long, slow, lapping surveys up and down every inch of his liquid body, swallowing and tasting with each intermittent blink. Just like ten years ago: all the way down to the birch-wood stick.

The more he spouted, the more it greased him for action. He cowgirled 'Trying To Get To You' front and reverse, then seized and spread 'One Night' by its ankles.

Just caaawl ma naym!'

History watched and wept for the Sixties – that scarlet fool – wasting its eyes and ears on *'oo!'*-ing moptops, hermits and other gormless billy goats, all cuckolds to rock 'n' roll when pulverised with such leonine majesty.

'Aw, get dirty, baby!'

Once pleasured he pulled out and slipped back in 'Baby, What You Want Me To Do' for the third time – this time pinning it to the floor and fucking it cross-eyed.

'Yup! Yup! Hep! Hep!'

He fucked it all the way up Sunset Strip, into the hills, screwing every hole in Bel-Air Country Club, then home down Hollywood

Freeway bucking and fucking back towards Burbank, his body broiling in fluids and a low rumbling 'Hmmummumm!'

And the cosmos softly throbbed.

He still wanted to do 'one more', but on his feet. Too late, he realised there was no guitar strap, forcing him to stand with one leg on his chair to prop it on his knee while Charlie crouched below, raising his microphone stand to catch his voice.

The song was 'One Night', again. A song about a man tired of living *'a very quiet life'*, forsaking it all for one night of fleshly sin. The R&B original by Smiley Lewis had been sung from the point of shame and remorse. The version tailored for Elvis in '57 changed the lyrics from red-light regret to sexual salvation. A song about escaping the squares' suburbia of milk, cookies, A-grades, twin-sets, sedans, lawn-mowing, pensions, golf and church, for the freaks' cuckoo-land of whisky, cigarettes, necking, mini-skirts, hotrods, twisting, discos, drugs and sex. 'One Night' was a carnal hymn to liberation. A song about the freedom to do whatever you wanted to do, to ride your machine without being hassled by The Man, to get loaded, to have a good time. To be free, at last.

This night, The Night, 'One Night' was His Song.

When he'd finished he could just about stand, staggering around to the front of the stage to sing to the tape of 'Memories'. He splashed down between two girls, Eros soaked to the black vinyl bone, giving it all of what breath hadn't yet evaporated from within. He ended the song just about on his feet. The final bell.

Ladies and gentlemen! The winner, by a clear knockout, and the new reigning Rock 'N' Roll Champion Of The World – Elvis Presley!

Then weightless once more, victorious, exhausted, wobbling through the heat and the noise to the unlit horizon off the studio floor from whence he came.

★

'He *came!*'

The gasp was Bill Belew's. The cum was Elvis'.

They'd carried him the last steps back to the dressing room, like a man who really had gone 12 rounds with Ali, ten of those bracing rope-a-dope. At first they thought it was just the leather steaming him alive like a human lobster. The underside of his jacket was sodden. Bill only had a short time to clean and dry it for the next show. They hadn't a spare. Then Bill collected his leather pants. They, too, were drenched in sweat. And something stickier. Bill poked a spot near the groin then held his blobbed fingertips to his face. The unmistakable milky white of life essence.

'Oh... my... God!'

Somewhere between three Rusty-romping 'Baby, What You Want Me To Do's Elvis had consummated himself.

It took Bill's whole wardrobe team and every spare hairdryer to clean everything in time for the second show, scheduled for 8 pm but knocked back due to the late running of the first. By then Elvis was showered, pilled, rehydrated, his hair restyled and his leather squeaking ready to be sluiced anew, knowing they were expecting the impossible. For a man having thus been resurrected to be asked to resurrect again. To once more be as Zeus' thunderbolt and strike the same spot, twice, in a single evening.

Impossible.

The band resumed their places on the stage, black towels now placed at their feet to dampen the overwhelming rattle of their boot-stomps, Hog Ears since swapping his upturned guitar for an empty case. The second audience was bigger, with more friends and more fans who'd successfully applied to NBC's advance ads before the Colonel could hijack any more tickets. There were more girls, younger, prettier, giddier, to be herded tight around the stage, including Elvis' 'little sis', Pat Parry, the English hairdresser who'd hung out with his Angels at his homes in Bel-Air.

'I've had a sneak preview of what is going to happen here...'

Robert the D.J. was finishing his warm up.

'May I say that you are going to *totally* have your minds blown...'

The low hum of yearning.

'Mr Elvis Presley!'

And out he slithered. Oestrogen Hiroshima. Sobs, mewls and high-pitched squalls past the pitch of sanity. It was the leather that did it. And the body, the bulge, the hair, the lips, the face, the eyes, the tongue, the cheeks and the sex beyond sex beyond sex beyond sex. 'Oh my God,' a girl whimpered, 'I'm gonna be sick!' Sick in the presence of the impossible. Time double-took and déjà vu combusted that the universe dare be this blissfully ridiculous.

The second show was even better.

It was better because the girls screamed like lovers in their throes and the harder they screamed the harder he threw them, slamming, throttling, slapping, tugging, strapping, biting, spanking, thrilling. The bolder ones passed him hankies which he returned freshly anointed with his saintly sweat, locking them back in their handbags, now keepers of sacrosanct Turin Shrouds to be sniffed, sucked, rubbed and worshipped in demonic privacy. And all undressed him in waking dreams of drooling-eyed madness, breathing as if already breached, ruined by his ruthless basilisk beauty.

It was better because he'd already shaken loose, and the looser he shook the sexier, wilder and funnier he vibrated. He dusted off the same old gags he'd used seven years ago on stage in Memphis on 'Elvis Presley Day', about 'Heartburn Motel' and *'Are you lonesome tonight, does your hair look a fright?'* Someone shouted a request for 'It's Now Or Never' and instead he hitched a wedgie in

'MacArthur Park', wibbling in the style of *Laugh-In*'s Tiny Tim. He hoped Steve got the joke, and just to make sure he did, he wibbled it again.

It was better because he played the same songs just as fierce and new ones even fiercer. He still sang 'One Night' like he was slow grinding Bardot and he still sang 'Baby, What You Want Me To Do', twice, both times burning Rusty up the Strip, round the Hollywood hills and back again. He still put the X-rated into Xmas with 'Blue Christmas', this time with an extra cracker of festive filth in Leiber and Stoller's 'Santa Claus Is Back In Town'. And then, from an infrared nowhere in the spectrum between Mars and Memphis visible only to his genius, he grasped 'Tiger Man'.

It was another old Sun record, a novelty Tarzan blues first recorded by Rufus Thomas Jr. in '53, the year before his own Sun debut. But how he grabbed it, right then, was a mystery. A mystery because musically and rhythmically it was also 'Mystery Train', Elvis' fifth, and best, Sun single which he might have easily played instead. But he chose to sing 'Tiger Man'. The sex roar of *'the king of the jungle'*. It wasn't even his song. He'd make it so.

He sang it, he screamed it, he possessed it and it possessed him with sulphur, blood and lust. Lucifer Christ, the High Executioner, still had one last bullet in his chamber. Cocked and aimed in the den of Perugia Way on a testy August night in 1965. The last words of the condemned: 'Why don't you go back to making rock 'n' roll records?'

Try this for a Memphis cherry-bomb, motherfucker!

'Cross my path, you'll take your whooooole life in your hands.'

The righting of the last wrong. His Revenger's Comedy was complete.

Even the closing 'Memories' was better because the girls either side of him, eyes agape and mouths agog, dribbled as one with his golden sweat, quivering Magdalenes at the feet of their risen saviour. A vista ripe for the sable tips of Raphael.

Just as before, he ended it on his feet, but when it was over instead of stumbling back to the dressing room he lingered there, smiling, nodding, purring, radiating, feeling. A feeling he hadn't felt for so long it would have hurt him to remember the last time he had. But it no longer mattered. Not now it was back again. The same feeling. Like saying 'hello' again to an old, old friend.

The feeling of what it was to be Elvis Presley.

THE ASCENSION

The next day, a Friday, was a new dawn. A new dawn for Elvis, for what remained of the Sixties, and for rock 'n' roll, separating its mortal past from a future of infinite reincarnations: where no fall is fatal and the dead may rise again; where crowns are lost in one battle to be reclaimed in another; where commercial prisons exist only to be broken out of; where yesterday's peach-canned Ken® is tomorrow's King of the Jungle. History had been his judge and would forever judge him on last night alone, regardless of how little would make it to the final edit. Even a little glimpse was glimpse enough from the mountaintop. The Promised Land of black leather, Echosonic twang, 'Baby, What You Want Me To Do', sweat, sex and 'One Night'. That was the Comeback.

But in the meantime, he still had a TV special to finish.

That morning Elvis was back on Stage 4 to film the gospel sequence, dressed more sinner than saint in a burgundy suit and scarlet neckerchief complementing the red pallet of its set: a half-built church with scaffolding rigs and wheelbarrows loaded with bricks around a mock art-nouveau stained glass window. Gene had been asked to design something appropriately religious with 'a negro feel' and instinctively thought of the 1963 film *Lillies Of The Field*, where Sidney Poitier played a drifter coerced by nuns to build them a chapel in the middle of the Arizona desert, hence the bricks and barrows. The scene opened with choreographer

Claude Thompson twisting spotlit contortions to Darlene Love's 'Somewhere I Feel Like A Motherless Child', prelude to the Reverend Presley's sultry sermon joined by Darlene and her fellow Blossoms, climaxing in the frenzy of 'Saved' as dancers leapt asunder in born-again convulsions of flailing limbs and flashing knickers.

The clothes, and the morals, loosened up that afternoon for another section of the 'Guitar Man' epic where Elvis, back in blue denims, had to mime 'Let Yourself Go'. The minimal script had mentioned only accompanying 'girls' and an 'interior set'.

The 'girls', now gathered, were a feather-boaed harem of pink heels, slit-skirts, chain belts, bikini tops, bare bellies, naked thighs, pebble-dashed in rouge, lashes like rakes, twiddling French cigarettes, flicking curtain-tassel earrings, chewing gum and drooping grapes, one of them flicking the pages of a Supergirl* comic.

The 'interior set' was *A Walk On The Wild Side* meets Hanna-Barbera: a tart-red Babylon of plantation shutters, chaise longues, ceiling fans and a brass bed possibly sprung for more than sleeping in.

The set was clearly a bordello. The girls, evidently, hookers.

Gene had designed it to be a bordello. Steve and the whole crew knew it was a bordello, just as the dancing girls knew they were playing hookers, including Susan who'd been cast to play the innocent 'virgin hooker' who catches Elvis' eye once he's done bumping off every other hipbone. They'd just been clever enough never to use the words on the page.

---

* The March 1966 D.C. *Action Comics* Vol 1. No. 335, featuring 'The Supergirl From Krypton', 'The Cave-Girl Of Steel', 'Supergirl's First Romance', 'Supergirl's Super-Pet', 'The Origin Of Super-Horse', 'Supergirl's Two Sets Of Parents' etc.

It took a not-nearly-so-clever NBC executive to blab the word 'bordello' on a memo to the sponsors to curse a bother of suits from Singer scampering onto the studio floor, unspooling their bobbins at the sight of so much muck and brass. Their concern, so they told Steve, was purely a professional matter of haberdashery: too much flesh on display and not enough stitched fabric. Bill and his wardrobe team had to quickly embroider agreeable solutions with extra scraps of chiffon before the suits from Singer, apparently satisfied, allowed taping to continue. The bordello remained a bordello, the hookers, a little less saucy, still remained hookers and Elvis remained happily entwined with Susan long after Steve had cried the last 'Cut!'

Saturday's main feature was the Return of the Black Leather Avenger. The arena segment: live before another studio audience, back in the same flesh-roasting suit on the same square underlit-stage, still in the round surrounded by fans on three sides but with the band and orchestra from the Western Recorders session taking up the fourth. Once again there'd be two tapings staggered at 6 and 8 pm, both running late, both before the same audience, every bleacher packed to capacity. Only this time Elvis would be alone, and on his feet.

He walked out with the fearless gait of the conquering hero to the same chorus of perfumed bedlam. Somewhere in its blitzkrieg of applause were the hands of Priscilla: in all the years she'd been with him, it was her first Elvis Presley concert. As Scotty had gone back to Memphis with his Gibson he'd borrowed a new guitar – a red Hagström Viking II – from the orchestra's Al Casey, more as a prop since it looked better than it sounded and no instrument was ever going to sound as divine as Scotty's humbucking Excalibur.

He warmed up by chopping a quick 'Heartbreak Hotel', then a snatch of 'One Night', before fireballing into the main medley of hits.

The running order had been shuffling all week, finally losing the two most recent contenders, 'U.S. Male' and a planned bookending 'A Little Less Conversation'. That left just eight breakneck skids through 'Heartbreak Hotel', 'Hound Dog', 'All Shook Up', 'Can't Help Falling In Love', 'Jailhouse Rock', 'Don't Be Cruel', 'Blue Suede Shoes' and 'Love Me Tender', nearly all crashing under the weight of so much unnecessary brass, strings and choral harmonies. To look at him Elvis was still the black knight of Shake Rag, but to listen was to hear the jackpot jangling excess of Las Vegas. Exactly as Tom Jones, in his Flamingo watusis and ancient Welsh wisdom, had prophesised. This really was what an Elvis could be in 1968.

In the eyes of every woman in the room he still looked like the most tempting proposition in the history of white knuckles. Priscilla knew he was. But her birthday watch was still ticking. So did Rusty, who wasn't there to hear Elvis spontaneously break into Their Song yet again, grunting 'Man! That's dirty!' as the band followed his lead, the girls wobbling ringside daring themselves to reach out and touch his leather as if afraid the faintest contact might zap them to a too-too-satisfied crisp.

The first time when he sang 'Love Me Tender' he caught Priscilla's eye and she his, and Cupid snivelled to remember a musical cigarette box of Christmases past. But she left to keep a charity dinner appointment before the next show when he changed the words to *'You have made my life a wreck'*, and Cupid belly-laughed, as he did.

The second show he was giddier throughout, yelling 'Moby Dick!' with his mic stand like a harpoon, whinnying Tiny Tim's 'Tiptoe Through The Tulips' and another absurd 'MacArthur Park'.

'Mah boy, mah boy,' he chuckled at himself. 'They're gonna put me away for a while.'

The two performances lasted barely half an hour apiece, ending in different pick-up shots for the big 'Guitar Man' medley, the second bringing in Gene's 'neon highway' design of coloured strip lights on a black background vanishing to a fake horizon, before the finale of a lip-synched 'If I Can Dream'. It was the first time his fans had heard the song. It demolished them, twice.

Their tears told Elvis everything he already knew.

They had only the Sunday left to finish every other scene, the original three-day schedule having already overrun.

The first two were a quick couple of links in the 'Guitar Man' medley with Elvis in blue denims on the previous night's neon highway.

The next set was Gene's most ambitious, paying homage to his beginnings in television working on *The Judy Garland Show* where its star performed before her name, 'JUDY', spelled out in towering block capitals made up of stacked lightbulbs. It was vintage Broadway, but so was Gene. His version used strings of red bulbs to spell 'ELVIS' in letters 24-feet high, held up by a rig of platforms allowing Allan and Chris' pitch of '100 Elvises' to stand shaking guitars in silhouette behind him. In rehearsal, the rig wobbled like a house of cards as soon as anyone moved. Not wanting the deaths of 100 Elvises on his hands, Gene modified the design to a stronger inverted T-shape and had it chained to the ceiling for extra stability. It still wobbled.

In execution the 100 Elvises only stretched to 89, mostly dancers, extras and any spare, remotely slim male who could follow Jaime Rogers' simple choreography for the show's 'Trouble'/ 'Guitar Man' opening gauntlet. Elvis wore a black shirt and red kerchief, sizzling into the lens in close-up, bayoneting the air with

Casey's red guitar, his name skyscraped in lights and his body echoed in 89 shaking shadowy clones. The Warrior King and his Shake Rag infantry.

It was *Jailhouse Rock* meets 'Jumpin' Jack Flash'. Elvis meets 1968. He looked like he belonged there.

The last scenes were all pieces of the main production number. Denim Elvis in a back alleyway with one of the bordello's pink madams, then more 'Trouble' progressing from a dive bar saloon to a discotheque and finally a supper club, each involving its own small set and change of jacket, from gold to black to trimmed velvet.

The saloon was Tanya's big moment to impress with her 'Little Egypt' belly-dance routine, trying, and failing, to keep the costume jewel from popping out of her navel as Elvis laughed 'mah belly, mah belly!' and mumbled fond memories of seeing Las Vegas's topless girl group, the Ladybirds.

In the discotheque, Elvis fudged a lyric, the camera catching a loud, comical 'Shit!' He fought back giggles for the next four takes. Until slate number 1015. *'So don't you mess around with me.'* They were the last words he sang. The special was done.

But the slate that really counted wasn't the last, but one of the first filmed earlier in the day in front of Gene's giant glowing red 'ELVIS', the letters floating in space like Belshazzar's feast. Slate 918. His third attempt singing live over the backing track of 'If I Can Dream'.

Elvis wore a blood-red neckscarf, white boots and Bill's specially designed white suit dominated by a double-breasted frock coat with flat Napoleonic lapels. He looked luminescent, as if beamed in from a higher plain. So white that Elvis, so bronze, appeared Cherokee, Navajo, Apache, Patuxet, Mexican, Puerto-Rican, Pakistani, Bangladeshi, Sri Lankan, Fijian, Bolivian, Syrian,

Egyptian, Moroccan, anything but a Southern Caucasian. A coloured man singing his song of freedom. Except he more than sang it. He shone it.

On the last note he spread his arms out in a crucifix then levered them like the wings of an angel, ready to be beamed back up again. Seven days earlier he'd sung 'If I Can Dream' writhing on a studio floor in deathly darkness. But this version, *the* version, was all light. The light of life and resurrection.

Elvis would never have to sing it again.

DECEMBER 3, 1968

The Tuesday following Thanksgiving. Three weeks away, America's Christmas countdown has begun. Displays in every department store window and gift guides in every newspaper: for him, a La-Z-Boy recliner rocker, valet stand, loafers, turtleneck sweater, electric shoe polisher and a 12-gauge shotgun; for her, a three-speed mixer, a quilted duster, a cruet set, an electric can opener, a Mince-O-Matic and a 'birdie-egg-blue' peignoir ensemble.

The days now getting shorter, and colder.

In the White House, Johnson's last month in the Oval office before the inauguration of Richard Nixon – the president-elect who could've been Bobby – who will soon change its drapes from landslide-white to tricky-gold and the nation from denial to despair.

In Atlanta, Coretta, the widow of Dr Martin Luther King Jr. assassinated not eight months ago, is being wiretapped by the Federal Bureau of Investigation concerned over her potential influence upon the growing anti-war movement.

In Vietnam, the U.S. military count beyond their 16,000th body bag that year.

In Florida, NASA prepares to send Americans into orbit for the second time in six months.

In pop, Diana Ross & the Supremes at number one with 'Love Child' having just nah-nah-ed off the Beatles' 'Hey Jude'. The witch-wailing *Cheap Thrills* of Janis Joplin's Big Brother & the Holding Company the number one album, Jimi's *Electric Ladyland* only a slight return behind with its version of Bob's 'All Along The Watchtower'. The week the Rolling Stones lay on their *Beggars Banquet* and the Monkees give *Head*.

In cinemas, Jane Fonda naked in space and Steve McQueen jumping Frisco street-lights in a Highland Green Ford Mustang. And for those that still care, Elvis Presley in another bucket of bland popcorn called *Live A Little, Love A Little*.

Still very much the 1960s.

For the work-whacked, slipper-footed, chop-fed and couch-anchored, at 8.30 pm they have a choice of entertainment. Red Skelton as 'Willie Lump Lump' singing and spoofing with Jane Powell. The cat burgling Robert Wagner in *It Takes A Thief*. An old black and white *Perry Mason* repeat. Comedy and chat with Merv Griffin. A documentary on African horticulture.

Or stick with channel 4, the sitcom *Julia* starring Diahann Carroll, until the stroke of nine. When in full living colour of the NBC peacock, the resurrection will be televised...

★

'Singer presents Elvis! *Starring Elvis Presley in his first TV special. His first personal appearance on TV in nearly 10 years brought to you by Singer – maker of the world's finest sewing machines and other fine products for home and industry. What's new for tomorrow is at Singer today!'*

★

In Los Angeles, Steve was watching at home.

It had been a tough five months since slate 1015. So tough Binder-Howe were no longer in business.

After finishing *Elvis*, Bones suggested they ought to expand the company with a new partner. Binder-Howe-Geffen. Their old pal, David, the one Steve first told about Laura Nyro, who now managed her. That Geffen.

A breakfast meeting was arranged at the Beverly Hills Hotel so all three could discuss the terms of the merger. Steve arrived on time. The time he'd been told to arrive. He found Bones and David were already there, already breakfasted, already an hour into negotiations without him. Steve hung around for as long as it took him to suggest where they could both stick the remaining danishes, then left. Binder-Howe was dissolved that afternoon.

He'd lost Bones, but he still had the feature film. The murder mystery, the one he'd been working on since before Finkel even offered him Elvis, the one being driven by producer Walter Wanger, his first since *Cleopatra*. The same Walter Wanger who died of a heart attack just two weeks ago. That Wanger.

'If you're looking for trouble...'

He smiled at Elvis on screen. Trouble. That had been Steve's story of '68, all right. Doyle Lott. Plymouth. Bones. Wanger. And trouble spelt C-o-l-o-n-e-l.

Steve had thought the clap of slate 1015 would be the end of it.

The Colonel still wanted Christmas.

The filming was over, the sets dismantled, the crew gone home, the lights turned out, the tapes edited, the sound mixed, the end titles added, all ready for broadcast.

The Colonel still wanted Christmas.

If the Colonel didn't get Christmas then NBC, as the Colonel reminded them, were contractually obliged to remake another in its place. 'A Christmas one.'

In all the footage on tape there was only one usable Christmas song. 'Blue Christmas'. Elvis had sung it in each of the sit-down shows. Adding it would mean losing 'Tiger Man' which to Steve felt like the Mona Lisa losing its smile. But it was all the compensation he and NBC had to offer. The Colonel accepted. 'Blue Christmas' would suffice. 'One li'l ol' Christmas song' is all he'd ever asked for in the first place. It was a matter of psychopathic pride.

Just as the Colonel put Christmas back in, the suits from Singer took the bordello back out. The network censor had passed the scene but when the corporate sewing circle saw the edit their bobbins unspooled yet again. The whole sequence – Susan, Supergirl and 'Let Yourself Go' – had to be chopped from the 'Guitar Man' medley. Steve had won his *Petula* fight with Plymouth and Chrysler, but Singer and their parental weight of General Electric was a sponsor spat too far. The bordello joined 'Tiger Man' on the lost riches of the cutting room floor. Even without the interference of the Colonel and the sponsor Steve had too much material and not enough airtime. He was forced to make further cuts, also sacrificing most of 'It Hurts Me'. In all nearly a day's worth of shooting had been wasted on scenes that would never make it to air. He pleaded with NBC and Singer to buy an extra half hour to make it a feature-length 90 minute special. They couldn't.

'There's somethin' wrong with ma lip!'

But Steve only had to look at his TV screen.

'I got news for you baby, I did 29 pictures like that.'

It had still been worth it.

It had been worth it if only to see Elvis' face when Steve screened it for him that fall. He watched it twice, once with his Angels yahooing behind him, once alone with Steve. When it finished the second time he turned to Steve and said, 'I'm never going to sing a song that I don't believe in any more.'

But it was the look as he'd said it. It wasn't just happiness, or pride, or defiance, or determination. A look as ageless as it was euphoric. The look of a man set free, at last.

There hadn't been a wrap party, but now the edit was complete Bill suggested they have one that night back at his apartment. When Elvis heard he asked if he could come along. Steve, ecstatic, offered to drive him there in his yellow Ford convertible, the Angels following behind in the stately Lincoln Continental. They cruised down Highland, past traffic heading for the Hollywood Bowl, Elvis in Steve's passenger seat, the roof down, a skin-pinching hallucination in the wing mirror of every gridlocked driver. Steve felt he was hallucinating too. It was like chauffeuring Jesus.

The two cars were the first to arrive outside Bill's apartment block. Steve led Elvis and his Angels up the stairs and rang the bell. There was no answer. They rang again. Silence.

Steve started to panic. Maybe he'd taken down the wrong address. He needed to find a telephone and call Bill. Elvis told him he had a phone in his car. In 1968 only Elvis *would* have a phone in his car.

Steve rang the number. It picked up. 'Hi, this is Bill...'

An answering machine.

Elvis shrugged an embarrassed smile. 'I'd probably better be going.' Steve nodded. Then Elvis took something from his pocket and placed it in Steve's hand. 'Here.' It was a piece of paper with a scrawled number. 'That's my direct line,' he hushed. 'You keep in touch, man. Call me, anytime you need.'

Steve stuck out a hand. 'Thanks, Elvis.' They shook. 'I will.'

Elvis gave one last wave from the backseat before his Lincoln faded into the new night of endless possibilities.

With slapstick timing, Bill and the rest of the crew arrived only a minute later. They still celebrated even without Elvis, whose number stayed folded in Steve's pocket. Until the day came when he decided to unfold it and try the number. Somebody who definitely wasn't Elvis answered. Steve asked them to tell Elvis that he'd rung. They said they would. Steve always did wonder if his message had even been passed on.

The black leather Lazarus pulsated on screen.

'Mah, boy, mah boy.'

They never spoke again.

★

'You're about to see the most gifted gift of them all – the Golden Touch & Sew sewing machine from Singer! The machine every woman dreams of owning… It's the most gifted gift you can give or get!'

★

In Snowland, the Colonel didn't need to watch it.

He'd gotten what he wanted. A Christmas song up Bindle's ass, his first slice of $1 million from NBC and his name in the *TV Guide* feature headline. The picture was of Elvis but the print screamed 'The Indomitable Snowman'. Most of its seven pages were a profile of the High Potentate 'born of carnival folk'. The foot-long hot dogs, the dancing fowl. It was all there in glossy black and white. He'd also made RCA take out full page ads, one an eight-year-old photo of the Colonel dressed up as Santa Claus next to Elvis. 'Season's Greetings from Elvis and the Colonel'. Another yellow snowball of frozen piss in Bindle's face. The magazine had wanted Elvis on that week's cover too, but the Colonel named too high a price. They had to pick another star of another special airing instead. Fate inked the rollers and irony turned the presses. The issue of *TV Guide* the week *Elvis* was broadcast had Rusty on its cover.

Elvis still won the ratings – over 40 per cent of the viewing public, the biggest of any TV special that year. None of it had been the Colonel's doing but all of it was the Colonel's blessing. The six figure offers were already making his billfold purr. More television. The London Palladium. Or a new $60 million luxury hotel being built in Las Vegas, the biggest on the Strip. The International. Stick the boy on stage, turn on the hotplate, make him dance 57 shows in four weeks, lie back and watch it snow half a million in greenbacks. Maybe. He'd just need to sleep on it and weigh up the zeroes first.

Either way the future was the Colonel's gold-plated chuck-a-luck to spin however he wanted. He almost owed Bindle and Finkel a favour. Almost.

His cigar belched an ashy laugh. '*Sonofabitch!*'

It was back in early July. A few days after he'd cleaned out his closet at NBC and sent the William Morris agents with their palace guard uniforms back to the hire shop. He had a chauffeur drive him home the 100 miles from Hollywood to Palm Springs. It was evening when he arrived back at his Las Palmas estate, the silhouettes of tropical trees against the cobalt blue twilight, the limousine winding onto North Vista Vespero towards the distant red glow. A glow that grew redder and brighter as they turned into his driveway of number 1166. Redder and brighter still once the Colonel stepped out of the car so he could see it properly, searching for the generator that was making the low fuzzy hum above the faint chirp of crickets, spotting it near a border hedge, his eyes tracing the cable leading to the five 24-foot-high letters outlined in red light bulbs illuminating his lawn. The ones designed by Gene, spelling 'ELVIS'.

The psychopath Andreas Cornelis van Kuijk threw back his head and howled his stony heart out to the desert stars above.

Finkel got the cane.

★

'*Who's the gift for?*'

'*It's a gift for me! A record album. A special stereo album. Singer presents Elvis. It's only one dollar 95 cents and you can get it only at your Singer centre. You gotta hear it! It's really a swell gift!*'

★

In Beverly Hills, Elvis was watching at home with Priscilla amongst the mock-Regency splendour and matrimonial debris of their Hillcrest TV lounge.

He was still working in Hollywood fulfilling the last of his movie contracts. There'd been a tinned-spaghetti western called *Charro!*, with a bearded Elvis pretending to be the Man With No Name. It dragged like a boring episode of *The High Chaparral* but for the first time in 29 films he didn't have to sing any songs, only the title theme. Now he was making his last for MGM, a weird period musical set in rural Iowa in 1927 that had been called *Chautauqua* until somebody pointed out nobody could pronounce it when it became *The Trouble With Girls*. He was handcuffed to one more in the New Year, his last as part of the NBC deal about an inner-city doctor and some nuns. But these would be the last three scripts he ever had to learn. From now on, he only had one part to play.

The role was spelled out for him when Steve called him to see the final edit of the TV special back in the fall. It was funny. All his life he'd been watching people on screen. More often at the Memphian, sat in his usual seat, front middle, surrounded by his Angels around him, Gary Pepper at the end of the row, local fans behind him, Krystal burgers, fries and shakes beside him, hollering up to the projectionist whenever he wanted to run a reel again. Watching Charlton Heston as Moses, Peter Fonda as Blues, Marlon Brando as Terry Malloy, James Dean as Jim Stark, Kirk Douglas as Spartacus or Peter Sellers as Dr Strangelove. He'd been humbled by each and every performance. But he'd never experienced anything quite like this.

It was damn near as perfect a part as Elvis had ever seen. And here it was again, on the same home TV screen he'd usually watch *Laugh-In* and *Star Trek*. It awed him. It moved him. It *was* him. All those years of peach-canned agony, whining about 'branching out' and 'somethin' more serious'. When all along, the greatest role of his life was staring him straight in his double-fuck face every time he passed a mirror.

'Mein Führer! I can walk!'

Himself.

★

'Wouldn't someone you know love a Singer big screen colour TV, or a Singer portable colour TV?'

'Very reasonably priced too! This portable − only $298!'

★

In Memphis, Gary Pepper was watching at home, the Chevrolet Impala Elvis had given him two Christmases ago still parked outside on Eva Street having never been driven.

The biggest Tanker that ever lived, Gary Pepper naturally thought it was the best hour of TV he'd seen in his life. Until the next hour. Straight after *Elvis* finished at 10, NBC broadcast another music special starring his and Elvis' favourite 'chick', Brigitte Bardot, rollicking on a Harley in thigh boots and being all sassy in a beret with a tommy gun like Bonnie Parker. Gary Pepper just about collapsed out of his chair. The sexiest man in the world today, followed by the sexiest woman. It just *had* to be the sexiest two hours in the whole goddamn history of television!

He really couldn't wait to tell Elvis how much he'd loved his show. *All* of it. To think it had been ten years since they sent him

323

into the Army. And now look at him – 1968, and *still* the King of Rock 'n' Roll. It boggled Gary Pepper's mind to think what he'd be doing in another ten years. By 1978, Elvis would probably be president. 'President Presley!' Man! That'd be *the most*! He'd need to tell 'the Big E' that one soon as he got home. It had to be any day now. Elvis always spent Christmas at Graceland. Meaning more midnights at the Memphian, sitting at the end of Elvis' row, laughing at his jokes, clapping whenever he clapped, watching the same reel over and over and over again. Gary Pepper sure missed those nights. Hell, he just missed his pal.

Everything was always so much better when Elvis came back.

TRANSMISSION

SINGER PRESENTS *ELVIS*
TUESDAY, DECEMBER 3, 1968
9.00 – 10.00 PM EST, CHANNEL 4 (NBC)

1. Show Opener
'TROUBLE' (Jerry Leiber/Mike Stoller)
'GUITAR MAN' (Jerry Reed)

★FIRST COMMERCIAL BREAK★

2. Informal #1
'LAWDY, MISS CLAWDY' (Lloyd Price)
'BABY, WHAT YOU WANT ME TO DO' (Jimmy Reed)

3. Arena Medley
'HEARTBREAK HOTEL' (Mae Axton/Tommy Durden/Elvis Presley)
'HOUND DOG' (Jerry Leiber/Mike Stoller)
'ALL SHOOK UP' (Otis Blackwell/Elvis Presley)
'CAN'T HELP FALLING IN LOVE' (Hugo Peretti/Luigi Creatore/George Weiss)
'JAILHOUSE ROCK' (Jerry Leiber/Mike Stoller)
'BLUE SUEDE SHOES' (Carl Perkins)
'DON'T BE CRUEL' (Otis Blackwell/Elvis Presley)
'LOVE ME TENDER' (Vera Matson/Elvis Presley)

★SECOND COMMERCIAL BREAK★

Elvis dialogue (taken from first informal sit-down show)

4. Gospel Medley
'SOMETIMES I FEEL LIKE A MOTHERLESS CHILD' (Trad. arr Earl Brown) ‡
'WHERE COULD I GO BUT TO THE LORD' (J.B. Coats)
'UP ABOVE MY HEAD' (Trad. arr Earl Brown)
'SAVED' (Jerry Leiber/Mike Stoller)
‡ *Lead vocal by Darlene Love.*

★THIRD COMMERCIAL BREAK★

5. Informal #2
'BABY, WHAT YOU WANT ME TO DO' (Jimmy Reed)
'BLUE CHRISTMAS' (Billy Hayes/Jay Johnson)
('TIGER MAN' (Sam Burns/Joe Hill Lewis))★
'ONE NIGHT' (Dave Bartholomew/Pearl King/Anita Steiman)
'MEMORIES' (Billy Strange/Mac Davis)
★ *Replaced 'Blue Christmas' in later non-seasonal broadcast, August 17, 1969.*

★FOURTH COMMERCIAL BREAK★

6. Guitar Man Medley

	Scenario
'NOTHINGVILLE' (Billy Strange/Mac Davis)	Road
('GUITAR MAN' (Jerry Reed))★	(Alley)★
('LET YOURSELF GO' (Joy Byers))★	(Bordello)★
'GUITAR MAN' (Jerry Reed)	Road
'BIG BOSS MAN' (Al Smith/Luther Dixon)	Amusement Pier
('IT HURTS ME' (Joy Byers/Charles E. Daniels))★	(Amusement Pier)★
'GUITAR MAN' (Jerry Reed)	Road
'LITTLE EGYPT' (Jerry Leiber/Mike Stoller)	Saloon
'TROUBLE' (Jerry Leiber/Mike Stoller)	Saloon/Disco/Club/Arena
'GUITAR MAN' (Jerry Reed)	Arena (with Road)

★ *Cut from original broadcast; only an edited section of the 'It Hurts Me' sequence featuring Jaime Rogers' karate dance was included, not the full song.*

★FIFTH COMMERCIAL BREAK★

7. Finale
'IF I CAN DREAM' (Earl Brown)

8. End Credits
'LET YOURSELF GO (Instrumental)' (Joy Byers)

Production Coordinators JOE ESPOSITO, LAMAR FIKE, TOM DISKIN
Costume Design BILL BELEW
Art Direction GENE McAVOY
Choreography JAIME ROGERS, CLAUDE THOMPSON
Special Lyrics & Vocal Arrangements EARL BROWN
Musical Direction & Arrangements BILLY GOLDENBERG
Music Production BONES HOWE
Writers ALLAN BLYE, CHRIS BEARDE
Producer & Director STEVE BINDER
Executive Producer BOB FINKEL

A Production of TERAM, INC PRODUCTION
and BINDER/HOWE PRODUCTIONS, INC.

Original soundtrack album available on RCA VICTOR
Monaural LP and Stereo 8 Track Cartridge Tape

BIBLIOGRAPHY

Adler, David, *The Life And Cuisine Of Elvis Presley*, Smith Gryphon, 1995

Angell, Callie, *Andy Warhol Screen Tests*, Abrams, 2006

Apollo, Fred, *The Fame Game: A Hollywood Agent Looks Back*, Xlibris Corporation, 2009

Babitz, Eve, *Eve's Hollywood*, New York Review Books, 2015

Bartel, Pauline, *Reel Elvis!*, Taylor Publishing, 1994

Belafonte, Harry with Michael Schnayerson, *My Song – A Memoir Of Art, Race And Defiance*, Canongate, 2012

Benner, Joseph S., *The Impersonal Life*, DeVorss & Co., 1983

Bernardo, Mark P., *Elvis Presley Memphis*, Roaring Forties, 2012

Bianculli, David, *Dangerously Funny – The Uncensored Story Of The Smothers Brothers Comedy Hour*, Touchstone, 2009

Binder, Steve, *'68 At 40 Retrospective,* JAT Publishing, 2010

Brown, Peter and Pat Broeske, *Down At The End Of Lonely Street: The Life And Death Of Elvis Presley,* Heinemann, 1997

Burns, Rebecca, *Burial For A King – Martin Luther King Jr.'s Funeral And The Week That Transformed Atlanta And Rocked The Nation*, Scribner, 2011

Cairns, Steve and George R. White, 'The King And Hi-Fi' article in *Record Collector*, Issue 298, June 2004

Charlesworth, Chris, *Caught in A Trap: The Kidnapping Of Elvis*, Red Planet Publishing, 2017

Coons, Virginia, 'Elvis TV Special' article in *Elvis Monthly*, No.106, November 1968

BIBLIOGRAPHY

Cosgrove, Stuart, *Memphis 68: The Tragedy Of Southern Soul*, Polygon, 2017

Davis Jr., Sammy, *Hollywood In A Suitcase*, Star, 1981

Dundy, Elaine, *Elvis And Gladys*, University Press of Mississippi, 2004

Emerson, Ken, *Always Magic In The Air: The Bomp And Brilliance Of The Brill Building Era*, Fourth Estate, 2006

Esposito, Joe and Elena Oumano, *Good Rockin' Tonight: 20 Years On The Road And On The Town With Elvis,* Simon & Schuster, 1994

Finstad, Suzanne, *Child Bride: Priscilla Presley – From Elvis's Teen Lover To Michael Jackson's Mother In Law,* Arrow, 1998

Fletcher, Tony, 'Visit to Memphis' article in *Elvis Monthly*, Vol.6 No.4, April 1965

Flippo, Chet, *Your Cheatin' Heart – A Biography Of Hank Williams*, Simon & Schuster, 1981

Folsom, J. Paul et al, *Physician's Desk Reference To Pharmaceutical Specialities And Biologicals*, Medical Economics Inc., 16th and 19th editions, 1961, 1965

Fortas, Alan with Alanna Nash, *Elvis, From Memphis To Hollywood*, Aurum, 2008

Gaar, Gillian G., *Return Of The King: Elvis Presley's Great Comeback*, Jawbone, 2010

Geller, Larry and Joel Spector with Patricia Romanowski, *If I Can Dream,* Century, 1989

Gerber, Gail with Tom Lisanti, *Trippin' With Terry Southern: What I Think I Remember*, McFarland & Company, 2009

Gibran, Khalil, *The Prophet*, Vintage Classics, 2013

Gordon, Robert, *The King On The Road,* Hamlyn, 1996

Guralnick, Peter, *Careless Love: The Unmaking Of Elvis Presley,* Back Bay, 1999

Guralnick, Peter, *Last Train To Memphis: The Rise Of Elvis Presley,* Back Bay, 1994

Hartman, Kent, *The Wrecking Crew*, Thomas Dunne Books, 2012

Henning, Susan, *'68*, Rainbow Rhapsody Press, 2008

Hoey, Michael A., *Elvis' Favourite Director: The Amazing 52-Year Career Of Norman Taurog*, Bear Manor Media, 2014

Hohn, Lou, 'Very Dodgem' article in *Elvis Monthly*, Series 4, No. 2, February 1963

Hopkins, Jerry, *Elvis*, Warner Paperback Library, 1972

Hutchins, Chris and Peter Thompson, *Elvis & Lennon*, Smith Gryphon, 1996

Innes, Winifred, 'Elvis TV Spectacular' article in *Elvis Monthly*, No.104, September 1968

Jones, Tom, *Over The Top And Back*, Michael Joseph, 2015

Jorgensten, Ernst, *Elvis: A Life In Music – The Complete Recording Sessions*, St Martin's Press, 1998

Jorgensten, Ernst and Peter Guralnick, *Elvis: Day by Day*, Ballantine Books, 1999

Juanico, June, *Elvis: In The Twilight Of Memory*, Little, Brown, 1997

Keogh, Pamela Clarke, *Elvis Presley: The Man. The Life. The Legend.*, Atria Books, 2004

Kiedrowski, Thomas, *Andy Warhol's New York City*, The Little Bookroom, 2011

King, Coretta Scott, *The Words Of Martin Luther King*, Fount, 1985

Klein, George with Chuck Crisafulli, *Elvis – My Best Man: Radio Days, Rock 'N' Roll Nights And My Lifelong Friendship With Elvis Presley*, Virgin, 2010

Kort, Michele, *Soul Picnic – The Music And Passion Of Laura Nyro*, St Martin's Griffin, 2003

Leary, Timothy with Ralph Metzner and Richard Alpert, *The Psychedelic Experience: A Manual Based On The Tibetan Book Of The Dead*, Penguin Modern Classics, 2008

Leiber, Jerry and Mike Stoller with David Ritz, *Hound Dog: The Leiber And Stoller Autobiography*, Omnibus Press, 2010

Lemani, Tanya, *Have Belly Will Travel*, America Star Books, 2007

Levy, Alan, *Operation Elvis*, Consul, 1962

Lisanti, Tom, *Fantasy Femmes Of Sixties Cinema: Interviews with 20 Actresses From Biker, Beach And Elvis Movies*, McFarland & Company, 2001

Lorentzen, Erik, *Elvis: The King Of The Jungle*, KJ Consulting, 2014

MacDonald, Ian, *Revolution In The Head: The Beatles' Records And The Sixties (Fully Updated Edition)*, Pimlico, 1998

Mankiewicz, Tom, and Robert Crane, *My Life As A Mankiewicz – An Insider's Journey Through Hollywood*, University Press of Kentucky, 2012

Miles, Barry, *The Beatles Diary Volume 1: The Beatles Years*, Omnibus Press, 2009

Miller, Albert B. et al, *Physician's Desk Reference To Pharmaceutical Specialities And Biologicals*, Medical Economics Inc., 22nd edition, 1968

Montague, Magnificent with Bob Baker, *Burn, Baby! BURN! – The Autobiography Of Magnificent Montague*, University of Illinois Press, 2003

Moore, Scotty with James Dickerson, *That's Alright Elvis: The Untold Story Of Elvis's First Guitarist And Manager, Scotty Moore,* Schirmer Books, 1997

Nash, Alanna, *Baby Let's Play House: The Life Of Elvis Presley Through The Women Who Loved Him*, Aurum, 2010

Nash, Alanna with Billy Smith, Marty Lacker and Lamar Fike, *Elvis Aaron Presley: Revelations From The Memphis Mafia,* HarperCollins, 1995 (republished as *Elvis And The Memphis Mafia*, Aurum, 2005)

Nash, Alanna, *The Colonel: The Extraordinary Story Of Colonel Tom Parker And Elvis Presley,* Aurum, 2003

Oates, Stephen B., *Let The Trumpet Sound – A Life Of Martin Luther King, Jr.*, HarperPerennial, 1994

Osborne, Jerry, *Elvis: Word For Word*, Harmony Books, 2000

Parker, Ed, *Secrets Of Chinese Karate*, Prentice-Hall, 1963

Pepper, Gary, the following articles printed in *Elvis Monthly*: 'Direct From Memphis', Vol. 1, No.3, March 1960; 'Operation Honouring Elvis In Elvisland', No.70, November 1965; 'Elvis Presley Coliseum', No.72, January 1966; 'Let's Have A Party', No.73, February 1966; 'It Hurts Me', No.74, March 1966; 'Such An Easy Question', No.75, April 1966; 'Elvis Is Back', No.78, July 1966; 'Spin Out', No.79, August 1966; 'Mess Of Blues', No. 82, November 1966; 'Just For Old Times Sake', No.83, December 1966; 'If Every Day Was Like Christmas', No.84, January 1967; 'Such A Night', No.85, February 1967; 'What'd I Say?', No.86, March 1967; 'The Rising Sun', No.87, April 1967; 'Ask Me', No.88, May 1967; 'Gary Pepper Reports On The Wedding of the Year', No. 90, July 1967; 'Long Lonely Highway', No.92, September 1967; 'Rock-A-Hula Baby', No.93, October 1967;

'Viva Las Vegas', No. 95, December 1967; 'Big Boss Man', No.96, January 1968; 'C'Mon Everybody', No.97, February 1968; 'City By Night', No.98, March 1968; 'Too Much', No.99, April 1968; 'What's She Really Like', No.100, May 1968; 'I Gotta Know', No.101, June 1968; 'I'm Coming Home', No.102, July 1968; 'My Wish Came True', No.104, September 1968; 'Your Time Hasn't Come Yet Baby', No.105, October 1968; 'Indescribably Blue', No.107, December 1968; 'Big Hunk Of Love', No.109, February 1969; 'Night Life Again', No.110, March 1969; 'Feelin' Groovy', No.115, August 1969.

Pierce, Patricia Jobe, *The Ultimate Elvis,* Simon & Schuster, 1994

Posner, Gerald, *Killing The Dream – James Earl Ray And The Assassination Of Martin Luther King, Jr.*, Little, Brown, 1998

Presley, Priscilla Beaulieu with Sandra Harmon, *Elvis And Me,* Berkley Books, 1986

Presley, Priscilla with Lisa Marie Presley etc., *Elvis By The Presleys,* Century, 2005

Racimo, Victoria and Kimberly Gatto, *All The King's Horses: The Equestrian Life Of Elvis Presley*, Regnery History, 2017

Randi, Don with Karen 'Nish' Nishimura, *You've Heard These Hands – From The Wall of Sound To The Wrecking Crew And Other Incredible Stories*, Hal Leonard, 2015

Schilling, Jerry with Chuck Crisafulli, *Me And A Guy Named Elvis: My Lifelong Friendship With Elvis Presley,* Gotham Books, 2006

Sharp, Ken, *Writing For The King*, Follow That Dream, 2006

Simpson, Paul, *The Rough Guide To Elvis,* Rough Guides, 2002

Thomas, Evan, *Robert Kennedy – His Life*, Touchstone, 2000

Tye, Larry, *Bobby Kennedy – The Making Of A Liberal Icon*, Random House, 2016

Vellenga, Dirk with Mick Farren, *Elvis And The Colonel,* Dell, 1988

Wallis, Hal and Charles Higham, *Starmaker: The Autobiography Of Hal Wallis*, Macmillan, 1980

Weingarten, Marc, *Station To Station: The Secret History Of Rock 'n' Roll On Television*, Simon & Schuster, 2000

Wertheimer, Alfred, *Elvis '56: In The Beginning*, Pimlico, 1994

West, Red with Sonny West and Dave Hebler, as told to Steve Dunleavy, *Elvis: What Happened?*, Ballantine, 1977

West, Sonny with Marshall Terrill, *Elvis: Still Takin' Care Of Business*, Triumph Books, 2007

Whitney, Dwight, 'The Indomitable Snowman Who Built Himself – And Elvis Too' article in *TV Guide*, Vol. 16 No. 48, November 1968

Williamson, Joel with Donald L. Shaw, *Elvis Presley: A Southern Life*, Oxford University Press, 2015

Worth, Fred L. and Steve D. Tamerius, *All About Elvis*, Bantam, 1991

Of the above titles, special mention must go to the works of Alanna Nash. Anecdotally, Alanna's epic oral history of the Memphis Mafia, first published as *Elvis Aaron Presley*, is still the best horse's mouth account by those who knew him. The chapters in this book concerning the psychopath Andreas Cornelis van Kuijk, alias 'Tom Parker', are indebted to her equally illuminating biography *The Colonel*.

Deserved credit must be given to the observational details of Elvis' movements in and around Memphis and Hollywood throughout the 1960s as recorded at the time by dedicated fan magazines. Namely, the legendary Gary Pepper's short-lived *The Tankcaster* (Memphis, Tennessee, USA), Rocky Barra's *Strictly Elvis* (Livonia, Michigan, USA) and Albert Hand's *Elvis Monthly* (Heanor, Derbyshire, UK). A selection of some of the specific articles consulted, and their authors, have been respectfully included in the above bibliography. The chapter 'Judas Writes' quotes Albert Hand's concerned editorial and Valerie White's letter of response from *Elvis Monthly* Series 5, Nos 4 and 6, April and June 1964.

Other archive periodicals consulted include: (USA) *Billboard, Boxoffice, Cashbox, Ebony, Jet, Los Angeles Times, Memphis Press-Scimitar, New York Times, Newsweek, Rolling Stone, TV Guide, Vanity Fair, Variety*; (UK) *Disc & Music Echo, Evening Standard, Melody Maker, Daily Mirror, New Musical Express, Daily Record, Record Collector, The Sun*.

With gratitude to the Newsroom and Humanities archives at The British Library, Euston Road, London, and to the invaluable research material provided by the following websites:

Elvis Australia – elvispresleymusic.com.au
Elvis Echoes Of The Past – elvisechoesofthepast.com
Elvis History Blog – elvis-history-blog.com
Elvis In Concert – elvisconcerts.com
Elvis Information Network – elvisinfonet.com
Elvis Presley News – elvispresleynews.com
Elvis Presley Photos – elvispresleyphotos.com
For Elvis CD Collectors Only – elvis-collectors.com
Keith Flynn's Elvis Pages – keithflynn.com
The Official Blog Of Graceland – blog.graceland.com
Scotty Moore Official Website – scottymoore.net

DISCOGRAPHY

During the early contractual negotiations, the Colonel reassured Steve Binder and Bones Howe that there wouldn't be a soundtrack album for Elvis' NBC special. As the producers of the musical material, Steve and Bones were automatically entitled to royalties from any such record and justifiably wary of being snowed.

The Colonel, naturally, snowed them.

The soundtrack deal between NBC and RCA had already been agreed before Steve and Bones were hired. As they were to bitterly discover months after the show was finished, essentially they'd given the Colonel a new Elvis album 'for free' – as had the network who handed over the tapes to RCA without charge.

When Steve and Bones later protested, the Colonel attempted to placate them each with a one-off cheque for $1500 pending signature of a legal waiver to surrender all musical copyright. Steve returned his to the Colonel unsigned with the torn cheque and a curt handwritten riposte: Bones' exact response isn't known. Neither of them ever earned a cent from any official disc related to the '68 Comeback.

★

Singer Presents Elvis Singing Flaming Star And Others
RCA Victor LP (PRS 279). Released October 1968.
Side 1: 'Flaming Star', 'Wonderful World', 'Night Life', 'All I Needed Was The Rain', 'Too Much Monkey Business' / Side 2: 'Yellow Rose Of Texas–The Eyes Of Texas', 'She's A Machine', 'Do The Vega',
'Tiger Man'

The show's first appearance on record was this slapdashed compilation of mostly soundtrack odds and ends from *Flaming Star, Viva Las Vegas, Easy Come, Easy Go, Stay Away, Joe* (which also supplied the cover image of a cowboy Elvis) and *Live A Little, Love A Little*. The album arose from NBC's sponsorship deal with Singer, given this exclusive branded Elvis LP only available in Singer electrical stores, limited to one-per-customer and retailing at a bargain $1.95. Worth the price if only for the Mephisophelean hysteria of 'Tiger Man', as taped at Burbank at the second 'sit-down' show of June 27, 1968. Which, strangely, meant his fans' first giddy taste of the '68 Comeback was a track absent from the coming broadcast itself.

The album was later rereleased on RCA's budget Camden label in March 1969 (CAS 2304).

'If I Can Dream' (b/w *'Edge Of Reality'*)
RCA Victor single (47-9670). Released November 1968.

The first single from the show (backed with a song from *Live A Little, Love A Little*). Every inch a comeback at 45 rpm, in the U.S. it stayed at number 12 for two weeks in February 1969; in the UK it did the same at number 11 in March 1969.

Elvis (TV Special)

RCA Victor LP (LPM 4088). Released December 1968.

Side 1: 'Trouble–Guitar Man', 'Lawdy, Miss Clawdy/Baby, What You Want Me To Do', Dialogue, Medley ('Heartbreak Hotel', 'Hound Dog', 'All Shook Up', 'Can't Help Falling In Love', 'Jailhouse Rock', Dialogue, 'Love Me Tender') / Side 2: Dialogue, 'Where Could I Go But To The Lord', 'Up Above My Head', 'Saved', Dialogue, 'Blue Christmas', Dialogue, 'One Night', 'Memories', Medley ('Nothingville', Dialogue, 'Big Boss Man', 'Guitar Man', 'Little Egypt', 'Trouble', 'Guitar Man'), 'If I Can Dream'

The official soundtrack album released in non-glorious mono straight from the TV tapes. Reaching number eight in the U.S. charts in late February 1969, it marked Elvis' first top ten album at home in over three years.

'Memories' (b/w 'Charro')

RCA Victor single (47-9731). Released February 1969.

The second and last single from the soundtrack, coupled with the title theme to his otherwise non-musical western. 'Memories' peaked at number 35 in the U.S. charts in April 1969.

★

Photos from the '68 Comeback continued to grace Elvis records unrelated to the show, most famously the sleeve of June 1969's *From Elvis In Memphis*, and the same year's double *From Memphis To Vegas* (its first half recorded live 'In Person' at the International Hotel). Tickets, flyers and press adverts for his maiden summer season in Vegas '69 also featured similar images of 'Comeback' Elvis.

Throughout the Seventies and Eighties, NBC outtakes and informal rehearsals were unearthed on various RCA compilations and boxsets. Probably the most significant revival of interest coincided with the 1985 HBO broadcast of *One Night With You*, allowing the viewing public to witness the unaired, unedited first 'sit-down' performance by black leather Elvis and his Blue Moon Boys of Burbank in its entirety (often cited as the obvious inspirational template to MTV's *Unplugged* series which began four years later). RCA's failure to release an accompanying soundtrack album remained a bootlegger's godsend well into the Nineties.*

It wasn't until the 30th anniversary in 1998 that the '68 Comeback was granted the reverential treatment it had long been missing in the digital age. *Memories: The '68 Comeback Special* (RCA/BMG 67612-2) was a wonderfully comprehensive double CD comprising, for the first time, the complete soundtrack to the show's many pre-recorded elements, the first '6 pm' sit-down show of June 27 (as seen on *One Night With You*), outtakes and rehearsals. Equally essential was its single-disc twin, *Tiger Man* (RCA/BMG 67611-2) of the full second '8 pm' sit-down show – the Second Second Coming – and, as such, immediately qualifying at the eleventh hour as one of the greatest live albums of the 20th century.

Two further aficionados-only limited CDs followed on RCA's new specialist Elvis collectors' label, Follow That Dream: 1999's *Burbank 68,* and 2006's *Let Yourself Go*. Both included rehearsals taped by Joe Esposito in the giggly informality of Elvis' Burbank dressing room as he prepared himself for the sit-down shows, supplemented by different sets of outtakes from the 'stand-up' shows and the Western Recorders sessions.

In 2008, RCA marked the ruby anniversary with an 'ultimate' four-disc boxset *The Complete '68 Comeback Special – 40th Anniversary Edition* (33275-2) amassing the original soundtrack album, the outtakes, the two sit-down and stand-up shows and the Esposito dressing room tapes, intended as the last word – last release? – on the '68 Comeback.

But we shall see.

---

* Confusing matters, though RCA did release a limited LP (with a free poster) to coincide with the broadcast stamped with the HBO logo and stickered '*One Night With You*', it was merely a lazy repressing of the original 1968 *Elvis (TV Special)* soundtrack album.

PERMISSIONS

PICTURE CREDITS

Cover

Front (Elvis Presley performing on the Elvis comeback TV special on June 27, 1968): Michael Ochs Archives/Getty Images.

Section 1

Page 1 (Gary Pepper and the Tankers wait for Elvis' return home in Memphis, March 8, 1960): AFP/Getty Images. Page 2 (top): ABC Photo Archives/Getty Images. Page 2 (bottom): Tannen Maury/EPA/REX/Shutterstock. Page 3: SNAP/REX/Shutterstock. Page 4: MGM/Kobal/REX/Shutterstock. Page 5 (top): Paramount/Kobal/REX/Shutterstock. Page 5 (bottom): Sipa USA/REX/Shutterstock. Page 6: LFI/Photoshot. Page 7 (top): WENN. Page 7 (bottom): AF Archive/Alamy Stock. Page 8 (Elvis behind bars in *Blue Hawaii*): SNAP/REX/Shutterstock.

Section 2

Page 1 (Dr Martin Luther King Jr mourner on the streets of Chicago, April 5, 1968): TopFoto. Page 2: Frank Carroll & Gary Null/NBC/Getty Images. Page 3 (top): Pictorial Press Ltd/Alamy Stock. Page 3 (bottom): Frank Carroll & Gary Null/NBC/Getty Images. Page 4 (top): Keystone Pictures USA/Alamy Stock. Page 4 (bottom): SNAP/REX/Shutterstock. Page 5: Kobal/REX/Shutterstock. Page 6 (top): Frank Carroll & Gary Null/NBC/Getty Images. Page 6 (bottom): Rex Features/Shutterstock. Page 7: Frank Carroll & Gary Null/NBC/Getty Images. Page 8 ('If I Can Dream'): Frank Carroll & Gary Null/NBC/Getty Images.

All picture research and layout by Simon Goddard, with thanks to Amazing15 Design.

THANKS

To Steve Binder for all his time, help and encouragement.

To Steve's fellow graduates of the Class of Burbank '68 for sharing their personal recollections, especially Frank DeVito, Susan Henning, Tanya Lemani and Gene McAvoy.

To the late Chris Bearde (1936–2017) who gave his last interview about Elvis for this book.

To the frethand of God, Scotty Moore (1931–2016), who I interviewed in 1999 with my trusted 'Tiger Man' Dominic Whiteland, and to Heaven's own hi-hat, D.J. Fontana (1931–2018).

To Nancy Whitehead for providing me with details about her friend and Elvis', the biggest Tanker that ever lived, Gary Pepper (1931–1980).

To Amelia Cone at Book Soup, West Hollywood, for leading me by the hand down Sunset Strip as it stood in the summer of '68.

To the blue suede crew at Omnibus – David Barraclough (one for the money), Chris Charlesworth (two for the show), and Imogen Gordon Clark (three to get ready). And to 'Diamond' Kevin Pocklington for takin' care of business.

And to Sylv – there in the dark, my beckoning candle.

THE AUTHOR

Simon Goddard was born in Cardiff in 1971. He grew up in Wales and Scotland and went to art school in the North of England before becoming a music journalist in London. His other books include *Ziggyology*, *Simply Thrilled* and the mock-picaresque biographical novel *Rollaresque* ('an excellent history of the early years of the Rolling Stones' – *The Times*). He is also the author of *Songs That Saved Your Life*, hailed by *The Guardian* as 'the best Smiths book', and *Mozipedia*, a *Mojo* Readers' Book Of The Year.

He is represented by The North Literary Agency.
thenorthlitagency.com